Mohamed Sheikh, Baron Sheikh of Cornhill in the City of London, was born in Kenya and brought up in Uganda, his parents originating from the sub-continent of India. He chairs businesses in the financial services and property sectors and has long been a leading figure in the insurance industry, and he also has an academic background. He and his company have received numerous awards and accolades and he is particularly involved in promoting inter-faith dialogue and undertaking humanitarian work. He has travelled widely overseas and has been awarded an Honorary Doctorate for his community work worldwide. He can best be described as a businessman, philanthropist, academic and a writer.

Lord Sheikh is a Conservative Member of the House of Lords and participates regularly in Parliamentary activities, holding senior positions in several All-Party Parliamentary Groups

He was made a Life Baron in 2006 and is a Freeman of the City of London. He founded and funds a registered personal and family charity.

This is Lord Sheikh's first book which is an acclaimed account of the life of Maharaja Ranjit Singh, a nineteenth-century leader of the Sikh Empire, who became a seminal figure in Indian history. This is the paperback version of the original book which was well received, all proceeds will be donated to a charity looking after orphans. His second book is titled *An Indian in the House* (2019) which is about the lives and times of the four trailblazers who first brought India to the British Parliament. He is now working on his third book, a historical novel based on events in mid-nineteenth-century India.

❦

EMPEROR OF THE FIVE RIVERS

The Life and Times of Maharaja Ranjit Singh

Mohamed Sheikh

BLOOMSBURY ACADEMIC
LONDON · NEW YORK · OXFORD · NEW DELHI · SYDNEY

BLOOMSBURY ACADEMIC
Bloomsbury Publishing Plc
50 Bedford Square, London, WC1B 3DP, UK
1385 Broadway, New York, NY 10018, USA
29 Earlsfort Terrace, Dublin 2, Ireland

BLOOMSBURY, BLOOMSBURY ACADEMIC and the Diana logo
are trademarks of Bloomsbury Publishing Plc

First published in Great Britain 2017 by I.B. Tauris
Reprinted by Bloomsbury Academic 2021
Paperback edition published 2023

Cover design: onethreefiveight.com
Cover image: Maharaja Ranjit Singh inspecting horses with
General Hari Singh Nalwa at Rambagh, Amritsar, c. 1832–35.
Gouache heightened with gold on paper. Courtesy of the Toor Collection

A catalogue record for this book is available from the British Library.

A catalog record for this book is available from the Library of Congress.

ISBN: HB: 978-1-3502-7436-5
PB: 978-1-3503-3713-8
ePDF: 978-1-7867-3095-4
eBook: 978-1-7867-2095-5

Typeset in Palatino Linotype by A. & D. Worthington, Newmarket

To find out more about our authors and books visit
www.bloomsbury.com and sign up for our newsletters.

This book is dedicated to my late father Mohamed Abdullah Sheikh and my late mother Kalsum Ara Sheikh who both immensely influenced my life.

CONTENTS

꒰ಜ꒱

PLATES

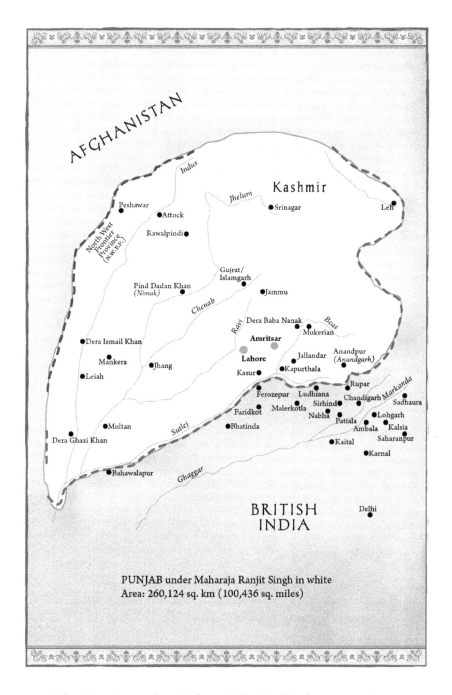

The Empire under Maharaja Ranjit Singh, 1799–1849

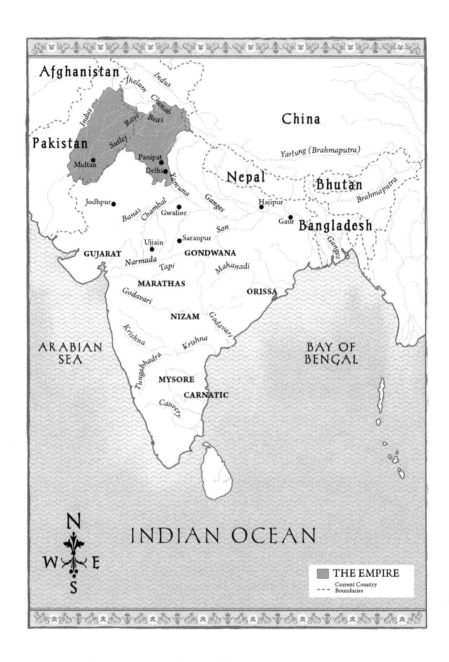

The Empire under Maharaja Ranjit Singh, 1838

PRINCIPAL CHARACTERS

Patrick Vans Agnew	British political agent
Syed Ahmed	Self-styled leader of the Jihad against the infidels in Hindustan
Yusuf Ali	An agent employed by the British to intercede with Ranjit Singh
Jean François Allard	French member of the Darbar
Lord Auckland	British governor-general of India
Paolo Avitabile	Italian member of the Darbar
Aziz-ud-din	Foreign minister of the Punjab empire and Ranjit's consistently closest adviser
Jung Bahadur	Prime minister of Nepal
Qadar Bakhsh	A member of the Darbar
Imam Baksh	Chief of police, Lahore
Sheikh Basawan	Muslim senior officer in the Khalsa army, as were Aziz Khan and Bakhtawar Kahn
Lord Bentinck	British governor-general of India
George Broadfoot	British army officer
William Brydon	British doctor who survived the retreat from Afghanistan
Alexander Burnes	British army officer appointed to explore Sindh
Misr Diwan Chand	General in the Khalsa army

Mokham Chand	Commander-in-chief of the Khalsa army whose son Moti Ram and grandson Ram Dyal also went on to serve in the army
Sansar Chand	Hindu ruler of Kangra and early ally of Ranjit
John Collins	British army officer who instructed Yusuf Ali
Lord Cornwallis	British governor-general of India
Claude August Court	French member of the Darbar
Lord Dalhousie	British governor-general of India
Bhawani Das	Finance minister
Devi Das	Keeper of financial records
Rani Dukno	Widow of Sher Singh
Prabhu Dyal	A Punjabi representative at the negotiations with Charles Metcalfe
Emily Eden	Sister of Lord Auckland and painter of a portrait of Ranjit
Neil B. Edmonstone	British chief secretary to the government in India
Lord Ellenborough	President of the Board of Trade, London
Lord Elphinstone	British envoy to Afghanistan
William Elphinstone	Commander of the British garrison in Kabul
Sir Henry Fane	Commander-in-chief, British army in India
Lieutenant Henry Fane	British army officer, nephew of Sir Henry
Alexander Gardner	Colonel of artillery in the Khalsa army
Mian Ghausa	Colonel of artillery in the Khalsa army
Josiah Harlan	American member of the Darbar
Jaswant Rao Holkar	Leader of the Marathas

John Martin Honigberger	Hungarian member of the Darbar
Baron Charles von Hügel	Austrian explorer
Imam-ud-din	Brother of Aziz-ud-din, custodian of the Fort of Lahore
Pandit Jalla	Childhood mentor of and later aide to Hira Singh
Rai Gobind Jas	Member of the Darbar
Banko Kahlon	Commander of the Ladakhi army
Raj Kanwar	Ranjit's second wife, from the Nakkai *misl*
Michael Katkoff	Russian newspaper editor who, along with Jemal al-Din al-Afghani, joined forces with Duleep Singh in an anti-British scheme
Chand Kaur	Wife of Prince Kharak Singh
Mehtab Kaur	Sada Kaur's daughter and Ranjit's first wife
Raj Kaur	Ranjit's mother
Sada Kaur	Ranjit's mother-in-law, from the Kanhaya *misl*
Sir John Keane	Commander of the Punjabi/British/Indian invasion force
Agar Khan	Ruler of Rajauri
Ahmed Khan	Ruler of Jhang
Attar Khan	Sitarist who played for Ranjit Singh
Azim Khan	Brother of Agar Khan
Dost Mohammad Khan	Barakzai ruler of Afghanistan
Fateh Khan	Leader of the Barakzai clan in Afghanistan
Hashmat Khan	Leader of a powerful Chattha clan who quarrelled with Maha and attempted to kill Ranjit in personal combat but, instead, was slain by him

Mohammad Akbar Khan	Afghan army officer, son of Dost Mohammad
Muzaffar Khan	Ruler of Multan
Nizam-ud-din Khan	Ruler of Kasur
Qutb-ud-din Khan	Brother of Nizam-ud-din Khan
Sarafraz Khan	Muslim member of the Darbar, as was his brother Zulfakar Khan
Sultan Khan	Raja of Bhimber
Balbhadra Kunwar	Gurkha general in the Khalsa army
Lord Lake	Commander-in-chief, British army in India
Bhajan Lal	Servant of Duleep Singh and influential in his master's conversion to Christianity
Sir Henry Lawrence	British Resident in India
Leili	Ranjit's much-loved Persian horse
Dr and Mrs John Login	Guardians of Maharaja Duleep Singh
Dr W.L. McGregor	British physician who tended to Ranjit Singh after his fourth stroke
Frederick Mackeson	British army officer
Sir William Macnaghten	Leader of Lord Auckland's mission to the court of Lahore
Shah Mahmud	One of Shah Zaman's two brothers
Aroor Mal	Amritsar's main banker
Charles Metcalfe	British envoy to the court of Lahore
Lord Minto	Successor to Cornwallis as governor-general of India
Yar Mohammad	Dost Mohammad's brother and governor of Peshawar
Ghulam Mohyuddin	A surgeon who administered to Ranjit at the court of Lahore
Moran	Dancing girl with whom Ranjit fell deeply in love

Hakim Muhammad	A personal physician to Ranjit at the court of Lahore
Bamba Muller	First wife of Maharaja Duleep Singh
Dr Murray	British physician who tended to Ranjit following his second stroke
Sir Charles Napier	British army officer
Nur-ud-din	Brother of Aziz-ud-din, Ranjit's personal physician and minister responsible for certain domestic matters
Sir David Ochterlony	British army officer sent to support Metcalfe when the negotiations with Ranjit Singh became tense
Leopold von Orlich	German member of the British army
W.G. Osborne	Military secretary to Lord Auckland
Pierre Perron	Frenchman employed by the Marathas in India
Henry Pottinger	British Resident in Cutch
Abdur Rahman	An occasional envoy for Ranjit Singh
Lakhpat Rai	Appointed by Maha as dewan, literally minister, but in his case *the* minister; murdered soon after Ranjit became ruler
Bhai Gobind Ram	Member of the Darbar
Ganga Ram	Overseer of accounts, along with Dina Nath
Jiwan Ram	An artist from Delhi who painted the Maharaja's portrait
Kirpa Ram	Devi Das's successor as keeper of financial records
Misser Beli Ram	Member of the Darbar
Archibald Seton	British Resident in Delhi
Muhammad Shahpur	Mufti in Lahore, along with Sa'adullah Chishti

Shah Shuja	Ruler of Afghanistan and brother of Shahs Zaman and Mahmud
Sahib Singh (1)	Bhangi ruler of Patiala whose bad rule in Lahore, along with that of Chet Singh (1) and Mohr Singh, led to Ranjit defeating all three of them
Sahib Singh (2)	An early ally of Ranjit, Sikh ruler of Gujrat
Sahib Singh Bedi	A venerated Sikh elder
Amar Singh Thapa	Leader of the Gurkhas
Atar Singh	Sandhanwalia sardar, as were Ajit Singh and Lehna Singh Sandhanwalia
Bhai Ram Singh	Member of the Darbar
Budh Singh	Maharaja Ranjit Singh's great-great-grandfather
Budh Singh Sandhanwalia	General in the Khalsa army
Charhat Singh	Ranjit's grandfather
Chet Singh	Aide to Maharaja Kharak Singh
Dal Singh	Ranjit's great-uncle, briefly Ranjit's first principal adviser and later a Khalsa army general
Desa Singh Majithia	A later administrator of Sada Kaur's estate
Dhian Singh Dogra	Prime minister of the court of Lahore
Prince Duleep Singh	Ranjit's child by Rani Jindan, later Maharaja of the Punjab
Fateh Singh Ahluwalia	Sikh leader and long-term close ally of Ranjit
Fateh Singh Kalianwala	Helped Ranjit to take over Kasur
Gulab Singh	Brother of Dhian Singh Dogra, as were Suchet Singh and Mian Udham Singh
Gurmukh Singh	Khalsa army paymaster
Hari Singh Nalwa	General in the Khalsa army
Hira Singh	Son of Dhian Singh Dogra

Hukma Singh	General in the Khalsa army
Hukma Singh Thanadar	A member of the Darbar
Prince Isher Singh	Ranjit's child, who died in infancy, by Mehtab Kaur
Jassa Singh Rămgarhiă	One of four men who challenged Ranjit following his capture of Lahore, the others being Jodh Singh of Wazirabad, Gulab Singh Banghi of Amritsar, and Nizam-ud-din Khan
Jawahar Singh	Brother of Rani Jindan
Prince Kashmira Singh	Ranjit's child by Daya Kaur, by whom he also had Prince Peshaura Singh
Prince Kharak Singh	Ranjit's first child, by Raj Kanwar, later Maharaja of the Punjab
Khushal Singh	Keeper of the royal palace, Lahore
Lehna Singh Majithia	Served the Darbar at high civil and military levels
Maha Singh Mirpura	Commander of Jamrud fort
Mahan Singh	Ranjit's father
Milkha Singh	Sikh ruler of Pindiwala and early ally of Ranjit
Prince Multana Singh	Ranjit's child by Rattan Kaur
Prince Nau Nihal Singh	Prince Kharak's son, by Chand Kaur who was proclaimed Maharani in 1840
Naudh Singh	Ranjit Singh's great-grandfather and founder of the Sukerchakia *misl*
Phula Singh	Ruler of the Nihangs
Prince Pratap Singh	Son of Sher Singh
Sahdev Singh	Son of Sher Singh
Prince Sher Singh	One of Ranjit's two other children by Mehtab Kaur, and later Maharaja of the Punjab; the third child was Prince Tara Singh
Suchet Singh	Uncle of Hira Singh

Surat Singh	Senior adviser from the Majithia clan, as was Amar Singh
Tej Singh	A Brahmin member of the Darbar (as was Lal Singh) and later commander of the Khalsa army
Thakur Singh	Member of the Sandhanwalia family who was instrumental in Duleep Singh's return to Sikhism
Zorawar Singh Kalhuria	General in the Khalsa army
James Skinner	British army officer
Henry Steinbach	Prussian member of the Khalsa army
Mai Sukhan	Attempted to resist Ranjit's capture of Amritsar
Sohan Lal Suri	Official diarist at the court of Lahore
George Thomas	English ruler of Hansi state in India
Vakil of Ahluwalia	A member of the Darbar
Vakil of Hyderabad	A member of the Darbar
Jean Baptiste Ventura	French member of the Darbar
Queen Victoria	Long-serving British monarch who became queen towards the end of Maharaja Ranjit Singh's reign in the Punjab and played a mixed role in the life in England of Duleep Singh
Captain P. Vitkevich	Russian representative in Kabul
Claude Wade	British envoy to the court of Lahore
Ada Douglas Wetherill	Second wife of Duleep Singh
William IV	Hanoverian British king
Shah Zaman	Saddozai clan ruler of Afghanistan at the time of Ranjit's accession

∽∾

INTRODUCTION

Northern Punjab, 6 July 1799: an oppressively hot day, with the monsoon expected soon. Ranjit Singh, still only 18 years old, was leading his army to take the ancient and holy city of Lahore, a major key in his campaign to unify the Punjab. He needed to hurry before the monsoon turned the surrounding plains to mud. He had one advantage: 6 July was the last day of the month of Muharram, when much of the population was commemorating the martyrdom of the two grandsons of the Prophet Mohamed (Peace Be Upon Him). That evening, Ranjit's troops crept into position and at dawn they blew up several gates and took the city by surprise. It – and his enemies – were at his mercy. Yet Ranjit, with a wisdom beyond his years, chose to act not with violence but with generosity. He assured the people that they would live in peace and freedom, and forbade his own forces from looting. To show his sincerity, he worshipped at the two main mosques, and then allowed his principal enemy, Chet Singh, to leave the city with his family. He had already demonstrated bravery and guile, remarkable attributes in one so young; this display of magnanimity marked him as a commander of remarkable calibre.

Clearly there is much about his character and achievements that demands explanation. Hence this book. But for a Briton to write about an Asian figure from two centuries ago presents challenges on several levels. Ranjit Singh hailed from a world very different from my own – inland Punjab, some 6,000 miles away. He grew up in conditions of extreme poverty and danger. He was a man of many, often conflicting, parts. Perhaps the most startling thing

1

about him was the contrast between his appearance – his one eye, his pock-marked face, his small size – and his prodigious talents. A European traveller, Charles, Baron von Hügel, described Ranjit as 'the most ugly and unprepossessing man I saw throughout the Punjab', while even Moran, a woman whom the Maharaja loved deeply, was uncomplimentary about his looks. Yet in his character he was truly admirable. He was perhaps best known as a warrior, yet he was also very much concerned with civil government and fair judicial practices. And he rose to fame at a very young age, being proclaimed Maharaja in April 1801 when he was still only 20 years of age. Admittedly, life expectancy was much lower then and youth and achievement often went hand in hand – but not on his colossal scale.

Ranjit Singh's greatness made this book a demanding enterprise. The scale of his achievements combined with the stories told about him made it difficult to distinguish between truths, half-truths and myths – a particular problem given that the South Asian traditions of historiography reflect an understanding of the relations between religion and kingship which differs greatly from that of nineteenth-century European and American commentators. For one thing, South Asian history-writing was informed by a cultural recognition of the ultimate, determining power of the Almighty in controlling the shared fate of mankind, and so historical texts often incorporated stories or even astrological passages which highlighted the exalted lineage and exemplary moral leadership of the ruler in question. The 'myths' contained in courtly chronicles of Ranjit Singh's reign often had a performative nature and were variously intended to project positive images of the majesty, masculinity and overall cultural authority of the Maharaja; or alternatively, to demonstrate the personal piety of the author (and even to cover any potential political dissent on their part). Unfortunately much of their meaning is not easily apparent to the modern-day historian, and often further confused when translated from their vernacular originals into the English language.

If religion, especially Sikhism, makes up a major strand of this story, secularism is another. India, which is proud to be a secular country, was helped to become so by great rulers from the past.

Akbar – the only Mughal ruler to earn the title 'the Great' – ruled India from 1556 to 1605 and benefited from the support of fine men of many faiths and ethnic backgrounds in his government, such as Raja Man Singh, an adviser at the court and a successful general, who was a Rajput Hindu. Two centuries later, Ranjit Singh, a Sikh, was similarly secularist in his high appointments. By choosing confidants from different traditions, Akbar the Great and Ranjit Singh were able to prove to their subjects that they cared about relations between the various communities.

A third major theme of this book is the way Ranjit Singh handled relations with the increasingly powerful British as they imposed their will on India. He did so in a way that won respect for the Punjab as an independent entity.

Early in the 1800s, a century before British imperial rulers began to negotiate with nationalist leaders in the Indian subcontinent, their forebears found themselves doing so on equal terms with a bold and energetic man who ruled just one portion of it, the Punjab. His ambitions included ruling over the 'Cis-Sutlej', the largely Sikh area 'this side of the Sutlej River' (from the point of view of the British). This worried Britain, which at the time was involved in a deadly struggle with Napoleonic France and feared French advances on British interests in Asia. The British wanted north-west India, including the Cis-Sutlej, to be well secured against any such threat. They decided to obtain Ranjit Singh's cooperation to get their way.

Initially, the British viewed this task as being unlikely to tax the ingenuity of the young representative, Charles Metcalfe, sent to negotiate with him. They felt that Metcalfe, a gifted 23-year-old who was already making his mark on imperial rule in India, had simply to impress upon Ranjit Singh the mutuality of British and Punjabi interests in resisting France, and make clear Britain's unwillingness for him to make any moves into the Cis-Sutlej. There should be no need for anything as formal as a treaty, which would suggest equality between British India and the Punjab.

At this time, Europeans took for granted their superiority over Asians. As his biographer John William Kaye made clear,[1] Metcalfe himself held the standard opinion of Britain's mission in India: to bring civilisation by extending imperial rule. So it was with surprise and irritation that Metcalfe found in Ranjit Singh a man who was at least his equal in the sophisticated art of diplomacy.

Metcalfe at first blew hot and cold, veering between pressing his superiors to invade the Punjab and professing Britain's unreserved friendship to the Maharaja. The situation was saved in part by what the two men had in common as human beings, particularly an underlying honesty and a certain humility. Each became committed to a constructive political outcome, for a breakdown posed dangers for both sides. In the end, the British got their way over the Cis-Sutlej, while Ranjit Singh obtained a treaty that effectively gave him freedom to act as he wished elsewhere in the Punjab.

And from that relationship grew a regard for Ranjit Singh's Punjab as a political entity. In the early 1800s Britain, the world's greatest naval and industrial power, was accustomed to ruling an ever-growing empire that was increasingly centred upon India. Yet after negotiating with Ranjit Singh, Britain felt obliged to respect the Punjab, almost at the heart of India, as a genuinely independent state. Punjabis, be they Indians or Pakistanis, Muslims, Hindus or Sikhs, may take pride in their forebear's supreme ability to impose himself on Britain, and on other foreigners, while building an expanding country with its own flourishing civilisation. As a result, the British maintained a grudging admiration for Ranjit Singh that lasted for 30 years, until the end of his life.

ॐ

1

THE FOUNDATIONS

It is a cliché that great leaders are made by the interaction of character and context. The context from which Ranjit Singh and his new state emerged was the historic Punjab – the clay that Ranjit moulded. It is with the Punjab that his story begins.

The Punjab's rivers – *ab* means both water and river – make the rather beautiful shape of a leaf, with the rivers as the veins and stem. At its northern tip, the leaf curls up into the Himalayan foothills, outliers of several tangled mountain systems – the Hindu Kush, the Karakorums and many minor ranges. Up here, tiny hamlets perch on hillsides or nestle in valleys. But most of the Punjab is flat, sloping from about 1,600 feet above sea level in the north to some 230 feet in the south-west, a drop of a mere 3.5 feet per mile. Its great rivers – the Indus and the five tributaries that give the region its name: the Jhelum, Chenab, Ravi, Beas and Sutlej – wander slowly across plains that freeze in winter and shimmer under a remorseless sun in summer, with temperatures up to 120° Fahrenheit in the shade. The rivers, meandering in broad, sandy channels, turn arid lands hardly reached by monsoon rains into well-irrigated *doabs* – the 'two-water' flat lands between rivers. The shallow river-beds bar large ships, but locals have always used small boats. Where the water does not reach, however, is semi-desert or desert. Higher and drier parts of the *doabs* support only low shrubs, where camels graze, and to the south, in areas away from river water, are barren tracts of shifting sands.

Water, canals, boats and farming: the combination made the Punjab's heartland a focus for civilisation, from the time of the Indus Valley Civilisation, the oldest in South Asia, dating back

5

to 2000 BCE. The land has always been a buffer-zone or target for conquest: the Greeks under Alexander the Great in the fourth century BCE, Hindus from northern India in the fourth and fifth centuries CE, the Turkish Shahiyas in the eighth and ninth centuries, Ghaznavids and Ghurids from Afghanistan, and finally the Muslim Mughals, who ruled in north India for 300 years and gave the region its name. They made Lahore their capital, and turned the ancient highway across north India into the great 2,500km artery known as the Grand Trunk Road. Dotted with caravanserais and shaded by trees, it ran from the Northwest Frontier through Islamabad and Lahore to Amritsar and Delhi, and beyond all the way to Kolkata (Calcutta). Described by Rudyard Kipling in *Kim* as 'a river of life such as exists nowhere else in the world', it allowed the flow of people, trade and armies, and so played a major role in the events described in this book.

Once hierarchical and dominated by caste, Punjabi society became more mobile under Turkish and Mughal rule. Artisans and service-providers moved from the countryside to towns to serve the new ruling class. New methods of irrigation extended crop-lands and supported new towns. By the early seventeenth century, merchants from Multan and Lahore were playing a crucial role in domestic and external trade. The spinning wheel, carding-bow and improved wooden loom brought about changes in weaving. Lime mortar made possible better brick-and-stone construction. Sialkot emerged as an important centre of paper manufacture. This was no industrial revolution: artisans still worked with elementary technology in a labour-intensive system of families bound by their caste, making the Punjab famous for hand-loomed carpets, shawls, rugs, glazed tiles and pottery. Most of the region's people worked in agriculture, as they do today; the Punjab is not only the breadbasket of Pakistan but is the most important wheat-growing region of the subcontinent.

Islamic law was introduced for the administration of justice under Turko-Afghan and Mughal rule. The Punjab already had a significant Muslim population, though by the sixteenth century many new ideas had begun to emerge or spread, such as Sufism – already widespread by the fourteenth century – and, particu-larly, Sikhism, which gained considerable ground among ordinary people as a new ethic that made no distinctions on the basis of birth. Its radical ideology had a special appeal for labourers, craftsmen, agriculturists, traders and shopkeepers. Their contributions enabled the Gurus to establish religious centres and new towns. The Sikh community's financial independence and strong organisation made it something of a state within the Mughal Empire.

The Punjab's long-established mixed population has bequeathed a rich cultural tradition of dance, music, folk ballads and a literature dating back to the Islamic poetry of Attar, a thirteenth-century follower of Sufism. But it also included an astonishing variety of different groups, divided by clan, religion and ethnicity. The Punjab in the decades before Ranjit Singh unified it was a patchwork of small clan-ruled areas known as *misls*, all with their own traditions and interests. To persuade and force such diverse entities into a single state was one of Ranjit's greatest achievements.

The Punjab between 1849 and 1947 was forcibly absorbed into British-ruled India. After partition in 1947, massive population changes swiftly occurred between newly formed India and Pakistan. Some 10 million people crossed over to what they hoped was the relative safety of a religious majority, most of them in the Punjab: over 5 million Muslims moved to the western Punjab, now in Pakistan, while nearly 4.5 million Hindus and Sikhs moved eastwards. Violence erupted on both sides of the border. About a million human beings died in the Punjab alone, with countless more innocent people injured. Maharaja Ranjit Singh, who had endeavoured to create a united country in which people were not discriminated against because of their religion, would surely have wept bitter tears had he known what would happen in the Punjab just over a century after his death.

Today, the old Punjab is divided between Pakistan and India, the Pakistani share being three times the Indian. The populations are very different. Almost all of the 86 million people in Pakistan's province are Muslims. By contrast, in the three Indian states most of the 24 million is Sikh (50–60 per cent) or Hindu. So in the Punjab as a whole, Sikhs are in a minority, as they were in Ranjit Singh's time, a fact that recalls the scale of his achievement.

എ

The Punjab's location and history of incursions led to the rise of the great religion that was central to Ranjit Singh's life. By 1500, Muslim invaders had in the course of 500 years converted about half the population of the Punjab to Islam, while the other half remained Hindus. Of course, many of those invaders had not been concerned solely with the Punjab. They were after an even greater prize: India, or Hindustan, whose disunity made it irresistible to predators. It was virtually inevitable that invaders from the west would ravage the lush and fertile Punjab on their way. Yet the Punjabi people were not blameless. They remained chronically unable to unite to keep foreigners out. Bands of them might unite against any one set of invaders, but such unity always collapsed once the invaders had gone.

In the late 1400s a young man called Nanak ruminated upon the inadequacies of his fellow Punjabis. What on earth could be done to bring the timeless sequence of invasion, plunder and death to an end and so give Punjabis a happier life? Nanak could see no way in which Muslims and Hindus could be brought together by appeals to reason and common-sense. Such appeals had been made many times but had always fallen on stony ground. The people needed something more.

He found his answer in his own religious outlook. Although brought up as a Hindu, he was attracted by the Sufi branch of Islam, whose disciples believed in converting infidels by persuasion not force. Nanak decided to focus on what Muslims and Hindus in the Punjab had in common: they shared the same land, and the same – often deplorable – conditions. In 1499, when he was aged 30, Nanak came up with what was probably the only possible answer: a new creed, Sikhism, with elements drawn from both the other two religions. He became Sikhism's first Guru, meaning teacher or master.

There are many points on which Sikhs and Muslims agree. Both groups believe in one God, Waheguru and Allah, and oppose idolatry. In Islam, the Prophet Mohamed (Peace Be Upon Him) bequeathed his followers the Qur'an and His way of life; Sikhism has a holy book known as the Granth. The Gurus encourage acts of charity, as does the tradition of *zakat* for Muslims. Worshippers remove their shoes and cover their head on entering mosques and Sikh temples, *gurudware*, and both sets of worshippers sit on the floor. Marriages in both Islam and Sikhism are supposed to take place only with the consent of both the boy and the girl. The *mool mantra* – the 'main chant' or 'root verse' of the Granth, said to be the first composition uttered by Nanak upon his enlightenment – equates with the Muslims' Kalima ('There is No God but Allah, and the Prophet Mohamed is his Messenger'), and some of the sayings in the *mool mantra* would be believed by Muslims as well as Sikhs.

Sikhism and Hinduism, too, have points in common. Both religions see Om as a sacred word; it is commonly used at the beginning of their mantras or sacred invocations. In Sikhism, as Khushwant Singh, one of Ranjit's biographers, has written, 'the concept of Om, which is somewhat elusive in Hinduism, is crystallised in Sikh theology and is given a status of symbol – the symbol of God. The singularity of God is expressed in the saying Ek Onkaar (There is one God).' [1] Both religions believe in the existence of the soul and its rebirth in different bodies. They have as their final aim the liberation of the soul from the bondage of matter or Moksha. They both adhere to the law of karma, or the law of cause and effect. They regard vegetarianism as virtuous. Sikhs celebrate Diwali, the Hindu festival of lights. The surname 'Singh' was also found among Hindu Rajputs. It has been argued that the Sikh *kirpan* (dagger) was adopted from the Rajput martial tradition. The turban was a common headdress of Indians and was not exclusively Sikh.

A man with a powerful message had no alternative but to spread the word himself. Nanak, who mastered Punjabi, Sanskrit and Persian, travelled all over India and beyond. He spoke before Hindus, Jains, Buddhists, Parsis and Muslims in temples and mosques and at pilgrimage sites. One place he visited in 1514 was the north-central Indian town of Gorakhmata, the abode of the devotees of Guru Gorakhnath, the eleventh–twelfth-century teacher of yoga. Here, Guru Nanak so impressed his listeners that Gorakhmata was thereafter renamed as Nanakmatta, and remains a place of pilgrimage today.[2]

Mecca, by contrast, was a long way from the Indian subcontinent. When Nanak arrived after his 2,000-mile journey he was so exhausted that he collapsed into sleep with his feet pointed towards the Holy Shrine. Jiwan, the night watchman, spotted this act of sacrilege and upbraided him, but once it was known that he was the legendary Guru, other pilgrims and holy men gathered at the scene. Again, Nanak's transparent sincerity won converts to his code of humility, prayer and truthful living.

Wherever he went he spoke out against empty religious rituals, the caste system and the sacrifice of widows (*sati*), and preached other tenets. Naturally, this could have offended followers of different faiths but he was careful not to actually *ask* his listeners to follow him. Rather, he stressed the ideals of equality, universality and social commitment. All men and women could join his path as equals. They then worshipped together in congregations (*sangat*) and ate simple food together (*langar*). Nanak taught that all spiritual and ethical norms and values were equally applicable to them.

Guru Nanak practised what he preached. He continued to attend Hindu services but when he visited Mecca he was accompanied by Bhai Mardana, a Muslim musician, and visited mosques. Naturally, he was up against enormous forces of resistance – adherents of a religion do not lightly abandon it, and those who do can find their liberty or even their lives abruptly ended. Religious conservatism is not easily overcome. And because Nanak lived in an age when news travelled at walking pace, many Punjabis would not hear of him for many years. But the magic of his new faith and its inviting nature enabled him to prevail.

Despite his ascetic lifestyle and the solitary nature of the task he set himself, Guru Nanak was a householder who married and had children. However, he eventually concluded that neither of his sons was capable of succeeding to his sort of life. Instead, Nanak chose a man called Bhai Lehna who had come to stay with him, who became known as Guru Angad.

Crucially for the development of Sikhism, by installing one of his followers as the Guru in his lifetime Nanak made the position of the Guru and the disciple interchangeable. This development led to Sikhism being established not just by Nanak and Angad but by further Gurus over the next 239 years (1469–1708). These teachers' main purpose was to promote the spiritual and moral well-being of their followers by setting an exceptional example of how to live a worthy life. They aimed to renew Sikh teachings, free minds from bigotry and superstitions, dogmas and rituals, and emphasise simplicity. Each succeeding Guru reinforced and extended the message, each one wove his own strands into the religious web (see box, pp 16–17).

Despite their meeting points, Sikhism does differ from Hinduism and Islam in various ways. Sikhs do not worship demi-gods, a man marries only one wife and all human beings are equal. Women are seen as equal not just in marriage but in all aspects of life. Sikhs are discouraged from fasting, from other forms of bodily suffering and from undertaking pilgrimages. Importantly, while devoting themselves to Sikhism, they do not regard their religion as inherently superior to any other. The teachings both help bind the people to a strict code and – in Ranjit Singh's time – morally empowered the Khalsa soldiers who developed into a determined body of men. Notably, the encouragement of equality meant that the Punjab was one part of India where the peasantry and lower castes were able to achieve political power.

The Sikh insistence on the equality of women is of particular significance, a truly remarkable position for any religion in any part of the world to adopt in the sixteenth century. Guru Nanak appreciated the unifying role of women in society and his historic role as the first Guru enabled him not only to work for their emancipation but to bind his successors to the same policy. Sikh scriptures categorically state that men and women together make society a composite, well-balanced whole, with each having a significant contribution to make. Marriage was viewed as a sacred bond between two equal partners, not merely a physical union of two individuals. The arrangement whereby, upon marriage, a man was given the name 'Singh' and a woman 'Kaur' was of immense significance to a woman, who was thus recognised as an individual who need not take her husband's name after marriage.

These egalitarian beliefs were applied from the start. Guru Nanak claimed Bibi Nanaki, his elder sister, as his inspiration and mentor. She supported him in his life's mission and became the first person he initiated into Sikhism. Guru Amar Das enhanced women's lives at a strategic level within the embryonic Punjabi state when he established 22 administrative units called *manjis*, or parishes. Four of the *manjis* were headed by women who, like the male appointees, enjoyed full decision-making powers within the parish. No other religion afforded women such a high status and influence. In addition, more than one-third of the 146 people whom the Guru trained as missionaries were women. Besides religious instruction, missionaries educated rural people, including women, in reading, writing and arithmetic.

Later Gurus maintained the egalitarian tradition. When Guru Gobind created the Khalsa in 1699, women were fully initiated too. The advent of the Khalsa meant that Sikh women could, and later did, lead armies into battle, as well as claim equality in socio-religious and political affairs. But while Sikhism was innovative in stressing the need for equality between men and women (and between men and men), equality did not automatically became established across the land. The inferiority of women was taken for granted by other religions, and female infanticide, *purdah* and *sati* continued to be commonly practised.

∽

The Punjab's location and the Sikh religion were two of the three foundation stones of Ranjit Singh's rule. The third was the confederacy of clans, the *misl* system (meaning 'like' or 'equal' in Persian), which originated when the Sikhs challenged the Mughal Empire in the early 1700s.

In 1705, Governor Wazir Khan of Sirhind, a border town on the Grand Trunk Road between Delhi and Lahore, had seized the mother of the Guru Gobind Singh and two of his children, and tried to force them to become Muslims. Failing in this attempt, Wazir Khan sentenced the two young boys to death by being bricked up alive together in a wall. Four years later, the Guru's champion, Banda Singh Bahadur, led a revenge attack. In a brilliant campaign, he took several Mughal cities including Mukhlisgarh, which he renamed Lohgarh (City of Steel) and which he made the first Sikh capital. This became his base for the assault on Sirhind, taken after a great battle in 1710 during which Wazir Khan was killed. Banda became ruler of the whole province of Sirhind, extending Sikh territory 150 miles eastwards.

Banda Singh Bahadur had breathed fresh life into Sikhism and taught Sikhs how to fight and conquer. But his success was brief. Imperial forces expelled him in 1713 and pursued him in a two-year campaign, culminating in Banda, his son Ajai Singh and hundreds of Sikhs being killed with the utmost cruelty.

By then the Mughal Empire was in terminal decline, pushed further to the edge by Nadir Shah, whose rise and fall is one of the most extraordinary in history. Born into a simple shepherd family in northern Persia, Nadir fought his way to power, reunited Persia and made himself Shah in 1736. After defeating the Mughal army in February 1739 and capturing the emperor Mohammad Shah, he entered Delhi, where in one day (22 March) his troops slaughtered some 20,000–30,000 Indians. He then seized the Treasury, removing the Peacock Throne, which soon became the symbol of Persian imperial might. Among the jewels he took was the famous Koh-i-Noor ('Mountain of Light') diamond. His troops left Delhi at the beginning of May 1739, with thousands of elephants, horses, camels and slaves who carried the booty. (Back home, in the grip of paranoia, he had many of his senior followers killed, until he was assassinated in 1747.)

The booty which Nadir Shah wrested from Delhi proved something of a curse. The Sikhs, who had hitherto been quiescent, now united and relieved the slaves of much of Nadir's loot and released many of them. The enterprise and bravery of the Sikhs won them new adherents, including many Muslim peasants who had been revolted by Nadir's savagery.

The Sikhs repeated these tactics during nine Afghan invasions between 1747 and 1769, under Ahmed Shah Abdali, who had fought with Nadir Shah and is considered by some the founder of modern Afghanistan. Abdali played havoc not only with the Mughal administration in the Punjab but with the Maratha Hindus who controlled their own little empire in northern India, and who had been and would again be a menace to the Punjab. Abdali assaults inspired Sikhs to resist. Their relatively small number, amounting to just over 100,000, became pre-eminent in a territory whose size was about the same in square miles. The historian Balwant Singh writes of the anarchy of this period being a 'God-send' to Sikhs whose 'reckless horsemen would roam at will from end to end of the Punjab ... gradually establishing their sway'.[3]

It was the collapse of the empire amidst the chaos of Nadir Shah's invasion and the Afghan assaults that allowed the *misls* to form and – eventually – for Ranjit Singh to rise. Each one was headed by a particularly bright and brave *misldar* who controlled a certain territory within which people were defended on payment of *rakhi*, a protection tax. Twelve *misls* came into existence, with a combined strength of some 70,000 horsemen. The strongest *misl*, the Bhangis, controlled Lahore, Amritsar and most of the western Punjab. Bhang, from which the name was derived, is hashish or hemp to which *misldar* Bhima Singh was said to be addicted. The other *misls* (of varying sizes) divided Sikh lands between themselves, rivalling each other, but generally – as warlords often do – agreeing on their territories and the boundaries between them. The *misldars*, met twice yearly in conference at the Harmandir Sahib in Amritsar, but behaved as a unified group only if faced with an external threat.[4] As the historian Indu Banga has put it, 'The Sikh dominions in the last quarter of the eighteenth century were remarkable more for internal strife than expansion.'[5] The situation was inherently unstable. Either one or a few *misls* would gradually take over the lot, or the system would collapse through its own weaknesses. As it turned out, a combination of both took place.

One of the local bosses, Budh Singh, was Ranjit's great-great-grandfather, and the first of his antecedents to become renowned for daring actions. His son Naudh Singh fortified their ancestral village of Sukerchak in western Punjab, located in today's Gujranwala District in Pakistan. Capturing land from the surrounding Afghans, Naudh Singh constructed solid territorial foundations for the Sukerchakia *misl* and, aggressive to the end, he died in battle in 1752. His eldest son Charhat Singh extended the domain. Charhat captured Gujranwala and then saw off the Afghan governor of Lahore so effectively that the latter had to abandon his armaments and food in his retreat, which enabled the third Sukerchakia *misldar* to grab more territory still. Although another Afghan force chased him away, he returned undaunted and won back what he had lost, and more. Like Naudh, Charhat died while fighting. Charhat's son Maha, or Mahan, who became *misldar* aged just 14, maintained his family's growing name for belligerence by capturing Hindu-controlled Jammu. Jammu's wealth enhanced Mahan's power yet further, and he successfully challenged the Kanhayas who had replaced the Bhangis as the strongest *misl*. This particular victory had important consequences for the career of Mahan's son, Ranjit, because the defeated Kanhaya *misldar* agreed to betroth his grand-daughter Mehtab Kaur to Ranjit.

Equally important, when the *misldar* died his daughter-in-law Sada Kaur, Mehtab's mother, would inherit the estates. It was exceptional for a woman to be a *misldar*. Ranjit's tough new mother-in-law was a fearless leader and had a character of steel; she would go down in history as one of Asia's most powerful women. Mahan died in 1792, leaving his *misl* to his son, Ranjit, then aged only 12.

Sikh Gurus 1469–1708

1. **Nanak**, the founder of Sikhism and the first Guru.
2. **Angad,** who succeeded Nanak in 1539, aged 35, was the first to start compiling the Sikh holy text – what we today know as the Guru Granth Sahib, beginning with the writings of Guru Nanak. He developed a new Punjabi script called Gurmukhi for this purpose.
3. At age 73, **Amar Das** was by far the oldest Guru upon his accession in 1552. He extended the fight against caste restrictions and untouchability. He strengthened the tradition of the *langar* by making all his disciples sit and eat their meals together. Amar Das introduced the Anand Karaj, the Sikh marriage ceremony that is not merely a legal contract but a fusion of souls. He abolished among Sikhs the Hindu requirement for a married woman to immolate herself on her husband's funeral pyre (*sati*).
4. **Ram Das** acceded in 1574. He founded the city of Amritsar and started the construction of the famous Harmandir Sahib (known today as the Golden Temple) there. Amritsar became both the capital and the holy city of the Sikhs. Ram Das composed the *Lawan*, a four-stanza hymn around which the Anand Karaj is centred.
5. **Arjan Dev**, the third son of Ram Das, acceded in 1581 and was the first of four Gurus who were all aged 18 or less at their installation. He supervised two great projects: he finalised the Adi Granth in 1604 (begun by Guru Angad) and completed the Harmandir Sahib. After the Mughal emperor Akbar died he was replaced by Jahangir, a man of a very different stamp. He took against Arjan (though not because of his religion) and had him executed. Arjan's killing meant he became the first Sikh martyr.
6. **Hargobind**, son of Arjan Dev, became Guru at the young age of 11 and remained in office for 38 years, longer than any of the other Gurus bar Nanak. His originality lay in arguing that non-violence could encourage evil and that people must be prepared to fight in order to protect the weak and the oppressed. He established a small army and was the first Guru to take up arms to defend the faith. Hargobind also introduced the Sri Akal Takhat Sahib, The Seat (Throne) of the Timeless One, in the Harmandir complex – a brave move at a time when only emperors were allowed to sit on a raised platform, or *takhat* (throne). He kept some 300 mounted followers in attendance, and a bodyguard of 60. Though imprisoned by the Mughal emperor at one point, he

became his valued companion, on one occasion killing a tiger that threatened the emperor's life.

7. After acceding at 14, Hargobind's grandson, **Har Rai**, spent most of his life in devotional meditation and preaching the teachings of Nanak. But he maintained the armed Sikh warriors and boosted the military spirit of the Sikhs in the face of opposition from the new Mughal emperor, Aurangzeb.

8. Har Rai's second son Guru **Har Krishan** was installed at the exceptionally tender age of five, but soon astonished the Brahmins with his knowledge and spiritual powers. After only three years as Guru he died while working with the epidemic-stricken people of Delhi.

9. **Tegh Bahadur,** 44 when he became Guru, believed in freedom of worship so strongly that Aurangzeb perceived him to be dangerous. The Emperor had Tegh Bahadur imprisoned in a cage, tortured and beheaded.

10. His son **Gobind Singh,** the tenth and last human Guru, acceded at the age of nine in 1675. He extended the martial work of Hargobind by creating the Khalsa (meaning Community of the Pure) and so formally made the Sikhs a military-religious order. All Sikhs were expected to be Khalsa or working towards baptism. During the ceremony, the initiate was instructed never to remove any hair; to avoid tobacco, alcohol and other intoxicants; to not eat the meat of an animal slaughtered the Muslim way (there is a longstanding debate about this: whether it was meant that Sikhs were meant to abstain from halal/jhatka meat, or from eating meat altogether); and not to commit adultery. It was Gobind who made the landmark decision to give male Sikhs the name Singh (lion) and females the name Kaur (princess). (Kaur is derived from Kanwar, meaning son of a king.) Gobind fought against Aurangzeb but sought reconciliation with Aurangzeb's successor, Bahadur Shah. He was assassinated by Afghan Pathans on the orders of a nawab suspicious of the Emperor/Guru relationship.

11. **The Guru Granth Sahib.** Shortly before his death, on 3 October 1708, Gobind performed an extraordinary act, which guaranteed Sikhism's enduring influence: he appointed the Granth as the everlasting Sikh Guru. Now expanded to include the writings of the Gurus following Guru Arjun, Guru Gobind Singh declared the holy text to be the supreme spiritual authority in a Sikh's life, rather than further human leaders.

2

RANJIT'S EARLY YEARS AND ENTRY INTO POWER

In 1782, George Forster, a civilian employee of Britain's East India Company, the enterprise upon which British rule in India was based, was told to report on the inhabitants of the Punjab on his way home to England. Forster travelled within the Punjab during the spring of 1783. Initially fearful of the Sikhs, he disguised himself as a Turkish traveller. His generally favourable impressions, published as a series of letters in 1798, included a particularly apposite comment:

> Should any future cause call forth the combined efforts of the Sikhs to maintain the existence of empire and religion, we may see some ambitious chief led on by his genius and success and absorbing the power of his associates, display from the ruins of their commonwealth the standard of monarchy.[1]

Ranjit Singh was only two years old when George Forster penned these words, but they describe his rise with prophetic succinctness.

Ranjit was born on 13 November 1780[2] in Gujranwala, in the north-east of today's Pakistan. This town in the Sukerchakias' domain took its name from its founders, the Gujjars, a centuries-old clan of uncertain origins. The boy was initially named Budh Singh, after his ancestor who first won the family fame. The name meant the Wise One, but when the news of his birth reached Mahan, who was returning from a successful battle, he gave his son a new and perhaps more suitable name: Ranjit, meaning Victor of Battles.

Ranjit's childhood was of the make-or-break kind. His father had little spare time for him, while his mother, Raj Kaur, was largely confined to the *zenana* (the inner apartments of a house, a practice of seclusion which Sikhs had borrowed from Muslims). Mahan Singh was away on a campaign at the time young Ranjit contracted smallpox; alarmed, he repeatedly sent messengers to enquire about the boy's condition. One of them had the appalling duty of reporting to Mahan that the smallpox had done its work so horribly as to blind his son in one eye. Grief-stricken, Mahan declaimed loudly that this blow was the will of Waheguru (a Sikh term for God). He drew strength from this and from recalling that another Sikh, Gujjar Singh, had been similarly affected yet had been a doughty warrior and a wise man. Henceforth, Mahan believed Ranjit could emulate Gujjar Singh.

One other significant experience for Ranjit was that of being taken by his father on what turned out to be his last military campaign. Mahan had sought tribute from Sahib Singh Bhangi of Patiala, who refused the demand and took refuge in the fortress of Sodhra, just north of Gujranwala. From there he called on people in nearby Lahore to come to his aid. Mahan besieged the fort but failed to take it and became ill during the winter of 1791-2. As if anticipating his death, he made Ranjit, then just 11, head of the Sukerchakias and returned to Gujranwala. Delighted at the news of Mahan's illness and Ranjit's succession at such a tender age, Bhangi summoned forces from Lahore to Sodhra. However, in a stunning exhibition of bravery and cunning, Ranjit intercepted the Bhangis before they reached Sodhra and defeated them. Mahan was fortunate enough to hear of his son's extraordinary achievement just before he died.

Mahan was a vital influence upon him. Ranjit learnt all about his father's fame and how he acquired it and was in awe of his achievements. But there was more to Ranjit's inheritance than the example of his father's military prowess. As the historian J.S. Grewal has demonstrated, the future Maharaja would begin his leadership of the Sukerchakia *misl* with a basic administrative apparatus already in place. Charhat and Mahan Singh had gone to some effort to recruit local *kardars* and *thanadars* to collect revenue and maintain law and order in their new territories, providing a steady flow of funds that would be an important financial support to Ranjit Singh's early campaigns.[3] Mahan Singh's former dewan (minister), Lakhpat Rai, was also still at hand to take care of administrative matters for the young Ranjit, and this relative sense of political stability was conducive to allowing the nascent elements of a new state to emerge, as opposed to the *misl* confederacy.

Though groomed for greatness, Ranjit Singh went through his childhood uneducated. He had a lifelong love of horses and was also practised in swordsmanship, as one of the earliest of the stories told about him attests. Mahan had punished Hashmat Khan of the Chattha family for mistreating his subjects. Burning for revenge, Hashmat plotted to kill Ranjit and saw his chance one day when his spies reported that Ranjit, who was only just into his teens, was out hunting. Hashmat Khan, fully grown and very much bigger than Ranjit, rushed to the scene, ambushed Ranjit and attempted to kill the boy while he was on his horse. But his sword did not hit flesh. Ranjit swiftly counter-attacked with his own sword and slew his assailant. He then beheaded Hashmat Khan and carried the trophy back to his hunting companions.

With Ranjit out and about and too young and untutored to know how to manage an estate, Lakhpat Rai increased his influence by acting in his stead. Raj Kaur was content with this arrangement but her brother wanted to obtain control for himself and intrigued with Sada Kaur, Ranjit's mother-in-law, to bring this about. Sada Kaur's powerful personality meant that she was an influential figure within both the Kanhaya and the Sukerchakia *misls*, and authority became vested in her, Lakhpat Rai and Dal Singh, Maha's maternal uncle, with Raj Kaur as a figurehead regent. But the triumvirate was soon riven with ill-feeling, with Raj Kaur rumoured to have been intimate with Lakhpat Rai.

☙

At the age of 15, Ranjit decided to take up the reins of rule. He had the good sense to retain Lakhpat Rai as dewan and Dal Singh as principal adviser. Ranjit Singh and his mother-in-law Sada Kaur remained in an uneasy alliance, but each realised the other's importance. They showed this in the summer of 1797 when

Ranjit had to help her against the remnants of the Ramgarhia *misl*. Having faced down what was left of it, Ranjit stayed at Lahore as guest of the Bhangis and took stock of the city's defences. All this boosted his authority and prestige – and confidence. In 1798, seeing the advantage of seeking an alliance with the Nakkai *misl*, he took the *misldar's* sister, Raj Kanwar, as his second wife, just as his mother had planned.[4]

The second marriage proved to be much more successful than that with Mehtab Kaur (see p 15), with the result that Mehtab decided to move back to her original family home in Batala, about 25 miles north-east of Amritsar. She receded into the background emotionally and politically, and the rest of her life was neither long nor happy (she predeceased her mother). As J.S. Grewal notes,[5] Ranjit's two marriages extended his political power-base, and his happiness with Raj Kanwar surely sustained Ranjit in making his first crucial political conquests.

Ranjit now faced a political crisis when Lakhpat Rai died unexpectedly. Ranjit dealt with the sudden loss of support by taking on his advisers' roles himself. This is not an unusual move by powerful figures seeking yet more power, and it worked. Ranjit Singh rode out the crisis by revealing or developing new talents.

Internally the Punjab was still divided among a powerful set of nobles and *misldars*. Externally, Shah Zaman had succeeded to the Afghan throne in 1793 and soon showed an interest in the Punjab. After limited success in two initial invasions, he occupied Lahore in January 1797, but almost immediately had to return to Kabul with a contingent to confront a rebellion by his brother, Shah Mahmud. As in the past, the Sikhs took advantage of the departing forces which had earlier behaved brutally in their advance towards Lahore and savaged them on their way home, while also throwing the weakened defenders out of Lahore – achievements that boosted Ranjit Singh's reputation as the 'Hero of the Punjab'.

However, the Afghans were too powerful and Zaman returned later in 1797, vowing vengeance. Many Sikhs fled into the hills. Even the sacred shrine at the Darbar Sahib in Amritsar was left with only a token guard. However, the resolute Sada Kaur stiffened spines by reminding her compatriots at Amritsar that they owed a duty to the people who paid them. Ranjit Singh and Dal

Singh supported her and the rejuvenated gathering agreed that the city and its shrine must be properly defended. They were strengthened in their resolve by Zaman's stupidity. Despite proclaiming that he would punish only Sikhs and leave other groups alone, his army grabbed provisions from the Muslims. Zaman managed to re-enter Lahore in November 1798 and to win over key people from the Muslim, Hindu and Sikh communities: Nizam-ud-din Khan of Kasur, Sansar Chand of Kangra and Sahib Singh of Patiala, leaving only Ranjit Singh unconquered. Zaman attempted to tackle him by proceeding to Amritsar but Ranjit met him some way outside the city. This succeeded, just as his similar daring had done against the Bhangis near Sodhra. Ranjit then invested Lahore and cut off Zaman's supplies. This inspired another act of stupidity on Zaman's part: he attacked the (unarmed) local populace. The erratic Afghan leader then appeared to retrieve his position by putting out peace feelers and engaging with a number of influential Sikhs; even Ranjit Singh felt obliged to send a negotiator to join them. At this point, Zaman faced new pressures. His scheming brother Mahmud was again stirring up trouble in Kabul, while Zaman's unpaid soldiers were threatening mutiny if they were not allowed to loot in Lahore. Caught between unacceptable options, Shah Zaman took the only way to save what he could of his forces: he set out west to return home.

Ranjit Singh was always keen to exploit an advantage and Zaman had just presented him with an excellent opportunity. He joined forces with Sahib Singh of Patiala and Milkha Singh of Pindiwala to attack the fleeing Afghan forces, and Sikhs once more established their rule in Lahore. To begin with, this meant a return to rule by the Bhangis rather than new government through Ranjit Singh, but this misrule would go on to serve his interests and, therefore, those of the mass of Sikhs. The three ruling Bhangi chiefs, Chet Singh, Sahib Singh and Mohr Singh, were inept and greedy and spent much of their time indulging themselves and quarrelling. People felt crushed under their demands for taxes. The situation was aggravated by their bad relations with two influential Muslim *chaudhris* (respected local worthies) who exerted great power in Lahore, and matters were brought to a head when Chet Singh had one of their sons-in-law imprisoned.

The exasperated population of Sikhs, Muslims and Hindus alike decided that the best way to improve Lahore's unhappy situation was to appeal to Ranjit Singh to move in and take over. Ranjit was in Rasulnagar when envoys arrived with this message. He listened to it carefully but non-committally. Afterwards he sent his envoy Abdur Rahman to Lahore to negotiate with the conspirators while he consulted Sada Kaur at Batala and took his own small armed unit to Amritsar, where his and her combined force of 25,000 men prepared to march on Lahore.

Despite confirmation from Rahman that the invitation from the Lahore leaders was genuine, Ranjit went on to exhibit a typical blend of dash and caution. It was July 1799, a bad time for a military expedition as the heat was oppressive and the impending monsoons would leave the land sodden. Although this very prospect prompted him to act quickly, rather than invade with overpowering force he chose to act with stealth, making use of 6 July as the last day of the month of Muharram. By the time the religious commemorations had ended, the city folk were so tired that few realised that Ranjit Singh was within a few miles of them. Ranjit had been assured that the city gates would be open to him in the morning. By sunrise on the 7th, Sada Kaur's contingent and those of Ranjit and other commanders were in place. Ranjit blew up some of the gates and then entered through the Lahore Gate while Sada Kaur and other detachments went in through the others. Taken by surprise, two of the despised Bhangis fled while the third, Chet Singh, took refuge in the fort.

Having taken Lahore by invitation and with care and cunning, Ranjit could now give free rein to his instinct for magnanimity. He issued a proclamation[6] assuring the people of peace and freedom while informing his own forces that looting was forbidden – one report had it that he backed this up with a warning that breaches of the order would be punishable by death. He worshipped at the Royal Mosque and then at the more frequently used mosque of Wazir Khan. He then allowed the hapless – and foodless – Chet Singh to leave the city, along with his family, with a grant. Such an act might have seemed weak coming from a lesser man, but all who knew Ranjit Singh appreciated that in his case it reflected boldness and strength.

His occupation of one of the Punjab's oldest and greatest cities was a landmark event in Sikh history. Lahore, which was mostly Mughal-built, became a vital midway point between Delhi, where the Mughals occupied the throne, and the Afghan border. But its emotional importance to Sikhs was at least as strong. Guru Ram Das, who founded Amritsar, was born in Lahore, while another Guru, Arjan Dev, was martyred there. Ranjit's occupation of Lahore also served to put firmly in the shade the once-powerful Bhangi *misl*. His conquest made him the strongest ruler in northern India and, despite the jealousy of other *misldars*, laid the foundations for a sovereign state. And all this happened while Ranjit was still scarcely more than a boy – an astonishing achievement for an 18 year old.

⍟

The fact that this boy-ruler had won control of Lahore was bound to ruffle the feathers of the older chieftains. They still wielded much power in their localities and felt that their age called for respect. They banded together to get rid of Ranjit. Sahib Singh Bhangi of Gujrat, Jassa Singh Rămgarhiă, Jodh Singh of Wazirabad and Gulab Singh Bhangi of Amritsar met at Amritsar, along with Nizam-ud-din Khan who had hoped that Zaman would retain Lahore. They decided to march on Lahore in the spring of 1800.

Characteristically, Ranjit Singh elected to confront them well ahead of their intended destination, but by then his job was at least half done by his enemies themselves. Gulab Singh, who was supposed to be leading the advance, spent much of his time with his concubines and then drank himself to death. The presence of Nizam-ud-din Khan caused friction because of his Afghan sympathies. The challengers soon became a disunited rabble.

Ranjit Singh met the main force at Bhasin, ten miles east of Lahore, while a force under Sada Kaur saw off the Ramgarhias at Batala. Ranjit again exploited every opportunity for further advantage. Having returned to Lahore to show the rejoicing citizenry that he had won his latest encounter, he marched on Jammu whose chief readily surrendered and presented him with tribute. Mirowal, Narowal and Jassuwal were also conquered, and Ranjit then took Sialkot where he placed his former adviser, Dal Singh, in chains. Quite why Ranjit chose to humiliate his father's uncle and his own former adviser in this way is unclear and is the less explicable when, as it turned out, he did not dispense totally with Dal's services. However, bad blood must have arisen between Ranjit and Dal's family, for Dal's wife combined with Sahib Singh Bhangi to see off an assault on the fort of Akalgarh. However, another fort, Dilawargarh, was taken and its chief paid off.

These latest skirmishes did not go unnoticed by neighbouring powers. Zaman despatched negotiators to talk to the rival Sikhs; an English adventurer, George Thomas, who ran a statelet called Hansi in the south-east towards Delhi, prepared to advance from that direction; and a French general, Pierre Perron, who was employed by the Marathas (second only to the British as a late eighteenth-century power in northern India), was approached by the Malwa *misl* for help. Once again, the venerable Sahib Singh Bedi came to his kinsmen's rescue. He hastened to Gujerat and insisted that the internal quarrelling must cease. His standing meant that the Sikhs obeyed him, including Ranjit Singh. Nonetheless, the young ruler took advantage of the new calm by capturing Akalgarh, which had defied him. His determination and bravery was rewarded by a stroke of good fortune: a year later Perron threw Thomas out of Hansi, thereby extinguishing another threat to Ranjit.

As well as displaying a quick-thinking military mind, Ranjit also showed political cunning by appearing to take Zaman's overtures seriously. He matched the Afghan's gifts and praise with even greater offerings and thus forced Zaman to take him more seriously than any other Sikh leader. On the other hand, once the news of this dealing leaked out, the anti-Ranjit sardars and the British became worried. The latter sent an agent, Yusuf Ali, to try and persuade the Sikhs to keep their distance from Zaman. In the first recorded official British despatch on Ranjit Singh,[7] the imperial authorities at Fort William in Calcutta noted that:

> [W]e deemed it expedient that a Native Agent should be dispatched to the Court of Runjeet Singh with suitable instructions for impressing that Chief with a just sense of the danger to which he would expose the interests of himself and of his Nation, by yielding to the insidious proposals of Zemaun Shah.

However, the arrangements were made by a middle-ranking lieutenant-colonel, John Collins, who failed to appreciate the political dimension of the mission. He despatched Yusuf Ali without gifts, which was discourteous, and armed only with advice which in the circumstances came across as a lecture. The Sikhs were rightly unimpressed. However, Sada Kaur took the visitor more seriously and summoned Ranjit Singh to Amritsar for a meeting on 22 October 1800. This was dangerous for Ranjit as the city was occupied by the Bhangis, but he went all the same.

At the meeting Ranjit agreed with Yusuf Ali that the Afghans could not be trusted, but another Sikh leader, Fateh Singh Ahluwalia, demurred, saying that Zaman had reached out with the hand of friendship and it would be wrong not to respond positively. To come to a firmer conclusion, Ranjit invited Yusuf Ali to meet with him in Lahore, which was an assertion of his own importance. Ranjit knew at least as well as Yusuf Ali how untrustworthy Zaman and the Afghans were, but he did not want to be seen doing Britain's bidding.

Meanwhile, Ranjit had been establishing government, civic life and security in Lahore. After three decades of Bhangi misrule and the upheaval of Ranjit's takeover, the city was desperately in need of peace and stability. Trusted people were appointed to government offices and charities were opened. In addition to the fort being well-manned, the city's defences were reinforced by a moat. Ranjit displayed his tolerance by taking care to accommodate Lahore's large Muslim community, decreeing protection for their legal system and appointing an imam named Baksh as the chief of police. Muhammad Shahpur and Sa'adullah Chishti were named as muftis.[8] The imam recommended the appointment of *chaudhris* to positions of responsibility around the city. This practice was subsequently adopted in the rest of the kingdom. In addition, assemblies of respected elders, *panchayats*, were established in villages to settle disputes and to handle some aspects of local administration.

These and other measures were vital in enabling Lahore to enjoy peace and security again. Ranjit Singh then enjoyed another stroke of good luck, to the delight of the city. His recent military adventures had come at a price and he thought he would have to raise money from the people, which would have been unpopular. However, a stash of 20,000 gold mohurs was found in the ruins of Budhu-da-Ava outside Lahore, a treasure which amply replenished the city's coffers.

Prestige and success bring their own rewards, and Ranjit Singh's fame now began to pay off in other ways: Lahore was inundated with people seeking work with the new regime. They included young men from the families of chastened chieftains, scholars, skilled craftsmen and, most important for Ranjit Singh's career, doctors. Ranjit Singh was obsessed with his health and liked to seek remedies for all his ailments, real or supposed. A doctor called Ghulam Mohyuddin, who treated an eye condition, brought with him his trainee-clinician son, Aziz-ud-din, whose charm and way with words mesmerised Ranjit. Having flattered the Maharaja by saying that new blossoms were bursting on the tree of his fortunes, Aziz-ud-din accepted Ranjit's prompt offer of employment with further flowery language. In contrast to Ranjit, Aziz-ud-din – a Sufi Muslim – was a well-read scholar, fluent in Arabic and Persian. He was also a poet. He became Ranjit Singh's principal confidant and foreign minister. Ranjit further favoured the Fakir family by employing Aziz-ud-din's two brothers, Nur-ud-din and Imam-ud-din.

By late 1800 Ranjit was so well entrenched in Lahore that assuming the title of Maharaja seemed increasingly appealing. He delayed in case some sardars disapproved, but soon appreciated the advantages of taking the title. The approval of the Punjab's peoples would help them to sink their differences and join together in an independent state. His decision was aided by the birth of his first child, Kharak Singh, to Raj Kanwar on 9 February 1801, which meant that Ranjit could now become Maharaja with a nominated heir. As usual Sada Kaur, who might have been disappointed that it was not her daughter who had produced the first boy, took the long view and supported Ranjit's decision as being in his, her and the people's best interests.

Ranjit Singh's coronation took place amid great splendour on 12 April 1801. The date was the first day of the Baisakhi festival, New Year's Day in the Hindu calendar, which was still widely used. Although Ranjit tried to limit the accompanying ostentation, partly in deference to his non-Sikh subjects, it was another land-mark day in Sikh history. Just over a century before, Guru Gobind Singh had promised them that *Raj Karega Khalsa* (The Khalsa shall rule). Now this promise was visibly fulfilled by an indige-nous Punjabi ruler ascending the throne with due ceremony. The poor were fed well, offerings were made to shrines and other holy places and prayers were uttered in *gurudware*. Poets recited their special verses, musicians played and sang their paeans and danc-ers gyrated. A special coin struck for the investiture paid tribute to two of the great Gurus – Nanak, the founding father of Sikhism, and Gobind – with a Persian inscription:

> My largesse, my victories, my unalloyed fame,
> I owe to Guru Nanak and Guru Gobind Singh.

At the special Darbar that was held in the Fort of Lahore, the revered Sahib Singh Bedi, who was descended from Guru Nanak, applied *tilak* to Ranjit's forehead. Courtiers and others then, one by one, paid homage and presented *nazrana* (gifts) and received *khilats* (robes) in return. Ranjit Singh then made a further gesture towards Muslims, the majority group in Lahore and in the Punjab, by visiting the local Shahi Mosque as a mark of respect and a signal of goodwill. Afterwards, he rode on an elephant through the cheering crowds, handing out gold and silver coins.

Ranjit did not allow the manifestations of loyalty or the splen-dour of the occasion to distract him from the realities of Punjabi life or overwhelm his modesty. Having already ensured that the coronation coins that had been issued did not bear his name, he dispensed with his right to wear his crown or sit on a throne. Instead, he continued to preside over the Darbar sitting cross-legged in a modest chair. Far from weakening his authority, these and other instances of his humility enhanced his status as a man apart and thereby strengthened his hold on the Punjab.

Having obtained sovereign political power, Ranjit Singh further consolidated Lahore's government. To prevent any return of the widespread crime in which the Bhangis had indulged, he had offi-cials placed at strategic points around Lahore. Having ensured that the majority of the citizens who followed the Muslim faith could continue to have recourse to Sharia law, he established separate courts for the minorities – Sikhs, Hindus and some Muslims – who preferred other systems.

Continuing in this even-handed way, Ranjit did not change the time-honoured method of obtaining revenue from land cultivators annually through the village revenue collector, whose activities were overseen by the keeper of fiscal records. The sums raised were not supposed to amount to more than half the value of the gross produce. At least as important as the cultivator's land rights was his right to dig and own a well. In this part of the world where water was scarce for much of the year, this right could not be overvalued and in practice it exceeded that of the proprietor or *jagirdar* whose well rights were nominal. For centuries these arrangements had allowed agriculture to flourish in the Punjab and Ranjit Singh saw no good reason to overturn them. He contented himself with ensuring that the system was not abused and that it raised sufficient money for his fledgling state.

Nor did he overlook people's physical welfare. A hospital that treated people without charge was established in Lahore and placed under the authority of Fakir Nur-ud-din, the Maharaja's personal physician. Nur-ud-din also looked after the upkeep of the royal palaces and gardens, was one of three custodians of the key to the Treasury, commanded the arsenal at the Fort of Lahore and helped Ranjit Singh to settle judicial appeals. The third brother, Imam-ud-din, was custodian of Gobindgarh Fort, and was also responsible for the royal stables at Amritsar. This range of duties shows the young Maharaja's determination to hand responsibilities to those best able to discharge them, whatever their religion.

The new Maharaja's careful balancing act in building a secular Punjab that embraced equality gave him a new ruler's first indispensable asset: a strong political base. No matter what else a leader goes on to achieve, all his or her gains are at risk if the home base is shaky or neglected. Ranjit Singh knew that his position was still far from assured, being surrounded by rivals within and enemies without. He had to cement his authority locally before he could safely add to it elsewhere. This awareness was far more than an instinct for self-preservation: he knew his next steps would have to be of a very ambitious military nature. He needed to be strong at home if he was to venture abroad.

REACHING OUT BEYOND LAHORE

Neither the glory of capturing the great Mughal capital of Lahore, nor the acceptance of the exalted title of 'Maharaja' would be enough to cement Ranjit Singh's position as the pre-eminent ruler of the Punjab. As the nature of his conquests would soon show, he was never content with simply being the leader of the minority of Sikhs. He had assumed for himself the right and the duty to govern everyone who inhabited the Punjab. Thus, if he was not going to appear as yet another notional ruler of Lahore, he had no choice but to use the prestige of his newly conquered capital and make a show of his might across the region.

Ranjit Singh had already made a profound impression as a warrior through qualities which have been well described as follows:

> He consistently provided first-rate leadership to his army. In the battles, he invariably set his subordinates an example of personal bravery and courage of high order. It is true that no man can rise to higher command without possessing courage. Actually a military leader must develop his quality of courage into mental robustness, which can withstand the mental stress and strain with which he will be assailed under difficult circumstances. He must be able at all times to take a dispassionate view of the situations and remain unaffected by favourable or adverse circumstances. A good military leader at all times maintains an unbiased view of the situation and must be able to judge the true value of the events in a calm and detached manner.[1]

But outstanding leadership qualities would not be enough to win battles. The resources had to be in place. By the end of the eighteenth century these had begun to develop in the army under three of the Gurus – Hargobind, Har Rai and Gobind Singh – who had forged a military tradition that was now embedded in Sikhism. Sikh soldiers could march to war knowing that their religion not merely permitted but encouraged them to fight in its defence. Yet at the outset of his reign Ranjit Singh's military forces were remarkably slender. There are no verified figures,[2] but the most generous estimate suggests that he had at his disposal no more than about 5,000 soldiers, mostly horsemen; a decade later the number had tripled. Another account shows that even by 1811 the number of infantrymen (2,852) and artillerymen (1,209) amounted to only just over 4,000.[3] There is general agreement on two points: first, that the initial number was small; and, second, that it grew significantly as Ranjit's reign went on. The small initial size meant that the young Maharaja had to find allies, as he had done when he combined with Sada Kaur to take Lahore.

After securing Lahore, his next target was Nizam-ud-din Khan of the Pathan (Pashtun) city and district of Kasur, a little to the south-east of Lahore. The two men had clashed before, and Ranjit wanted a quick military solution. Nizam-ud-din fought off one assault in 1801 and the following year Ranjit made a more determined attack. Nizam-ud-din met him head-on outside Kasur's border, but was forced back and surrendered, accepting Ranjit as his sovereign and agreeing to pay a large indemnity. Much of this success with the Pathans was due to Ranjit's aide, Fateh Singh Kalianwala, who took three of Nizam-ud-din's brothers hostage to ensure that he honoured the surrender terms. Although Kasur was not finally annexed to the Maharaja's dominions until 1807, Ranjit had at least neutralised it.

Ranjit Singh then turned his attention the other way, to the north-east state of Kangra (now the Indian state of Himachal Pradesh) which was much further away from Lahore, beyond Amritsar in the Himalayan foothills. Kangra's ruler, Sansar Chand, had allied himself with Afghanistan's Shah Zaman. Able and ambitious, Sansar Chand had taken firm control of Kangra since acquiring it in 1785 and had brought the hill chiefs to heel.[4]

They supplied men for his army. Sansar Chand coveted the fertile areas of Hoshiarpur and Bijwara and hoped to neutralise the British to fulfil his ambitions. However, in 1801 he overreached himself by encroaching upon Sada Kaur's territory, Batala. Forces under Fateh Singh Ahluwalia were hastily assembled to intercept him before Ranjit Singh arrived on the scene and sent the enemy packing. Ranjit exploited this success by taking the wealthy towns of Nurpur and Naushera from Sansar Chand and giving them to Sada Kaur, an act that helped shore up their relationship.

Ranjit Singh also made sure to establish a solid and lasting friendship with Fateh Singh Ahluwalia, who had already given him substantial help and who ruled lands on both sides of the Sutlej. In April 1801 he and Fateh publicly exchanged turbans at Tarn Taran, where Ranjit bathed in the sacred waters surrounding the temple. A few days later Ranjit acknowledged Fateh even more symbolically by receiving him at a full Darbar with gun salutes. The pair went on to win over neighbouring Muslim landowners, who offered Ranjit 400 fine-bred horses as tribute.

In 1802 the two men captured several statelets beyond the Jhelum river, well to the west of Lahore. Daska, Chiniot and Phagwara were also acquired, the last being given to Fateh. Ranjit also determined to kill off the ambitions of Sansar Chand once and for all and expelled him from Hoshiarpur and Bijwara. Fateh would continue to prove a very useful ally to Ranjit Singh until they fell out in 1826. However, as with Kasur there was a delay (until 1809) before Kangra formally became part of Ranjit's empire.

Nizam-ud-din Khan then attacked some villages outside Lahore. Ranjit responded with ruthlessness followed by magnanimity. Instead of going to the villages, he brought heavy artillery to bear on Nizam-ud-din's main base of Kasur, knowing that Nizam-ud-din would rush back there. It worked: Nizam-ud-din surrendered. Then, having re-emphasised his ability to deploy a massive show of force, he pardoned Nizam-ud-din for a second time. The ruler of Kasur kept his post, though not for long because soon afterwards he was assassinated and succeeded by his brother Qutb-ud-din, who had had a hand in the killing. This usurper then tried to defy Ranjit Singh but was subdued.

Having brought within his influence territory to the near

south-east of Lahore, and an even greater amount to the north-east, the Maharaja now determined on a still more ambitious plan – to attack Multan, the loyalty of whose rulers had swung towards Afghanistan. Multan, in the south-west, rich in bazaars, mosques, shrines and tombs, is one of the most ancient cities in the subcontinent. Known as the City of Sufis from its large number of Sufi saints, it was not only completely in the opposite direction from Ranjit's recent conquests but was much further away, being over 150 miles from Lahore and not far from the stem of the Punjabi 'leaf'. The Afghans would take a dim view of this encroachment in an area that was proving increasingly loyal to them. In addition, the town was well defended. Not surprisingly, Ranjit's advisers begged him to desist. He would risk disaster taking on a fortified place whose inhabitants and neighbouring Muslim tribes could be expected to resist fiercely. However, the Maharaja was adamant, and marched his troops towards Multan.

In this case, as often, fortune favoured the bold. The advancing troops had a much easier task than anticipated and, having reached Multan's outskirts, they shelled the fort in the town's centre, rendering the town indefensible. Muzaffar Khan, the Nawab, submitted and agreed to pay an indemnity, and to forward future revenues to Lahore, not Kabul. The whole operation further secured Ranjit's growing reputation as 'the Lion of the Punjab'.

Again, just as he did not initially take formal possession of Kasur and Kangra, Ranjit Singh did not permanently occupy Multan. Such a step would have been beyond his resources at this stage. It was enough to show that he could harass and subdue Multan's defenders, if only temporarily. But this sort of hit-and-run exercise left him less than satisfied and in December 1802 he resolved to capture one big, symbolic prize – the holy city of Amritsar.

Amritsar was arguably the most important city for Ranjit to acquire as an assertion of his kingship over his growing dominion. Although it acknowledged Lahore as the region's largest city, Amritsar was the Punjab's most important economic centre. It was the commercial gateway to northern India and a hive of trading activity in silks, spices, tea, hides and – as Ranjit well knew – armaments. But far more important to Sikhs was Amritsar's religious status. Nowhere else had the standing of this sacred place where Sikhs bathed in holy waters and made offerings. As an empire-builder, Ranjit Singh had to acquire it.

As with earlier attempts to gain territory, he was aided by division within. Amritsar was under the control of about a dozen quarrelling families whose armed tax collectors harassed businesses by squeezing whatever they could from them. Resentful locals, well aware of Ranjit Singh's praiseworthy policy in Lahore, made clear that they wanted him to do the same with Amritsar. Matters came to a head when Aroor Mal, the city's main banker, begged Ranjit to take over and establish civic order. Late in 1802, he did so, aided by forces under Sada Kaur and Fateh Singh Ahluwalia. They methodically picked off the disunited sardars one by one until Mai Sukhan, the widow of the Bhangi *misldar* and the only one to put up much resistance, was bought off with a pension.

Amritsar joyously welcomed the Maharaja, increasing his fame and prestige. Ranjit justified the hopes that the city placed in him. He brought Amritsar under a single administration and made it his summer capital, spending four months a year there. He enhanced the city's high commercial status and made it a city of gardens and religious establishments (*akharas*). His rule in the region was strengthened militarily by obtaining the powerful fort at Govindgarh and its five big cannons. These included the huge Zam Zama ('Taker of Strongholds') gun, a fabulous weapon 14 feet 4.5 inches long with a 9.5 inch bore, one of two produced in Lahore in 1757, probably the largest ever made in the subcontinent. It had already seen action many times with half a dozen owners.

During his reign, Ranjit Singh had the domes and the outer upper walls of Amritsar's Harmandir Sahib ('Temple of God', also known as the Darbar Sahib) plated with gold taken from Mughal buildings in Lahore, from which it derives its present alternative name, the Golden Temple. (Amritsar's vast Maharaja Ranjit Singh Panorama complex, opened in 2006, includes a painting of Ranjit, accompanied by his ministers, supervising the gold-plating work.) He also funded the building's superb marble-work. At various times he and other members of the royal family presented the holy place with gold-plated doors, a gold umbrella with a peacock encrusted with sapphire and pearls, a string of pearls, a headband of pearls and a canopy made from rare cloth embroidered with gold and silver.

Ranjit's acquisition of Amritsar also won him the services of a gifted soldier, Phula Singh, whose thousands of Nihang ('crocodile' in Persian) followers had been important and possibly decisive in securing Amritsar for Ranjit Singh. The Nihang was an order of celibate warriors created by Guru Gobind Singh to serve and protect the Khalsa. Renowned for their martial skills and fight-to-the-death courage, they were supposedly named after the way crocodiles seize their prey. Thereafter, Phula Singh allied himself to the Maharaja and generally provided further good service, save for one or two occasions when his zeal strained Ranjit's patience. Ranjit disliked fanaticism, but Phula Singh and his Nihangs would prove extremely useful additions to his army.

There was a further and unexpected bonus to the expedition. Deserters from the East India Company were among those who flocked to the Maharaja's colours. Even more important than their numbers, Ranjit Singh noticed their discipline – it was the first time he had seen soldiers march in step and assemble in formation following crisp, shouted instructions. Ranjit determined to borrow from this tradition. He not only employed the men on attractive terms but, with typical forward thinking, sent some Sikhs over to serve the British and learn more from them. All in all, the taking of Amritsar had proved hugely advantageous.

One other development of more personal importance made 1802 a highly significant year for him. He met and fell in love with a Muslim dancing girl called Moran. This young girl of spirit and charm captivated Ranjit – still only 22 – with the heady emotional force that first love inflicts on young men. Ranjit had never before experienced the romance or the close companionship that she gave him. Their combination was almost overpowering for Ranjit, the more so as he had been an only child. The pair were so uninhibited together that, with Ranjit being of high status, they had to meet in secret near to Moran's village of Makhanpur between Amritsar and Lahore.[5] Once when she was on her way to meet him there, her slipper fell into a canal. Moran was annoyed by this inconvenience, so Ranjit had a bridge built across the canal for her to walk on.

As well as being his first love, she was possibly the love of his life, for he risked his reputation over her when they were seen riding together in a drunken state on an elephant. The Sikh priests decided they could not put up with this sort of behaviour unbecoming of their Maharaja. They summoned him to the Golden Temple and sentenced him to a public flogging. Ranjit Singh did not object to this extraordinary decision, but calmly accepted it. His humility won over the judges. They reduced his punishment to a fine and one notional stroke across his back. Nonetheless, Moran remained the apple of Ranjit's eye. Although she did not exert political influence, she quickly persuaded the Maharaja to produce a coin in their joint honour. It bore the effigy of a dancing girl and the word *mor* ('peacock') in the shape of a peacock's tail.

Moran's influence was lasting. Ranjit never lost his affection for her. Fakir Syed Waheed-ud-din, a descendant of Aziz-ud-din and his two brothers, has recorded the Maharaja's reaction at the start of the Rupar summit of 1831 when the British governor-general, Lord Bentinck, escorted Lady Bentinck from the boat.[6] Despite this being a moment of high importance – the first meeting between two chiefs of state, when first impressions mattered greatly – Ranjit's first thought was of Moran. The Lahore diarist Sohan Lal Suri wrote, 'The Maharaja said that at that moment he was reminded of Bibi Moran, for he had exactly the same kind of love and unity with her and could not bear separation from her even for a moment.'

Nonetheless, his passion to rule always overrode that of romance. In 1811 Ranjit sent Moran away to Pathankot in the far north-west.[7] She was reported to be still living there in 1835. This suggests that he found her lively and independent manner too much of a distraction from governance and conquering. Yet she is believed to have always remained the Maharaja's favourite. A mosque near Lahore was named after her, as was a village near Amritsar. The village of Pul Kanjari where Ranjit had the bridge built for her is now being promoted as a tourist attraction. The publicity surrounding this venture has even created a swell of feeling in favour of the village being renamed Pul Moran.[8]

Moran is portrayed in only a few images, and these show her as studious, even dull-looking, seated and with her hands raised to her chin in silent devotion – hardly a fair reflection of the feelings she aroused in a Maharaja who liked to have fun and who found in Moran a challenging spirit. Yet this image reflects the role of women generally in political life under Ranjit Singh. As Waheed-ud-din notes,[9] Moran and certain family relatives apart, women generally in his time played no prominent part in Punjabi politics. The revolutionary Sikh stress upon equality was not quite so revolutionary in practice.

In 1803, Ranjit Singh resumed his military activities. Having secured Kasur, Kangra, Multan and Amritsar, he turned to the south-west, to Ahmed Khan of Jhang who was refusing to pay tribute. Helped again by Fateh Singh Ahluwalia, and taking advantage of a prevailing civil war in Afghanistan, the Maharaja's troops smashed into the town and plundered its riches. Ahmed Khan fled, not realising that the victor was not actually after Jhang for his own personal greed but to obtain its loyalty. Once he had absorbed this fact, he was allowed to return as a vassal. His allies who ran Uch, Sahiwal and Garh Maharaja ended up in similar positions, giving Ranjit Singh an empire that now stretched some 450 miles from Amritsar.

☙

One of the many remarkable facets of Ranjit Singh's character was that he took a keen interest in administration and developed his own set of beliefs on how his Punjab should be governed, despite leading an outdoors life of riding, hunting and warring, and despite his lack of formal tutoring. Yet Ranjit's early interest in the intricacies of governance strongly suggests that adults around him ensured that he knew what his role as ruler would entail.

His leadership qualities made up for his lack of formal education. Fearless and decisive, he gave his followers confidence in his instructions. He knew, with a skill that amounted to genius, how to match the right men to the right jobs. In military matters, his boldness, magnetism and tireless spirit combined with a commitment to good planning and avoiding waste of lives as well as ammunition. As a nineteenth-century European commentator quoted by T.R. Sharma put it:

He always knew exactly how far he should go. However large and far-reaching his ultimate design might be, immediate measures were always practicable. He made each step secure before he took the next, never challenging an enemy till he felt the chances of a contest would be in his favour.[10]

But reshaping the army was no easy matter. The Khalsa had existed for more than a century and had strong and highly conservative traditions. Though he managed to get new recruits to wear the Sepoy cap and all soldiers to adopt a decent uniform, on other matters he was less successful. For example, older soldiers refused to exchange their turbans for caps, and scorned the notion of being paid money.[11] To them, it was enough to serve as a soldier and have a patch of land (a *puttidar*).

The fact that at the start of his reign Ranjit commanded a small force of no more than about 5,000 men, mostly horsemen, was another source of tension. One way in which Ranjit wanted to modernise the army was by boosting the numbers of infantrymen.[12] The cavalrymen were aghast at this idea and attempted to block it by mocking new foot soldiers. Ranjit faced them down by giving the infantrymen prizes, even *jagirs*,[13] and he went out of his way to praise them on parade. Budding recruits among the watching public got the message. Aided by the advantage that the infantry gave in battle, this section of the army had become popular and accepted within a decade.

Ranjit also decided to augment the artillery. At this time, before Punjabis had seen the British army in action, very few indigenous people understood the art and science of gunnery. He allocated vast sums of money to training and to foundries. Once again, the revolutionary scale of his intentions dismayed the old guard. The infantry comprised mainly Hindus, Gurkhas and Afghans.[14] In correcting the imbalance, it was important to move slowly and avoid antagonising any one group by seeming to favour another. The Sikh element did not become pronounced until about 1818, 16 years after his accession.

One example of how he ensured early improvement was through the selection of appropriate commanders. Fateh Singh Ahluwalia had been vital in the taking of Amritsar; now he enlisted the support of Mokham Chand, whom he had noticed in action in 1803. In 1806 Mokham Chand became commander-in-chief of the Sikh forces, an office he would perform brilliantly until his death in 1814, having taken a major role in increasing Ranjit's political and military power. (Mokham Chand's son Moti Ram and grandson Ram Dyal also went on to serve in the army.)

On the non-military side, Ranjit Singh devoted much time and energy to civil administration, with somewhat controversial results. One nineteenth-century British commentator, who served as a civil servant in India after Ranjit Singh's time, bluntly dismissed Punjabi administration as 'a simple process of squeezing out of the unhappy peasant every rupee that he could be made to disgorge',[15] while in the 1920s an Asian commentator asserted that Ranjit was primarily a conqueror who made no bold administrative innovations.[16] Others are more positive. Radha Sharma concludes that the Maharaja wielded an extraordinary command over all departments.[17] Sir Alexander Burnes, a British observer whom we shall come across again, noted that the Maharaja conducted all the affairs of his kingdom with energy, vigour and consideration.[18] Finally, another Asian observer described Ranjit Singh's government as 'a pure and unmitigated despotism'[19] – not a damning criticism, but (as is clear from his commentary) a recommendation for transforming the Punjab into a military monarchy.

How to strike the right balance? Let us begin by surveying the situation at the time of the Maharaja's accession. Until well into his reign, the Punjab was mainly governed through the 12 *misldars*, each of whom appointed his own officials and army commanders. These were usually granted *jagirs* rather than paid in cash. They collected land revenue, but showed little interest in civil and financial administration,[20] which they mostly delegated to their Hindu accountants and managers, while the law remained the Mughal system handled by Muslims.

In the previous chapter, we have already observed how the Maharaja derived many benefits from inheriting the basis of an administrative structure from his father and grandfather. Ranjit Singh's determination to unify the Punjab certainly created a more centralised governing system, as the power of the other *misls* diminished. By 1805 Ranjit had taken advantage of the *misls'* decline to annex two territories in the Rachna Doab and in the Jalandhar Doab.[21] In so doing he developed vassalage, which had long existed, into a major instrument of power, acquiring vassals by the score.[22] Only a few chiefs felt independent enough to attend a conference of the Panth's leaders in Amritsar to discuss the threat posed by the arrival in the Punjab of Jaswant Rao Holkar, the one remaining Maratha chief, who had fled from Lord Lake, commander-in-chief of the British army in India. From then on, the *misldars* became subordinate, appointments of local officials and provincial governors being increasingly made in Lahore.

This last factor serves to make a significant point about administration in the region at this time. The whole area had long been ravaged by one marauding invader after another. For 60 or 70 years before Ranjit's time, the Punjab itself had been in turmoil. None of the Punjabi provinces was within his control at the start. Then for much of his time as ruler the area he ruled was expanding. This semi-permanent state of disruption and transition made the task of creating orderly administration a daunting one.

To begin with, Ranjit worked from his main base, the Lahore Darbar. The purpose of the Darbar was threefold: to allow ministers and courtiers to advise, to be heard and held to account; to afford the common people access to the Maharaja; and to act as a focal point for the Punjab as a political entity. As often as possible, the Darbar convened daily, sometimes in the capital, sometimes just outside it, in places like the Musamman Burj, an octagonal tower in the Lahore Fort, the nearby Hazuri Bagh gardens (in which he built a white marble pavilion) and the splendid Shalamar Gardens which had been erected by the Mughals in the mid-1600s (and which are now a UNESCO World Heritage Site). Sometimes the Maharaja held them in the shade from trees or on open ground under a canopy.

Ranjit Singh appeared at these sessions unassumingly dressed in plain silk or in white muslin. He also wore little jewellery. He did not preside from his throne, preferring to sit cross-legged in a low, ordinary chair. He did not display a royal emblem on his turban. Notwithstanding his status as Maharaja, his modesty was entirely in keeping with the republican nature of Sikhism, and in total contrast to the way in which Oriental potentates normally presented themselves.

Yet within this remarkably modest setting the court was an impressive picture of grandeur. The Maharaja's chair might have looked modest but it was laced with gold. He liked his advisers to be expensively dressed, adorned with gorgeous jewels. The Darbar canopy was formed of Kashmir shawls inlaid with silver, while equally sumptuous shawl carpets covered the floor. A Briton, General Sir Henry Fane, visited Punjab in 1837 to attend the wedding of Ranjit Singh's grandson, and was guest of honour at a special Darbar there as the highest-ranking British representative. He compared the spectacle to a gala night at the opera.[23] Where the occasion called for any special display of pomp the scene was even grander. A huge encampment of tents in crimson and gold stretched as far as the eye could see. The Maharaja would leave his tent amid booming cannon fire, ranks of horsemen glitteringly arrayed would move majestically towards elephants bearing important dignitaries, and column after column of troops in a blaze of colours would appear in the distance. Beyond them would be a sea of ordinary people, there to catch what they could of the drama. As the horses drew towards the elephants, everyone's eyes naturally fell upon the main character astride his own elephant, less ostentatiously attired than those around him, his innate modesty amid majesty making them feel proud to serve him.

Ranjit prepared himself well for the Darbar. After rising early, he devoted time to outdoor exercise, in all weathers, and religious observances, before he turned to official matters, speaking with advisers. He had intelligence officers distributed around his domains so that information could be brought to his advisers promptly, the news being read to him every morning. Alongside his modest appearance, Ranjit was keen that etiquette and decorum were established for Darbar sessions so that ministers, advisers and common people alike could have an opportunity to be heard. None spoke without an indication from him to do so. Only a very few people were allowed to sit on chairs near to him. Ordinary people would bow and make customary offers of gifts – cash, fruits, shawls, horses, swords and pistols – which became a useful form of state income. Courtiers and visiting tributaries, too, were expected to arrive bearing gifts.

At the same time, Ranjit Singh's wish to limit formality extended to him being addressed merely as 'Singh Sahib', which was a term applicable to any Sikh noble.[24] Some of the older chiefs occasionally just called him 'Brother'. It was some time before he accepted being called by his actual title. He frequently reminded his courtiers that the Guru – the holy writ – was the true king and that he was only the Guru's humble servant. But despite his being content with informality, the courtiers invariably addressed him with a studied respect.

To begin with, official business was conducted through verbal orders, in Persian. (In later years, Ranjit used Hindustani in discussions with the British.[25]) The quality of discussion and decision-making was high from the start. One reason for this was the presence of Aziz-ud-din. Ranjit employed the polished Aziz-ud-din in many crucial diplomatic negotiations, and over the years he became the kingdom's most respected statesman. In 1803 an astute dewan called Devi Das was appointed to keep the records of major financial transactions, and his efforts smoothed the way for Kirpa Ram, another dewan well-versed in finance, to develop a more sophisticated system from 1805.

The unique difficulties of being the ruler of a new and rapidly growing kingdom were eased by Ranjit's willingness to immerse himself in detail. He dealt with some relatively basic business such as approving civil and military accounts as well as more strategic matters such as settling revenue allocations and appointing officials.

In the afternoons, after a short post-Darbar siesta, the Maharaja would listen to readings of the Granth for an hour and a half before inspecting troops, receiving petitions or discharging other tasks with which only he as Maharaja could deal. Ranjit followed much the same routine every day (scorning any possible assassination attempt).

In all this he seemed to be able to forget his unprepossessing countenance – his swarthy, pock-marked complexion, disfigured face, broad head, large forehead, short arms and small hands. He was so short that he sometimes needed an attendant to help him up on to a horse. Moran was reported to have teased him about his appearance by asking him where he was when God had been distributing good looks. 'Looking for my kingdom,' replied Ranjit, unfazed. None of this affected Ranjit's authority in the Darbar. His animated and occasionally fiery manner, his energy and his decisiveness made his looks irrelevant.

ↄ

Ranjit Singh's appeal lay in his directness. He was fearless, never embarrassed, animated, always full of questions, particularly with foreigners, and energetic. He was never more alive than when on a horse. He once rode 102 miles in a day. In a display of horsemanship, he would canter up to someone holding a lemon and slice it in half without touching the person with his sword. That he was held in such awe was in large measure due to his riding skill, which was of supreme importance at a time when horses were vital for hunting, travel, agriculture and transporting men, equipment and supplies to war. True, elephants were of use where lions or tigers roamed, and an elephant's size and slow gait conferred grandeur. But no animal was more important than a good horse. Indoors, he had other less attractive habits. He enjoyed watching dancing girls. Like other Asiatic monarchs, he kept a large number of them and paid handsomely to ensure that they were always on hand. The women did more than just dance.[26] Ranjit, who became notorious for his drinking bouts, plied them with money and drink which caused them to quarrel and fight, much to his delight. He would ply his guests with concoctions of brandy, musk, opium, plants and herbs, or made from raisins and ground-up pearls. The effects were worsened when his drinking bouts were accompanied by no food except fat quails stuffed with spices. Many suffered accordingly.

Yet Ranjit Singh was also a religious man who devoted hours each day to religious affairs.[27] After rising and saying prayers, he would bathe and dress and then go to the prayer room to listen to the first recitation.[28] Wherever he might be, a compartment was set aside for these purposes and to safeguard the Granth. The readers were well looked after, being allocated a *jagir*, property and abundant daily rations. Occasionally, Ranjit would have two slips of paper placed on the Granth, one stating what he would like to do and the other showing the opposite. Someone would be asked to retrieve one of them for him. Ranjit would then accept whichever of the two was presented as a command from God. He ensured that soldiers' Granths were closely guarded on expeditions. All in all, he had a profound reverence for all that was holy or spiritual.[29]

He gave generous funds to religious buildings, Sikh, Hindu or Muslim. Ranjit set aside land for a Muslim shrine, Ismail alias Wadda, near to the Shalamar Gardens, often visited religious sites, and venerated the Jawalaji and Kangraji temples in the Kangra region. He celebrated the monthly Sankranti festival by visiting Amritsar and offering the Sikh prayer Ardas at the Darbar Sahib. Afterwards, cows, horses, buffalos, gold and silver were distributed to the poor and needy. Such distributions were also made on the autumn Diwali day (the Sikh and Hindu Festival of Light) and the Hindu Dusserah day.

All this was accompanied by stories of kindness. He cherished children, and liked to feed birds from his own hand. He would release a captured tiger cub rather than kill it. Foreign dignitaries were impressed by the fact that he abolished slavery, which was still widely practised in Asia and across the world, and did not impose the death penalty – an exceptional position to take at the time, and one of the finest aspects of his rule.[30] This was not pure humanity: it had a political purpose – to reduce inter-faith friction. It did not mean that his punishments were always mild, for he allowed corporal punishment and mutilation and tolerated capital punishment by one of his provincial governors.

But another far more important aspect of Ranjit's religious faith was its tolerance. Unlike either Islam or Christianity, Sikhism was not a missionary religion. Sikhs believed utterly in their religion and were only too happy for others to join them, but they did not try to coerce anyone to do so. Nor did they view non-Sikhs with contempt. This attitude underpinned Ranjit Singh's entire religious outlook. He regarded everyone in the Punjab as equal before the Universal God (Ik Onkar). And his people knew it. Whatever opinion the non-believers might have of Sikhism, those who served under Ranjit could trust him. As a result, many served for long periods, such as Gurmukh Singh, a Sikh who was in office from 1780 and remained army paymaster for all of Ranjit's rule, and the three Fakir brothers, who were also there almost from the start.

Historians also have to note Ranjit's more intimate relationships, because several of his many wives, his children and an adopted child were of occasional significance in Punjabi civil and military affairs while he was Maharaja, and had quite dramatic significance after his death. Ranjit Singh had in his harem over 40 women, which in Asian monarchical circles was conservative. Five of the wives are known to have produced children, though only two princes are considered by historians to have been formally acknowledged by the Maharaja as legitimate sons: Kharak Singh (the only one known to be Ranjit's actual son) and Duleep Singh. Mehtab Kaur reportedly bore him three sons, Princes Isher (who died in infancy), Sher and Tara. However, some accounts suggest that Mehtab was barren and that the offspring were actually those of Mehtab's mother, Sada Kaur, and conceived through her concern to maintain her influence over Ranjit. Be that as it may, Raj Kaur definitely gave birth to Kharak, Ranjit's first child whom he later appointed as his heir. Three so-called junior queens also had sons. Rattan Kaur reputedly bore Prince Multana Singh; and Daya Kaur produced Princes Kashmira and Peshaura Singh. Finally, in 1838 Rani Jindan gave birth to Duleep (see Postscript). Some of these children played significant roles in Ranjit's life, but of others little is known.[31]

Prince Kharak, the nominated heir, was born in 1802 and turned out to be a grave disappointment, being unimaginative and unadventurous. He inherited his father's physical ungainliness, which would not have mattered if he had possessed his other qualities. But the boy had none that mattered. He was quite pious, which aroused a certain admiration, but lacked guile, and the art of statecraft was quite beyond him. He also became dependent on opium. His limitations weighed heavily upon the Maharaja's shoulders. Two instances of Kharak's naivety illustrate why Ranjit and court officials worried about his capacity to take over as ruler.[32] In the first, which evidently occurred late in Ranjit Singh's life, the Maharaja was trying to encourage Kharak to pay attention to affairs so as to be in a better position to handle them on his accession. To make the point that the time might not be far off, Ranjit said, 'Look at my grey beard, my son.' But instead of grasping his father's meaning the prince simply felt the beard and said, 'By God, it has all gone grey.' On the second occasion, Kharak was inspecting the royal stables in the company of Nur-ud-din and asked the keeper of the stable if one of the horses there had been killed in the Battle of Naushera. Despite his inadequacies, Prince Kharak went on several military expeditions of which he was nominally in charge. And he benefited by being married to a dauntless woman called Chand Kaur, who bore Prince Nau Nihal Singh, a favourite of Ranjit's.

Sher Singh, born in 1807, had a livelier spirit and more gumption than his older half-brother. Bright and a good soldier, he (like Kharak) was allowed to sit on a chair in the Darbar. A devotee of field sports he was popular both at court and with the army, and after 1820 his father allocated to him several civil and military assignments. He had weaknesses, being of capricious temperament and short on political tact, but overall he was tough enough to eventually become Maharaja. He also had some of Ranjit's generous instincts. However, he could not weather the storms that blew around him and everyone else in the wake of Ranjit's death and was killed in 1843, three years after Kharak died. Sher's brother Tara led a much quieter life outside of state matters and perhaps as a result lived on for over 20 years after his father's death.

∽

Ranjit also doted on Hira Singh, son of Raja Dhian Singh Dogra who became the Punjab's prime minister. Born in 1818, Hira Singh's upbringing took place virtually under the Maharaja's eye. Bright, handsome and with a winning manner, the boy excelled in riding, swordsmanship and musketry. Not surprisingly, therefore, Ranjit grew to like and admire him. As a young boy his gracious manner impressed everyone, the more so when he spoke. In later life, Hira Singh was the only person at court who was allowed to speak without the Maharaja giving a signal.

4

ENTER THE BRITISH

The first decade of Ranjit Singh's rule was marked by considerable success. Internally, he consolidated his rule by suppressing several *misls* – the Nakkais who were near Lahore, the Faizalpurias on either side of the Sutlej, and the Dalle-walias in the Jalandhar Doab. In terms of foreign affairs, a major development secured the young Maharaja's standing. In 1805 the British forced the remaining Maratha leader Jaswant Rao Holkar into the Punjab, and the Punjabi government feared a British inva-sion. Luckily the governor-general, Lord Cornwallis, hesitated and Ranjit Singh took advantage of this to mediate between him and Holkar. In the 1806 Treaty of Lahore Ranjit's government agreed not to 'hold any further connection with' Holkar. The terms appeared to put Ranjit in his place but in fact the treaty confirmed his status as head of an independent state. It also amounted to a warning to Holkar, whom Ranjit loathed.[1]

The following year, the British again expressed goodwill,[2] noting that 'the approach of the Rajah of Lahore towards the north-western confines' of British territories 'is not likely to occa-sion any agitation or disturbance'. They had reason to be cautious, for events had turned against them internationally. Only two years had passed since the Royal Navy had beaten the French at the Battle of Trafalgar, but France was still the main force in Europe and beyond. Napoleon Bonaparte had made peace with Russia, and Russia was now antagonistic to Britain. She joined Napole-on's Continental System of trade discrimination against the British Empire, and instigated war between Finland and Sweden in order to force Sweden, too, to join the anti-British system. Russia was an enemy of Persia, and so the Franco-Russian rapprochement inspired Britain to approach Persia. This resulted in the preliminary Treaty of Tehran of March 1809, by which Britain agreed to train and equip Persian infantrymen and to pay a subsidy should Persia be invaded by a European power, or to mediate if that power was at peace with Britain. Although Russia had made peace overtures, which the British supported, these developments strengthened Persia's determination to continue fighting Russia.

Fearing that Napoleon harboured aggressive intentions towards India, the British backed up their activity in Persia with missions to Afghanistan and the Punjab. In June 1809, Lord (Mountstuart) Elphinstone secured a treaty in Kabul that served to allay British fears about a possible French invasion. British diplomacy in this massive area – from Persia to India – appeared extraordinarily successful. In the space of just three months, three countries had signed friendly agreements with Britain: Persia in March, the Punjab in April and Afghanistan in June. The diplomatic drive was the opening of what later would come to be called the Great Game, the long, stealthy struggle mainly with Russia to maintain and expand British influence across southern Asia, with indigenous peoples as the supporting cast. The British wanted to keep the two states of Persia and Afghanistan well disposed and untouched by the blandishments of Russia and France.

Uncertainty ruled. For instance, while the Persian situation became even better for Britain after 1809, the Afghan treaty proved stillborn when the ruler Shah Shuja was overthrown by forces loyal to his brother Mahmud. But Afghanistan's leaders were notoriously unpredictable: Mahmud had had his other brother Zaman blinded to keep him out of power. The wretched Zaman, though defeated by Ranjit Singh, was treated far worse by his own family. In fact, Zaman later obtained sanctuary from Ranjit.

The result of the third British mission to the Punjab was a landmark in Ranjit Singh's career. Despite being untutored in diplomacy, he performed with skill throughout the negotiations. He did not get his way completely, but nor did they, and he achieved an enhanced standing for himself and his country, winning respect from the British for resisting their attempts to coerce him.

The agreement that emerged was also a big stepping-stone for

Charles Metcalfe whom in 1808 Lord (Gilbert) Minto, Cornwallis's successor as governor-general of India, had picked as Britain's envoy to the court of Lahore. Metcalfe was one of the most brilliant young men of his age. Indian-born, he had lived and been educated in England before returning to India to work in the East India Company. He studied Oriental languages and was appointed political assistant to General Lake, joining Lake's expedition against Holkar. Metcalfe's physical stamina and diplomatic skills were remarkable. At 23, four years younger than Ranjit, he was the man to limit Ranjit's territorial ambitions. During the Second Anglo-Maratha War of 1803 to 1805, some Cis-Sutlej states had pledged allegiance to General Lake. As a result, Britain's north-western Indian frontier was extended to the Jumna (sometimes known as the Yamuna, or the Jamna). British attention then began to switch to the Cis-Sutlej region which lay between the Sutlej to the north, the Himalayas to the east, the Jumna and the Delhi area to the south and the Sirsa area west of Delhi.

Early in 1808 Ranjit Singh and Minto had exchanged letters of goodwill, although Minto had taken a superior tone which the British never seemed to realise was bound to annoy a man who regarded himself as at least their equal. At the start of his letter Minto had said, 'The report which the Right Honorable Lord Lake made of your character and conduct when he had the pleasure of meeting you, impressed this Government with a high sense of your good qualities.'[3] In February, Archibald Seton, British Resident in Delhi, suggested to Minto that Britain should respond to a plan by Ranjit Singh to bathe in the river Ganges in eastern India by receiving him with 'acts of kindness and consideration'.[4] Although the Maharaja cancelled his plan, he remained in British minds when several Malwa chiefs came to visit Seton seeking protection. The British turned them down. Ranjit Singh then invited the chiefs to Amritsar and assured them that he would not annex their territories. He had no wish to provoke the British but was suspicious of their intentions. He assumed they desired to extend their land in his direction. They were wooing not only him but the Afghans, the bane of the Sikhs. And he did not share Britain's worries over Russian and/or French intentions towards the subcontinent. He knew that the British were, in part, making overtures to him because they had no choice: they needed to traverse the Punjab in order to reach Afghanistan.

British protestations of sincerity were made by Neil Benjamin Edmonstone, chief secretary to the government in India, when he proposed Metcalfe's mission. Edmonstone's letter to Ranjit Singh affirmed:

> Although the relations of friendship have at all times subsisted between the British Government and you, especially since the march of the British Troops under the command of the Right Honourable Lord Lake into the Punjab, and the conclusions of engagements with you ... yet [we are] desirous of improving, in a still greater degree, the foundations of mutual harmony and good understanding.[5]

Edmonstone also wrote to Metcalfe with instructions, but without setting out specific negotiating positions beyond asking Metcalfe to obtain Ranjit Singh's cooperation over British troops marching through the Punjab. He indicated that it was pointless to take up fixed positions because it 'was impossible ... to anticipate the demands which might be made'. The chief motive for the mission was the 'intrigues and extortions of the French Embassy in Persia'.

Ranjit Singh proved up to handling Edmonstone's intimidating tone. His reply, in Persian and received by the British on 6 July, began solicitously, referring to 'my desire for a joyful meeting ... I am praying to Heaven to receive agreeable accounts of your Lordship's health and welfare ... It is the wish of my heart that, the foundations for a sincere and cordial friendship ...' and so on. If the British liked Ranjit's welcoming words for Metcalfe's mission, their eyebrows would have furrowed when they came to his preferred basis for an agreement. His first stipulation was that, 'The Country on this side of the River Jumna, with the exception of the stations occupied by the English, is subject to my authority – Let it remain so.' Second, 'Whoever is my Enemy shall be the Enemy of the English.' Third, 'The reports of interested persons, until duly investigated, shall produce no misunderstanding between [us].' Fourth, 'Whoever shall be an Enemy of this state and of the British Government shall be expelled by the joint endeavours of both states.' And fifth, 'The relations of amity and friendship, as established by Treaty, shall continue daily to improve from generation to generation.'

These points illustrated how carefully the Darbar had considered Britain's overtures. The Punjabis had decided that the British initiative must receive a positive response, since the British had said nothing threatening and they were already a big regional power. However, the Maharaja was equally concerned *not* to receive Metcalfe without making clear his expectations. First, his notion of the territory adjacent to British India that came under his authority extended beyond the Sutlej and up to the Jumna, save for the British 'stations'. Second, if the British wanted to offer friendship then they themselves could side against the Punjab's enemies – and the most obvious enemy was Afghanistan with which the British also wanted friendship. Ranjit Singh was keen to avoid their Afghanistan policy impacting badly upon his Punjab. Ranjit's third point was aimed at people such as the Malwa chiefs who had sought British protection. He knew he still had many existing and potential enemies; again, the British could help him to neutralise them. His fourth stipulation would make that all the more certain. Finally, he wanted not just an agreement but a treaty.

Edmonstone affected to be unconcerned by Ranjit's letter. On 11 July he replied with gratitude but said that, as Metcalfe was going to negotiate with the Maharaja, there was no need to address specific matters in his response. He also wrote to Metcalfe saying that there was no cause to readdress the river boundary issue as 'the case has been specifically provided for' in his letter of instructions. In fact it had not, and an anxious Metcalfe was not about to go to the Maharaja without seeking a more solid basis to the negotiations. He pointed out that Ranjit Singh 'occasionally makes incursions upon the territories of his neighbours … and sometimes pays an unwelcome visit to the petty states between the Jumna and the Sutlej'. Metcalfe wanted a ruling that he should not accompany Ranjit on such visits lest that appear supportive of his claim to the territories. Edmonstone wrote back on 11 August to say that Minto had agreed that Metcalfe should always 'apply to Government for orders' if Ranjit Singh should ever visit 'the neighbouring Chiefs'. Metcalfe was clearly not being given total freedom to act as he wished.

Armed with a briefing on Ranjit Singh and his administration, the tenor of which was broadly favourable towards the Maharaja, Charles Metcalfe arrived in the Punjab early in August. Ranjit had meanwhile arranged some actions which were designed to put Metcalfe in his place as a subordinate. First, he had Imam-ud-din welcome Metcalfe in Patiala, halfway between Delhi and Lahore and some way from Metcalfe's ultimate destination, so as to show that the Maharaja's rule reached beyond the capital. Simultaneously, invitations went out to several Malwais to meet with the Maharaja in Lahore. Metcalfe was not amused by the latter initiative and warned the Malwa chiefs not to incur British displeasure. He himself received some Malwais, who fanned the flames of ill-feeling by telling him that Ranjit was planning to attack the British as well as them. Imam-ud-din's assurance that there was no such plan did not mollify him. The envoy's suspicions increased when he was still not received by Ranjit Singh but by Mokham Chand and Fatch Singh Ahluwalia. By the time he at last met Ranjit himself near Kasur on 12 September, Metcalfe's mood was sulphurous. He made clear his opinion that as His Majesty's Government's representative he had been received with scant courtesy. He complained, too, that his mission force had been badly placed on a dry river bed.

The Maharaja, having already made his point, was soothing in response. He embraced Metcalfe and other members of his retinue and presented them with gifts. No business was conducted at this initial encounter but, tired from the journey and somewhat disorientated by Ranjit's earlier actions, Metcalfe was careless enough while at Kasur to again meet some Malwais. That in turn displeased the Maharaja who abruptly told Metcalfe that he expected him to depart within days, adding that his 'affairs of state must be attended to'.[6] This ultimatum added to the distaste which Metcalfe was showing in his reports to Calcutta.[7] After the first meeting with Ranjit he had written to Edmonstone complaining that 'the Rank and Dignity of the Government which I have the honour to represent, required that the Raja should come ... to meet the Mission ... He did not come into my wishes in that respect.'[8] On 18 September he apprised Edmonstone of 'an extraordinary

instance of [Ranjit's] suspicion and disrespect'. Metcalfe continued to keep his seniors closely informed, reporting not just on the
talks but on aspects of the Punjab, its rulers and institutions.

Metcalfe sensibly kept the bigger picture of relations between
Britain and the Punjab uppermost in his mind. Reflecting that
'a disputatious Correspondence would be a bad introduction',[9]
he sent a message saying he would call on Ranjit on the 18th.
Relations between them improved over the course of two meetings. Metcalfe set out Britain's position, which was, essentially,
that France had designs on Afghanistan and the Punjab against
which the regional governments should unite. In response, Ranjit
Singh warmly noted that an alliance with Britain had 'long been
the wish of my heart' and went on to ask when the French were
expected to invade. Metcalfe could not say when and so Ranjit
calmly concluded, 'In that case, there is time for us to think things
over'.[10] Some of the accompanying sardars then asked about the
British view of Shah Shuja and Holkar, to which Metcalfe replied
in effect that neither man would fall in with France.

The next day, Ranjit's advisers pressed the British to accept
a formal alliance and recognise Ranjit Singh as sovereign of all
Sikhs. Metcalfe could not go that far because it would have been
tantamount to recognising the Maharaja's claims to lands beyond
the Sutlej and would override those Malwais who were looking to
the British for protection. He tried to evade the issue by saying it
was Punjab-orientated whereas he was there to discuss matters of
mutual interest, but Aziz-ud-din said that the matter of a common
frontier was most definitely a mutual interest. Metcalfe again
made an evasive response by saying that the British had fixed
their boundary and had no wish to exceed it, but that merely gave
Aziz-ud-din the opportunity to ask where it *was* fixed.

Put on the spot, Metcalfe's lack of detailed briefing from Calcutta
now showed, as he was forced to think on his feet. He floundered.
His mission had established a military camp at Karnal, which
was some 300 miles south-east of Lahore. Apparently because of
that placement he told Aziz-ud-din that the border went as far
as Karnal. But that only allowed another sardar, Prabhu Dyal, to
say that Karnal belonged to Gurdit Singh, an old friend of Ranjit.
Metcalfe then fell back on attacking French villainy, but that left

his hosts unimpressed. Mokham Chand expressed irritation over the British not initialling an agreement with the Maharaja before sending a mission to Kabul, thus exposing the dangers of Britain having sent virtually simultaneous missions to Persia, Afghanistan and the Punjab. Because these countries were not well disposed towards one other, there was always the risk of the strategy coming undone through resentment on the part of one or more of them.

On the following day, Ranjit himself tried to pin Metcalfe down on the British attitude towards the Malwa states. Once again the envoy tried to slide out of a substantive response but showed some exasperation, telling Ranjit that if he continued to press the point rather than see the benefits of vagueness, he risked the governor-general simply deciding on the Sutlej as the frontier. Metcalfe was also rash enough to say that if the Maharaja wanted to press territorial demands against Afghanistan the British would not interfere. That angered Ranjit and he decided on drastic action. Without informing Metcalfe he broke up his camp and set out for Faridkot, south and east of the Sutlej, where the local chief had revolted. Given Faridkot's position beyond the Sutlej, the move was also something of a challenge to the British. Metcalfe, who followed in Ranjit Singh's wake, asked when negotiations could resume. Still annoyed, Ranjit said he would be in Faridkot for only eight days, which he hoped would suffice to complete the talks. He insisted on seeing precise proposals.

Cornered, Metcalfe provided three: joint action against the French; passage for British troops through the Punjab to the Afghan frontier to meet the invaders; and a British base and intelligence facilities in the Punjab to support action beyond the Indus. This was in keeping with his general instructions but, being of an extra-territorial nature, the demands were not acceptable to the Punjabis. They sent back counter-proposals: most-favoured-nation status (so undercutting any similar offer to Afghanistan); recognition of Ranjit Singh's sovereignty; that the British would not treat with disaffected chiefs or ally themselves with Multan and Bahawalpur, which was even further to the south; and that the Sikh–British alliance would exist in perpetuity.

None of these counter-proposals, save perhaps for the last,

fitted well with prevailing British strategy, and the Punjabis had not even said anything about joining with the British against a French invasion. But Metcalfe should not have been surprised. Not only were the Punjabis' assertions consistent with their territorial interests but they saw no reason to believe in French designs against the Punjab. With Metcalfe unable to accept the proposals, Ranjit moved his forces further into the Cis-Sutlej and forced Metcalfe to follow him again. When next the pair met the mood was tense but, fortunately, it was also frank. Having to act on his own authority more than he expected, Metcalfe's basic honesty (a quality Ranjit Singh always appreciated), plus Ranjit's underlying desire to befriend the British, kept the talks going. To the reiterated demand for recognition of the Maharaja's authority, Metcalfe replied that that would have presented no problem had there been full confidence both ways. Sensing an opening, Ranjit said he assumed Metcalfe had told his government that such confidence existed. Metcalfe replied hotly that, to the contrary, he had described the Darbar's attitude as jealous and suspicious. After further tense exchanges, Ranjit said generously that he did not doubt British sincerity except over their position regarding his suzerainty over all Sikhs. More provocatively, he said his people must wonder what had been gained from the six weeks of talks. Metcalfe naturally replied that he could say exactly the same thing.

The Maharaja's caravan moved on even further, heightening Metcalfe's annoyance. When the negotiations resumed Metcalfe again dragged out the French bogey but was told bluntly that if France had aggressive intentions in this part of the world, they were against the British, not the Punjab. There was, therefore, an impasse. Ranjit Singh moved yet further into the Cis-Sutlej, towards Ambala, and was joyfully received wherever he went.

Despite the Darbar's settled views about the French, Calcutta now tried to back up Metcalfe in his warnings about them. On 31 October Edmonstone sent Metcalfe a letter for Ranjit Singh in which he said that the

> object of [the] mission ... was to warn you of the danger which unknown to you, menaces your country, and to propose to you

to unite with the British Government in a system of measures ...
to repell [sic] it ... My friend, the justice and moderation of the
British Government are well known to you and to all the Chiefs
of India ... The British Government entertains no designs against
your Territories – On the contrary, it is the wish and the interest of
this Government to improve the relations.

The British simply wanted the Maharaja to be aware of 'the great
danger with which [his Territories] are menaced'.

The letter was just as obtuse as Edmonstone's first one of 20
June, being patronising, dismissing the Darbar's non-belief in
a French threat and offering no concessions to Punjabi wishes.
It could not hope to lift the negotiations out of the ditch into
which they had fallen. But for their part, the British, too, felt frustrated. They had taken the initiative and gone out of their way to
obtain Ranjit's friendship, even though their main concern was
with French machinations, not Ranjit Singh. Yet he was making
Metcalfe dance to different tunes as and when he pleased. Ranjit
Singh was playing a dangerous game, for the British were stronger
than he was – and they were about to make him aware of it.

∾

The British decided to take the Malwa states under their formal
protection. After all, several states had asked for this and so they
could at least secure that part of northern India. Troops would
forestall any further military actions in the area by Ranjit Singh.
While they were being assembled, Metcalfe should carry on negotiating with him as though nothing untoward was happening.
This duplicity could have stemmed from what some authors have
argued was Britain's ultimate objective: to liquidate all indigenous
states and take the entire subcontinent into its empire.[11] However,
1808 was long before the British decided to extend their rule over
the whole of India. The British deceit of that autumn could just as
well be blamed on the uncertainty that Ranjit Singh had created.

Ranjit now moved back westwards, to Amritsar. Metcalfe
followed him there, arriving on 10 November with a message from
the governor-general expressing surprise and concern that Ranjit
Singh desired the subjugation of chiefs who had long been consid-

ered to be under the protection of Britain as the ruling power in the area. Lord Minto also played a useful card that Ranjit had gratuitously given the British in 1805. When the Punjab appeared at risk of invasion by Lord Lake in his pursuit of Jaswant Rao Holkar, the Maharaja, in his attempt to mediate between them, had, with an unusual lack of care, suggested the Sutlej as his eastern border. Minto now pointedly reminded him of that offer and indicated that he expected Ranjit to give up what he had acquired since the commencement of Metcalfe's mission.

Ranjit remained outwardly calm. He returned to Lahore and received Metcalfe on 17 December. On the 21st the Darbar gave its response to Minto's virtual ultimatum, arguing that the British had not complained about the acquisitions before and had in addition indicated a disinclination to become involved north and west of the Jumna. Similarly, the British had rebuffed the request for protection from some Malwais while accepting that others had acknowledged Ranjit's suzerainty over them. The British now declined to accept such views. Ranjit Singh declared his disappointment, but matters were now moving outside Metcalfe's control. A task force charged with supporting the steelier political stance over the Cis-Sutlej was nearing its station on the river. The force was led by Lieutenant-Colonel Sir David Ochterlony, who had first seen service in India 32 years previously.

This move inevitably alarmed the sardars, and the atmosphere between them and their British guests became even more charged when Ranjit allowed it to be known that he was consulting Mokham Chand, his principal military adviser. Angered, Metcalfe somewhat hypocritically accused the Maharaja of seeking war. He would have felt even more inflamed if he had known that Mokham Chand was all for taking the British on. As Metcalfe became increasingly frustrated that Ranjit was not acceding to British wishes, his personal opinion of the Maharaja deteriorated sharply. In a dispatch to Calcutta he said that following his arduous tour Ranjit had been resting in the arms of 'his favourite mistress', though of course without adding that he had been doing much the same thing himself with a local woman.[12] Metcalfe's bitterness meant that he had no qualms about the new anti-Ranjit policy, which he had been central to inspiring.

Ranjit accepted Mokham Chand's advice to reinforce forts with men and provisions, but Mokham Chand could not guarantee that they would beat their better-trained opponents. That gave Aziz-ud-din the opportunity to argue for conciliation. Torn between these choices, Ranjit Singh concluded that he had no alternative but to accede to British demands over the border, but would do battle with them if they crossed it.

Relations between him and Metcalfe continued to see-saw. On 14 January 1809 he wrote telling Metcalfe that 'the sole object of this Government is the establishment of friendship',[13] to which Metcalfe replied on the 15th saying that 'the British Government entertains the most friendly sentiments towards the Maharaja; there is nothing whatever unfriendly in contemplation of the establishment of a Military Post on [the right side] of the Sutlej ... there is no intention whatever of advancing beyond that river, or of making conquests on [the left side]'. However, he concluded this superficially amicable message with a blunt challenge: 'Let the Maharaja be satisfied on this head and if the Maharaja will not be satisfied with this declaration, I am without remedy.' The young Englishman's *amour propre* had been grievously wounded by Ranjit's taunting actions in proceeding majestically through disputed territory in the Cis-Sutlej. He clearly thought that the Maharaja would do more than simply challenge. His anger now overcame reason, and he recommended that British forces should invade the Punjab. On 22 January he backed up his advice by telling Ochterlony that Ranjit had himself taken the field. It seemed that the envoy's impetuosity was about to prevail. British forces prepared for action. If they had invaded, Ranjit Singh might well have been defeated, his power limited, perhaps his reign ended.

Then out of the blue came one of those strokes of luck that sustained Ranjit throughout his life. Far away in Europe, Napoleon moved troops into Spain and so turned Spain into an enemy. The British quickly appreciated the magnitude of Napoleon's error, which would fatally undermine his empire. Accordingly, they realised that the perceived French threat to British interests in Asia had disappeared. On 30 January, Ochterlony was told that the 'reduction or subversion of [Ranjit Singh's] power ... is no longer of the same importance to our interest'. Nor was it necessary to force him to drop his 'old conquests' in the Malwa states.

Despite Calcutta's signal to relax, on 9 February Ochterlony declared the Malwa chiefs to be under protection and called for Darbar forces to return to the west side of the Sutlej. By now under enormous mental pressure – Sada Kaur and an uncle were among those Malwais who had welcomed the British – Ranjit Singh said he would accept all the demands bar the yielding up of Faridkot. To his credit, Metcalfe did not bridle at that but said he would consult Calcutta, albeit for tactical reasons – the delay would enable talk of a treaty to be put on hold – rather than amicability. The Maharaja sensed his continued mood of disdain and tried flattery by comparing him to Aristotle, but it did no good.[14]

Although Ochterlony's instructions meant that he should now take a peaceable position overall, he was not ordered to halt his march to the Sutlej, which continued. This led to a strange occurrence that according to one writer created disharmony between him and Metcalfe.[15] It began when some sardars met with Ochterlony at Nathi and told him of the difficulties they had experienced in trying to persuade Metcalfe to reach out more to the Maharaja. Ochterlony agreed to forward their complaint to Calcutta and report back. Already irked by the softening of British policy towards Ranjit, Metcalfe objected to Ochterlony's action. Minto then wired a reprimand to the embarrassed military commander who felt obliged to resign his commission. (The episode placed a black mark against Ochterlony's name.[16] Thereafter, he never reached high rank. Towards the end of his life Ochterlony complained at being 'unjustly treated' and 'disgraced' by the authorities.[17]

Neither the more relaxed British attitude towards the Punjab nor dissension between their civil and military wings meant that Ranjit Singh's problems with them were over. On the contrary, an outbreak of violence made things worse. In Amritsar on 25 February, Shia sepoys from Metcalfe's escort offended some Nihangs by interrupting Sikh prayers in front of the Golden Temple. The Nihangs attacked, the sepoys opened fire, and many Nihangs were killed or wounded. Ranjit Singh immediately realised the seriousness of the situation and calmed tempers by hastening to the scene and sending apologies to Metcalfe.[18] His initiative did not prevent

Ochterlony from deciding that if any further trouble broke out he would cross the Sutlej. However, the slow speed of communications at this time now came to Ranjit's aid. The British report of the incident to Calcutta crossed with two treaties drafted by officials there in the light of the change in policy. Their initiative led to a breakthrough. The draft treaties offered perpetual friendship and most-favoured-nation treatment, both of which Ranjit Singh wanted. On the other hand, other clauses did not recognise his sovereignty beyond the Sutlej, though he could keep troops to the east of the river to guard his lands there. That was much less than he desired.

In the Punjab, the pro-agreement policy prevailed over any momentary irritation over the Nihang episode. However, disagreement over Faridkot continued, which further rattled Metcalfe so much that he again turned to warlike language and in the Darbar's opinion created unnecessary delays. As late as mid-April he and Ranjit were still at loggerheads. On the 17th Metcalfe, replying to a Ranjit complaint, said petulantly that he did 'not well understand what you are pleased to write on the subject of the Treaty'.[19] The Maharaja came back stiffly the following day: 'I have only to observe that a great deal of discussion and argument produces great delay.' But he then became more amicable – 'My friend – When one of two friends … ' – before becoming brighter still by saying, 'the Treaty is a great comfort to me – Be pleased to visit me tomorrow, I cannot describe my anxiety to see you.' The Maharaja must have felt like an athlete who had run a tiring race but could now at last see the finishing line.

His faith was justified. The historic treaty was signed in Amritsar on 25 April. After all the hard work and tension, both sides celebrated the success of the negotiations with a week of parties. Between them – and between some bouts of irritation – Ranjit Singh and Charles Metcalfe had shown statesmanship, diplomatic skill and shrewdness combined with high intelligence.[20] In his long career as a high imperial official, Metcalfe had no further close contact with Ranjit.

ભ્

This narrative has described the 1808/09 negotiations in close detail for two main reasons. First, the long-established European tradition of recording events in detail means that this particular passage of Punjabi history can be empirically examined, whereas much else that happened in Ranjit Singh's era was either not so well chronicled or else the accounts vanished after the British took over the Punjab.[21]

Second, some observers viewed the outcome of the Treaty of Amritsar as a setback for Ranjit, and this analysis allows us to come to some conclusions about the controversy. Those who see the treaty as a setback argue that the British mainly secured greater territory for themselves and extinguished Ranjit's dream of a state extending into the Cis-Sutlej region. Although Ranjit secured British friendship and their agreement not to meddle in matters north and west of the Sutlej, these achievements appeared to be inadequate compensation against those of the British. There is enormous force to this argument. Ranjit Singh was a Sikh who led Sikhs and had as much right to want to rule Sikhs in the Cis-Sutlej as anywhere else. Yet he was prevented from doing so – and prevented, moreover, by a relatively tiny number of people from a country thousands of miles away who neither ruled the subcontinent directly from home nor dominated it by weight of numbers. There was a widespread and largely justified view, too, that they felt an underlying contempt for the 'natives' with whom they were negotiating. It is impossible to read some of the British communications to and about the Maharaja without sensing an unseemly superiority in tone.

However this analysis also suggests counter-arguments. For one thing, the British did not simply leave Ranjit Singh alone to run an existing territory but accepted his ambitions to extend that territory, if necessary by force. That meant that the Punjab could be unstable for years to come, and parts of it could erupt into war involving people who not only might look to the British for help but whose interests might appear important to Britain. Even so, the British went on to abide by the terms of the treaty. Given the history of invaders tearing up agreements and trampling across the Punjab without concern for the inhabitants, for a regional power to stand by its word not to do so was exceptional and, therefore, praiseworthy.

Two more minor arguments have received less currency. The first is that not everyone in the Cis-Sutlej desired Ranjit Singh's rule, and some found the tales of his war-winning exploits frightening rather than attractive. Sikhs were in a minority in the area, just as they were in the Punjab generally. This point has been little noted by most observers on the history of Sikh power between the late 1700s and the 1840s, as commentators have rather stressed how Sikhs – certainly Ranjit Singh – did not discriminate against non-Sikhs and drew much support from them. But the British and others in the region were entitled to view the Sikhs' overall lack of numbers as a factor in wishing to limit the extent to which they would accede to Ranjit's Singh's wishes. In addition, many of the leaders of the Cis-Sutlej states were Sikhs too, such as the Rajas of Patiala, Nabha and Jind, but were themselves jealous and wary of Ranjit Singh's power and did not want to be subsumed into his growing empire, as had been the case with other Sikh *misldars* in western and central Punjab. They therefore sought British protection as a guard against the Maharaja's ambitions (though they were equally wary of Company aggrandisement).

The other minor but still significant argument concerns the symbolic nature of the negotiations leading up to the treaty and its signing. This should not be underestimated as a potent factor in the esteem or fear in which Ranjit Singh continued to be held not just among people in the Punjab but outside it, too. At this time Britain was the world's foremost naval and economic power and had long been a major player in world counsels. It also had excellent land forces. For Ranjit Singh to have played host to one of Britain's representatives and have him trailing round the country after him looked very impressive indeed, and the appearance of equality between these two principals was preserved to the last for all to see. Broadly, the Treaty of Amritsar was to Ranjit Singh's credit and advantage, despite the closure to him of the Cis-Sutlej.

THE SECOND DECADE

A t the time of the Maharaja's initial negotiations with Britain, a considerable number of semi-autonomous small states still existed in the Punjab. Fortified by the treaty, Ranjit Singh set out to incorporate as many of them as he could.

The Maharaja's expeditions towards the end of the first decade had been audacious. In 1808 he had obtained a variety of territories, including Ambala which was well to the east, Ludhiana midway between Ambala and Amritsar, Ferozepur south of Kasur, Hoshiarpur to the north and Wazirabad north-west of Lahore. Each of the five was some way from the others but he became even more ambitious afterwards. It has been said that Ranjit Singh lost so much face through being checked by the British that he decided immediately to restore his standing by going for the significant prize of Kangra, Sansar Chand's territory in the western Himalayas.[1] He was certainly acquisitive in 1809, and not just over Kangra. Although he had made a point of attacking Jammu soon after taking Lahore, in 1809 the area was taken over completely. But Kangra was more important. The turbulent politics of the region gave Ranjit a handy reason for action. Gurkha forces were attacking Kangra, and Sansar Chand appealed to both the British and Ranjit for support, while the Gurkhas under Amar Singh Thapa also sought British help. The British rebuffed the pleas, honouring the terms of the Treaty of Amritsar, while the Darbar also refused help to Sansar Chand unless he first agreed that Kangra came within Ranjit Singh's domains.

By now besieged by the Gurkhas, the 43-year-old Kangra ruler concluded that submission to Ranjit Singh was the lesser evil.

The slippery Sansar then tried to retain his fort by promising to hand it over to Darbar forces once the Gurkhas had left, but Ranjit forced him to yield by arresting his son. On 24 August Punjabi forces took over the fort, but the Gurkhas still refused to give up what they had gained. Ranjit now showed further examples of his ruthlessness, military acumen and magnanimity. Rather than do battle and spill unnecessary blood he let the Gurkhas exhaust their supplies and then attacked them as they departed. Knowing that hunger would have weakened them, he supplemented artillery fire with an infantry attack. He then left his command post and rode into battle with his men. Finally, Ranjit allowed the Gurkhas to continue their departure and had his men help them round up what was left of their supplies. He even chastised a few Sikhs who grabbed some equipment for themselves. As usual his eye was on the bigger picture. Having squared the British, the Gurkhas had been the only remaining threat to the Punjab. Now that had ended – for good, as it turned out. On 24 December Ranjit formally acquired the fort and then returned to Amritsar with his authority enhanced (or restored if one accepts the view that the British treaty had harmed it).

Other conquests soon followed. He took Gujrat (north-west of Lahore) in 1809, and Pak Patan, 130 miles south-west of Lahore, followed in 1811. Rajouri was subdued over 1812 and 1813. However, Bhimber, which was further north than any of Ranjit's existing territories, proved harder to crack. He attacked it in 1811 because its Raja, Sultan Khan, allied with the defeated Raja of Gujrat and refused to submit. For once the Maharaja seemed to have underestimated an opponent. Despite Bhimber being in Kashmir, which meant its invasion would signal Ranjit's intent to take Kashmir as a whole, he sent only a modest army under Aziz-ud-din to subdue the Sultan. Possibly, he did so precisely *because* attacking Bhimber could reveal his wider intentions and he did not wish to cause premature alarm. Be that as it may, the invading force was sent packing. A more formidable army under Mokham Chand then overcame the defenders and Bhimber was split into a number of administrative units to keep the Sultan in check. However, in 1812 he killed one of the leaders and so once again Darbar forces invaded. This time they resorted to unscrupulous methods and lured Sultan Khan into accompanying them back to Lahore, where he was first feted but then imprisoned. Bhimber was finally annexed in 1815. The episode serves as another example of Ranjit Singh's willingness to be ruthless when more accommodating actions failed.

As noted, Ranjit's forays did not necessarily result in immediate annexation, nor were they always intended to do so. Had he invariably set out with the intention of annexation he would not have occasionally chosen some areas, such as Multan, that were far from his main base in and around Lahore. His strategy is revealed most clearly when the sequence of annexations is superimposed on a map. By about 1807 he had acquired a swathe of land west and east of Lahore which stretched beyond the Jhelum and almost as far as the Indus in the first direction and to the Sutlej in the other. By 1813 he had gained about half as much again in land bordering his southern flank and more in the north-west up to the Indus. Then between 1818 and 1821 Ranjit almost doubled his existing territory by wresting country to the southern tip of the Punjab and another pouch to the north a little beyond Srinagar. He augmented all this by capturing the great stretch between the Gomai river in the south-west and Leh which was some 550 miles to the north-east. Finally, he took the eastern piece between Leh and Beas. Looking at it this way illuminates the calculation behind Ranjit's moves.

Through the first and second decades of the 1800s, Ranjit Singh continued reducing the *misls*: the Bhangais in 1806, the Ramgahias in 1808 and the Nakkais in 1810. In 1811 Kanhaya authority was largely eclipsed. A special element of ruthlessness was applied against the Nakkais and the Kanhayas. Sada Kaur, the Kanhaya *misldar*, was, of course, the Maharaja's mother-in-law. Now she found her powers further clipped, though she kept her lands. Ranjit's guiding light of empire-building came before family attachments.

The capture of Kangra had a knock-on effect in the hill territories at the base of the Himalayas. In 1811 Kotila fort, in 1813 Haripur, in 1815 Nurpur and Jaswan and in 1818 Datapur all fell to central forces. But Ranjit Singh had rather more challenging territorial issues to handle besides the hill states. Afghanistan was one.

Hardly had the ink dried on the treaty that Mountstuart Elphinstone had signed in Kabul than the Barakzai family, who had the real power there, overthrew Shah Shuja and reinstalled Mahmud on the throne. Shuja left for the Punjab hoping to obtain Ranjit's support, thereby placing him in a dilemma. The Maharaja had no love for the powers that be in Afghanistan, but the country was a long-standing foe of the Punjab and so Ranjit was unable to warm much to Shah Shuja either. He was especially worried that Shuja might try to exploit the feeling for Afghanistan that existed in Multan and sent forces south to attack the city. The Nawab, Muzaffar Khan, appealed for British help but for a second time they cited the Treaty of Amritsar and refused. Nonetheless, although the Punjabis took the city, the fort proved invulnerable and the savage heat finally defeated the expedition. Ranjit Singh suffered three failures against Multan, in 1810, 1816 and 1817, before finally overcoming it.

Amid this time of conquest, in 1812 there was an occasion of great joy and happiness, the wedding of 11-year-old Prince Kharak. The boy was not yet officially the heir – Ranjit did not make him so until 1816 – but he was nonetheless clearly regarded as the most important child. The magnanimous Maharaja was content for opponents as well as allies to attend the ceremonies. Thus, Sansar Chand was invited, as was Muzaffar Khan who, mindful of Ranjit's continuing depredations over Multan, deputed a relative to go along instead. David Ochterlony represented the governor-general. His presence afforded Ranjit the opportunity to ingratiate himself with the British. To the alarm of some sardars such as Mokham Chand, he escorted Ochterlony around the innermost sanctum of the fort at Govindgarh. Then at Lahore he aroused more concern by showing him around the fort; Ranjit even pointed out its weaker aspects. The two men were so full of mutual admiration that they spoke of joint operations against Multan and Kashmir.

The outcome justified the Maharaja's diplomacy. There was no doubting his admiration for the European interlopers, but equally he was not interested in glad-handing them without purpose. As Ranjit would have hoped, Ochterlony went back singing his praises and secured Lord Minto's approval for a gift of muskets which Ranjit wanted.² Although Minto baulked at the idea of joining Ranjit on major expeditions, that, too, was fine by Ranjit. It meant that the British remained loyal to their new ally in Lahore and would not interfere with the expeditions. Ranjit had mentioned joint action only light-heartedly to Ochterlony, but he was set on mounting them as soon as he could.

An opportunity arose immediately after the wedding ceremonies. The Barakzai leader Wazir Fateh Khan sought to punish Kashmir and Attock, which were subject to Afghan sovereignty but felt no affiliation to that country. The Wazir also wanted to capture Shah Shuja who had now taken refuge in Shergarh in Kashmir. Fateh Khan offered Ranjit an equal share of the spoils, though there was no agreement for Fateh to have Shah Shuja. Nonetheless, all this worried Shuja's family who in desperation offered Ranjit their one valuable possession, the famous Koh-i-Noor diamond, if Punjabi forces would go into Kashmir and not just leave the province to Fateh. Ranjit, doubting the Wazir's sincerity, accepted the family's offer. The Darbar then considered how to enforce an assault on Kashmir and Attock. Crack forces were sent to secure the Punjabi approaches to Kashmir. This prompted Fateh to invade, and so Ranjit demanded to know what he was doing in the Punjab. The crafty Wazir sought a meeting with Ranjit at which he intended to have him killed if he did not participate in joint action. For whatever reason, when they met Ranjit agreed. Possibly he felt the Darbar forces could not achieve the ambitious aim alone. He might even have realised that the men whom Fateh had brought with him were ready to fall upon him if he was uncooperative. At any rate, Ranjit was now fulsome in his willingness to help. He suggested marching through safe territory that was already under his control and put up Mokham Chand and Dal Singh, his best generals, to lead the Punjabi contingents.

The Wazir's army set off at a suspiciously rapid rate at the end of 1812. Mokham Chand soon worked out that they meant to reach Shergarh first and spirit Shuja away, but Ranjit Singh counselled him to stick to the agreement with Fateh Khan. In a loyal act which showed part of the secret of the Punjab's success under Ranjit Singh, Mokham Chand backed his hard-pressed Maharaja not through blind obedience but by insuring against what he rightly feared could happen. He found a quick route to Shergarh and reached it in the nick of time before Afghan forces arrived. Having jointly stormed the fort, the Afghans then looted while the disciplined Darbar forces went to find Shah Shuja. The Wazir showed his true colours by refusing to share the plundered treasure after the Punjabis refused to hand over Shah Shuja.

Ranjit Singh now decided that Fateh Khan needed putting in his place. He persuaded the anti-Wazir governor of Attock to hand over his town to him. Ranjit thus not only stole a march on Fateh Khan but secured a very important conquest. Attock was considered to be a gateway to south-central Asia. It was under the Hindu kings of Kashmir until the end of the ninth century when it passed to the Afghans. As a result, it had subsequently been considered dangerous to the Punjab. Now it was lost to the Afghans, which greatly pleased Ranjit. It meant adding another bit of the Punjab to his domain, and moreover a strategically placed one. It was also the first set-piece victory by Punjabis over Afghans. The Darbar forces had manoeuvred brilliantly to cut the Afghan supply lines in order to take the town. Again, this fine action by his commanders was an indication of the secret of Punjabi success. They were so well-motivated and so obedient to the overall cause that they could act independently of Ranjit Singh who was overseeing governmental affairs in Lahore. News of the town's capture reached him there late in the night.[3] Overjoyed and despite the hour, he ordered cannons to be fired in celebration. The capture of Attock also pleased the British, who still feared the prospect of an attack through Afghanistan into India.

Having settled affairs with the Wazir (who nonetheless was threatening vengeance), Ranjit Singh now faced more difficulties, this time with the family of Shah Shuja over the Koh-i-Noor, the story of which runs through the history of the Punjab.

છ

Jewellery was not one of the Punjab's main industries but it was an important aspect of all the subcontinent's cultures. Maharajas and jewels go together in the mind's eye: the wealthiest Maharajas were covered with fabulous necklaces and armlets of pearls, diamonds, rubies and other gems. The passion had ancient roots.

The diamond-mining industry in India, which was the world's first, is at least 3,000 years old. In Greece and Rome, historians spoke of India as being the source of their diamonds. So it is no surprise that India produced one of the most famous stones, the Koh-i-Noor. The earliest history of this uniquely large, pure white diamond is not known and therefore the stuff of many legends. Some say the Koh-i-Noor was found in a river bed in 3200 BCE. The slight historical evidence suggests that the it originated in Golconda in the south Indian state of Andhra Pradesh, which was one of the earliest diamond-producing regions. The first written account of what appears to have been the Koh-i-Noor dates from about 1526 when Babur, the first Mughal Emperor, referred in his memoirs, the *Baburnama*, to an oval diamond whose extraordinary value he thought would suffice to feed the world for two days. Babur said the stone had belonged to an unnamed Raja of Malwa in 1294, that it was seized from the Raja and that it stayed with successive Delhi rulers before passing to Babur himself in 1526. Babur's source is unknown; perhaps it was hearsay. Moreover, his record of the stone's weight – about eight *mishquals* (1 *mishqual* = 96 barley grains) – served to generate endless debate. It is generally agreed that the earliest *known* weight was around 190 carats, i.e. around 38 grams, but sources vary and there was no standard carat until the early twentieth century, so it might well have been heavier when first discovered. After it was acquired by the British in 1849 it was recut, so that it now weighs just under 109 carats. In 1739 the Persian Nadir Shah plundered Delhi and carried off the Koh-i-Noor as part of the booty (he allegedly gave the jewel its name, exclaiming at its size). It became the property of Ahmad Shah Abdali, who was Shah Shuja's grandfather. Shuja had somehow got hold of the stone despite it being disputed between his fractious brothers Mahmud and Zaman.[4] The deposed Afghan leader then offered it under duress to Ranjit Singh.

Accounts differ over precisely what happened next, but most agree that, with Shuja rescued and the danger past, the Shah and his family now realised the enormity of their gesture over the priceless diamond and sought to reverse it. Khushwant Singh[5] has asserted that they not only denied that the precious gem was with them but said it had been sold. Such a claim would have been preposterous and provocative, but apparently viewing this instance of human frailty as understandable, Ranjit dropped his demand for the diamond and offered the family a *jagir*. *Jagirs* were granted as maintenance for an individual or family that was loyal and subservient to the Maharaja. If Ranjit Singh believed that they had had to sell the diamond due to financial difficulties, then it would have been incumbent upon him as their 'protector' to arrange for them to have something to live on. Thus in this case, the *jagir* offered was more in the nature of a pension than a reward. Incredibly, the family rejected this and, exasperated, Ranjit then had Shuja imprisoned.

When, at last, Shah Shuja agreed to hand over the stone on a particular date – 1 June 1813 – Ranjit met with him at Mubarak Haveli. Another account[6] claims that at their meeting Shah Shuja appeared unwilling to part with the great stone and so Ranjit Singh furiously demanded it. Cornered, Shah Shuja had it handed over, Ranjit pocketed it and then quickly left the meeting. Later the Maharaja wore the Koh-i-Noor on state occasions, first on an armlet, then fixed to his turban. The stone normally accompanied him wherever he went under a strong guard, and was otherwise kept securely in a place known only to a very few. The Koh-i-Noor remained in Sikh hands for over 36 years before the British took it.

෯

Shah Shuja's narrow escape from capture and possible death or serious injury at the hands of the Afghans, followed by his surrender of the magnificent gem, left him embittered and he cast around for some way to regain his lost status. Later in June 1813, his relatives secretly advised Fateh Khan that if he attacked Lahore he would find the city fairly defenceless. Inevitably, news of this treachery got back to Ranjit Singh who, livid with anger, questioned the relatives, but in vain. He asked Shuja for an explanation but the ex-monarch simply – and unconvincingly – blamed *them* for sending the message to Fateh Khan of their accord. Punishment was duly meted out to all concerned. Shah Shuja later escaped from Punjabi custody and disappeared for several years.

Although gaining Attock represented a strategic and salutary victory over the Afghans, perhaps the more so because it had been bloodless, the acquisition immediately became a problem as Fateh Khan wanted vengeance. At first Ranjit Singh tried to soothe him through gifts; then he changed tack and said he would discuss the town's ownership but only if the Afghans assisted him in capturing Multan. Fateh Khan had earlier said that he would do just that but now he reneged on the offer and decided to expel the Punjabis. Once again the latter under Mokham Chand rose to the challenge of relieving Attock which was surrounded. Mokham's main assistants were Hari Singh Nalwa and Mian Ghausa. Aged 22, Hari Singh Nalwa, who had been orphaned at the age of six, was, like Mokham Chand, of Khatri background. He was to become one of Ranjit's greatest and most feared commanders.

Mokham Chand took the initiative and moved his army into a position between the Afghans and the River Attock. This drastically reduced the Afghans' water supply, so they had no choice but to fight quickly or face defeat. They attacked. Having displayed one of the key ingredients of military success – initiative – Mokham now showed another: leading by example. He had his elephant's legs chained so that it could not retreat in the face of the Afghan onslaught and thereby held his ground for all to see. The Punjabis' artillery fire kept the Afghans at bay and so the ensuing battle of attrition became one that only the Punjabis could win. At the Battle of Haidru in July, they decisively routed the Afghans, who were too desperately thirsty to resist any further.

This success over Afghan forces did not make Ranjit Singh complacent. He knew that Fateh Khan would look to destabilise him again at the first opportunity. Ranjit reckoned the blow would fall in Kashmir and so decided on a pre-emptive strike to capture the province, something that was in any case one of his priorities. However, the Maharaja encountered opposition in the Darbar over timing. Although part of the summer and all of the autumn were still ahead, Mokham Chand feared that an assault on Kashmir might drag on into the winter, with disastrous consequences. Despite Mokham's high standing, Ranjit Singh decided to override him and attack. He even rubbed salt into the wound by appointing Mokham's 20-year-old grandson, Ram Dyal, to command the expedition.

Ranjit himself led the task force to the invaders' base camp in

Sialkot, 78 miles north-west of Lahore and at the foot of the Kashmiri mountain ranges. However, Mokham Chand's anxieties about their prospects now proved justified. A problem with territories with extreme seasons is that no one can know when the weather will turn really nasty. In late 1813, winter came early, before the Punjabis had even started their attack. All they could do was ensure that their supplies were plentiful, undertake reconnaissance activity and plan for a spring or summer assault. To cope with the increased scale of the operation, Ranjit called up several more experienced military leaders. Since Mokham Chand was now seriously ill and unable to participate, the Maharaja decided to lead one portion of the force into action while the other stayed under Ram Dyal. But just as the two-pronged operation was about to start, the 1814 monsoon season opened with typical force, impeding vision and turning the hard ground to slimy mud. The drenching rain held up the Maharaja's force, though Ram Dyal pressed on and received a lucky break: Agar Khan, the ruler of an important Kashmir town, Rajauri, showed Ram Dyal a way to proceed towards a fortress called Baramgulla. His assistance gave Ram Dyal the opportunity to capture the place, which he did on 20 July.

But that was the army's only success on this expedition. Although they continued to advance, when they came across Afghan forces in high positions in the mountains even an injection of an additional 5,000 men still left Ram Dyal unable to take the main prize, the Kashmiri capital of Srinagar. At the same time, Ranjit Singh's force was held at Poonch. It ran short of food and suffered an outbreak of cholera, which allowed the Afghans to win a moral victory by driving Ranjit Singh back. Fortunately for his country's reputation, Ram Dyal was able to foil attempts by Azim Khan, Agar Khan's brother, to dislodge him. But even that meant a stalemate. Again fortunately, Azim Khan preferred to see Ram Dyal leave unmolested rather than be beaten and so, after an exchange of gifts and friendly references to Ranjit Singh from Azim, Ram Dyal's forces returned home with an honourable draw to their name. However, in the context of the expedition as a whole, the Darbar had suffered an upsetting reverse.

But Ranjit Singh's lucky streak soon revived. That same year, war broke out between the British and Nepal. The Gurkhas sought help from the Punjab. These were the same people who, five years earlier, had tried to persuade the British to attack him. The Darbar viewed the request with contempt. Far from agreeing to help the Gurkhas, the Punjabis decided to offer support to the British. As it happened, the latter had gained the upper hand with the Gurkhas and so they could afford to decline the offer, allowing Ranjit Singh time to reflect on his embarrassing setback over Kashmir. He thought it through unsparingly. Many of the troops had been bested – how and why could that have happened? Ranjit knew he could not simply blame the weather. One answer was that many soldiers lacked experience of prolonged mountain warfare. One way of correcting the problem was to use the knowledge and experience of deserting Gurkhas who were trying to secure service with the Punjabis. The Maharaja also concluded that a degree of maladministration had been at work. Accordingly, he directed Ganga Ram, an accountant, and Dina Nath, to oversee military accounts. (Coincidentally, both were Kashmiris.) Finally, Ranjit felt that some of the statelets en route to Kashmir needed securing if the Punjabis were to succeed next time. As a result, Bhimber, Rajauri and Kotli were all taken and fortified by Khalsa forces. These operations did something to restore morale among men who had had an unusual reversal in a major attack.

In between his ruminations upon the failure in Kashmir and the taking of the hill states, Ranjit Singh and the kingdom of Lahore suffered a major personal loss. This was the death of Mokham Chand on 29 October 1814. Ranjit took this hard. Their recent difference of opinion over the timing for attacking Kashmir was as nothing compared to the broad support that this loyal and able Hindu general had provided even before becoming commander-in-chief of the army in 1806. His wisdom and experience could not quickly be made up, while his personal standing – almost like that of a father to Ranjit Singh – was irreplaceable. Mokham's son was accorded his *jagir* while his brave grandson Ram Dyal, who had performed so well in adverse circumstances in Kashmir, was confirmed in his senior military command.

If the first part of the 1810s had been only partially successful in military terms, the second part made good. Ranjit won three further major victories before the decade was over. Two of them occurred in 1818, the first being Multan. As it was well to the south, Multan could be dusty and sweltering, but it had exploited its fertile position near to the Ravi river to become a wealthy farming and trade centre. Having tried and failed to capture the place before, Ranjit now assembled a huge army of 20,000 men under Misr Diwan Chand, a newcomer to high office. Some other sardars resented Diwan Chand's sudden rise to prominence, so Ranjit appointed Prince Kharak as formal leader of the expedition. Highly detailed preparations were made to ensure success this time. Supply and communication lines from Lahore were secured, despatch riders positioned close to the route, and the formidable Nihangs made part of the main force, crucially as events turned out. The Zam Zama gun was sent down south.[7] Muzaffar Khan readily understood that all this meant he would have to fight to the finish.

While the battles outside and within the city were won relatively easily, taking the fort again proved hard. Its valiant occupiers held out from March until June. Two feats of Nihang bravery provided the breakthrough. First, they crossed the dry moat and mined a section of the wall; the resulting devastation induced Muzaffar to put out peace feelers, only to backtrack once he saw the attackers' terms. Ranjit Singh, overseeing operations back in Lahore, was irritated by this turn of events and sent mocking messages to the front, whipping his men into a state of frenzy for a decisive attack. The Nihangs then performed their second act of glory by charging through a hole in the wall: the astonished defenders were driven back until they could retreat no more. As well as increasing the wealth of the expanding state, the final defeat of Multan extinguished Afghanistan's sway over the Punjab once and for all.

The surrender was swiftly followed by the monsoon, which nearly cost Ranjit his life. He impulsively rode into the Ravi and almost drowned. That was in late September. Nonetheless, as an indication of the ceaseless pace of his life, less than three weeks later he took to the field again, leading an attack in the north-west, against Peshawar, which was even further from Lahore than Multan.

This action was triggered by the assassination of Wazir Fateh Khan by one of Mahmud's sons. The murder infuriated the Barakzais and Afghanistan descended into civil strife. This worried the Darbar because it made their border with Afghanistan even more unstable. But with the Afghans caught up in attacking each other rather than in guarding their country, it also offered an opportunity to extend the Punjabi frontier further in their direction. Even though the army was still recovering from its exertions in the south, the Darbar boldly decided the time was ripe for a new conquest. This time Ranjit Singh decided to lead from the front throughout, nominating Hari Singh Nalwa and Phula Singh as his principal aides. Nalwa had shown repeated military brilliance, while the fiery Phula Singh and his Nihangs could be counted upon to deliver awesome acts of bravery.

The expedition hit a setback 40 miles from Peshawar. An advance party that was searching for suitable points for the army to cross the swirling Attock river was massacred by Khattaks (Afghan Pathans). The killings angered Ranjit Singh not just because of the loss of life but because the territory came within his domains – the Khattaks paid tribute to him – and so counted as treachery. He had his troops lined up and then, having thrown gold coins into the river as an offering, he plunged in on his elephant. This inspired his men to ride or wade in after him and cross the choppy waters. Mortified, the Khattaks surrendered and Ranjit's soldiers were allowed to loot their settlements before moving on towards Naushera, halfway to their final goal. The scattering of the Khattaks frightened the Afghan governor into fleeing Peshawar and the Punjabis marched into the city without firing a shot. This time they were forbidden to loot; Ranjit had promised the citizens that they and their possessions would not be touched.

The attack on Peshawar illustrated several of Ranjit Singh's ingredients for success. First, he himself led the mission. Though he sometimes delegated the role of leader (as at Multan), he could not risk allowing his reputation as a warrior to lose its lustre. Secondly, he had shown his contempt for foul play by allowing his soldiers to plunder Khattak towns and villages. His men might have been disheartened had he not granted them that leeway following the scouts' deaths. But, thirdly, the Maharaja had demanded a higher standard of behaviour and thereby made an attack on Peshawar bloodless and much easier. The inhabitants had done him no harm so, in contrast to the actions of many foreign armies elsewhere, he saw no reason to employ savagery against them. And they felt no temptation to try and fight off the attack. Far from it; many welcomed the legendary Maharaja. The conquest had deep historical significance: no leader from the south-east had ruled Peshawar for some 800 years.

Having entered the city, on 19 November 1818, Ranjit left before December – and almost immediately found once again how tenuous his authority was. Dost Mohammad Khan, the 25-year-old new Barakzai ruler in Afghanistan, overthrew Ranjit's appointed governor in Peshawar and reinstated his brother, Yar Mohammad. Dost Mohammad then went to Lahore and offered monetary compensation and an acceptance of Ranjit Singh's suzerainty over the city. The Maharaja agreed to this. Dost had shrewdly counted on him not waging a war over the city just to enforce a particular chief upon it. This new Afghan ruler would become a thorn in Ranjit's side towards the end of his reign in the Punjab, and continued to be a key player in the region for 45 years until his death in 1863.

One reason why Ranjit Singh drew a line at Peshawar for the time being was that he wanted to deal once and for all with Kashmir. He had Lahore, Multan and now Peshawar, albeit without formal annexation as yet. He had been Punjabi ruler for almost 20 years. Kashmir, the fourth province, increasingly appeared as a challenge to him to prove his authority there.

A challenge indeed. Kashmir's hills and mountains lay between the Afghans and the Gurkhas, who would surely not be relaxed about Ranjit Singh moving in. It had been Muslim-ruled for almost 500 years, with a Muslim majority (a fact that makes this beautiful, fertile land a source of continuing dispute between India and Pakistan). And finally the Punjabis were haunted by the memory of their two rebuffs in 1812–13 and the even more decisive one in 1814.

So in seeking again to take Kashmir, Ranjit Singh faced a formidable task. The authorities there heard of his intentions and in March 1819 they asked David Ochterlony, now the Resident in

Delhi, for a British alliance. The British being uninterested, they asked for Kashmir to be formally taken under British protection. Ochterlony rebuffed them, citing the 1809 treaty in his defence. Thus, for a third time the British had stood by their word to Ranjit Singh, which was another reason for him to feel the friendship should be honoured.

The Kashmiri rulers then panicked and roughed up their size-able Hindu and Sikh minorities lest they spread support for an invasion. That was a mistake. Among the Hindus who fled was a senior minister who encouraged Ranjit to invade. Agar Khan, chief of Rajauri, also urged him to do so. Having already imprinted his rule on several adjoining areas, and with the winter behind him, Ranjit Singh resolved to attack. He had Prince Kharak and Misr Diwan Chand lead two forces while he himself took charge of a support base. In the actions that followed, the untrustworthy Agar Khan reunited with the Afghans, which left Ranjit needing to find someone else to take the invaders through the tortuous moun-tain passes. Ingeniously, he got Sultan Khan, the deposed ruler of Bhimber who had been languishing in gaol, to agree to do that. With Sultan Khan's help, Prince Kharak advanced while Diwan Chand, the day-to-day commander, battled with Afghan units and then rested the men, tired from skirmishes at high altitude, before wading into Afghan forces at Shupaiyan. The routed Afghans fled into the hills. The triumphant Darbar forces at last entered Srina-gar, the capital, early in July 1819.

こ

In 1935 the British-run Punjab Government Record Office published a book comprising 193 diary extracts in the form of letters.[8] Translated from Persian, these invaluable documents contained a wealth of minute detail of daily life at the court of Ranjit Singh between the years 1810 and 1817 (with one from 1822). They were discovered in 1932 in Poona, to the south of the Punjab on the west coast of India, but they contained no evidence of who had compiled, sent or received them, or why they covered only eight years of the Maharaja's long reign (with a single extract from a ninth year). The person who was named as the informant was Khushal Singh, keeper of the royal palace, though he was not always in the Maharaja's favour. The transcribed revelations of Ranjit Singh's character and methods adds to and confirms historians' understanding of proceedings at the Darbar, and of the life of the Maharaja. A few quotations illuminate aspects of Ranjit's character and rule.

Three of the entries illustrate Ranjit's concern with his health. We should not belittle his worries, for he lived in a time when sophisticated medicines were still in their infancy and in a part of the world where many diseases were rife. In addition, he led a determined, warring life that exposed him to constant danger. Moreover, his consumption of powerful alcoholic drinks might have increased his anxieties. It is of interest that this man with an iron constitution was nonetheless preoccupied with his body:

1810, Thursday 22 November: To-day the Noble Sarkar awoke early in the morning and came out to the Saman Burj where his staff of officials ... made obeisance. He showed his pulse to Hakim Muhammad Ali Khan who administered an aperient to him. The Noble Sarkar issued an order that no one might go inside his apartments without his permission.

1811, Wednesday 9 January: Yesterday the Noble Sarkar remained inside the zenana until the day had advanced one quarter and a half, and remained lying all this time in bed on account of the pain of the boil known as bubo imposthume, while Ghulam Mohy-ud-Din Khan, the surgeon, kept on treating him.

To-day he rose early ... [After] Sirdars made obeisance [he] showed his pulse to the physicians, and took some medicine and cold refreshing drink.

1812, Saturday 29 March: The Noble Sarkar applied medicine ... to his tooth, felt a little relief ... Raja Sansar Chand came in and enquired after the health of the Noble Sarkar who showed him great respect, made him sit on a chair and talked to him all about the pain in his tooth. Kanwar Kharak Singh ... said that if the Noble Sarkar permitted him he would march ahead. The Noble Sarkar replied that he should march ahead on the day following the next, which was considered auspicious.

An entry from 1813 shows how much Kashmir was exercising the minds of the Maharaja and his advisers:

> 1813, Wednesday 30 June: ... To-day [the Noble Sarkar] woke up early in the morning ... The sirdars ... expressed their hope that Kashmir, too, would likewise be shortly conquered ... The Vakil of Hyderabad was called in and the Noble Sarkar talked to him in privacy for four hours. The Vakil said that it was impossible to establish any control over the country on the other side of the river Attock without the co-operation of the Noble Sarkar, because, though the troops with Hazrat Muhmad Shah were inconsiderable, yet that country was ... difficult to manage. The Noble Sarkar said that after the establishment of control over the districts of Attock and Kashmir, arrangements would be made for the administration of those districts also.

An entry from the following year offers two fascinating examples of his demeanour in a crisis:

> 1814, Thursday 2 June: ... Fateh Singh Ahluwalia came, accompanied by Chaudhary Qadar Bakhsh. The Noble Sarkar said to him in private that he had no confidence in anybody except him and Diwan Mukham Chand. The Raja replied that the Noble Sarkar should have no fear in the least, that he was always ready to sacrifice his life and to do all he could for his good according to his wishes ... The officers of the army were urged to sacrifice their lives in the expedition to Kashmir, and promised that by the grace of God they would be given twice as many Jagirs as they already possessed, after its conquest.

It is breathtaking that he should tell Fateh Singh Ahluwalia that he has no confidence in anyone except him and Mokham Chand when there were many other trustworthy courtiers around. One wonders just how publicly Ranjit made this stark comment. Clearly he spoke loudly enough for the chronicler to hear, and one can only imagine how someone as reliable as, say, Aziz-ud-din would have taken such an apparently slighting remark. The other interesting point is how Ranjit expected his officers to be willing to die for the cause and to think of the favours they could expect to receive if they came through it.

An entry from 1815 reveals Ranjit's ruthless side:

> 1815, Friday 28 July: Hukma Singh Thanadar reported the capture of fifteen thieves. The Noble Sarkar ordered their ears and noses to be cut off and [that] they be banished from the town.

His order to mutilate a band of thieves is the only known time during his rule when he acted in this fashion, a rare reminder that notions of justice were much more peremptory in his day than now and he was not always as liberal as his reputation – based on his opposition to capital punishment – suggests.

An entry from 1816 demonstrates something that pervades the entries as a whole, indeed his whole reign: Ranjit's control of detail as well as grand strategy.

> 1816, Monday 22 April: Two horses and two camels and a letter sent by the ruler of Punchh, arrived. In reply the Noble Sarkar wrote him to send the revenue tax expeditiously, and paid twenty-five rupees to the bearer who had brought the letter, the horses and the camels. He was also warned that, in case of delay, the amount of the revenue tax which had already been paid, would be forfeited. Mehr Chand, the Vakil of Ahluwalia, stated that his master, the Sirdar Bahadur, wanted a temporary loan of five thousand rupees, and the Noble Sarkar told him to take a 'Hundi' from Sujan Rai Darogha.

There is evidence here to support those writers who attribute the collapse of his kingdom after 1839 to the difficulty of replacing Ranjit's personalised rule.

An 1817 entry shows how Ranjit Singh was not going to be intimidated by a brusque letter from Britain's Sir David Ochterlony:

> 1817, Tuesday 15 July: A letter from General Ochterlony Sahib Bahadur arrived from his army with four horsemen, and intimated, 'One, named Ram Dass, an employee of Alexander Sahib, had taken some thousands of rupees from him and had run away to his own place. It is reported that he is staying with

the Noble Sarkar. He has some papers of the government of the Company with him. I am sending herewith four horsemen, with whom the Noble Sarkar must send him back, because the relations existing between us and the Noble Sarkar are identical. In case this is not possible the Noble Sarkar must take possession of the money of the Company from him and send it to him (Ochterlony)'. On hearing this the Noble Sarkar wrote to him in reply to send one of his accountants, so that he might realise his claims from that person after arriving at an agreed figure.

The entry from 1822 offers a glimpse of how openly disdainful Ranjit had become towards his formidable mother-in-law, Rani Sada Kaur:

> 1822, Monday 10 June: … Rama Nand was ordered to show to the Noble Sarkar the account-papers of the realizations made from the country of Rani Sada Kaur.

Relations between her and Ranjit had been deteriorating for some years. Three episodes from years long after they had attacked and captured Lahore illustrate the point. She had not supported Ranjit during his tortuous negotiations with Charles Metcalfe in 1808–9; she had not attended Prince Kharak's wedding in 1812; and she had prevented Sher Singh and Tara Singh, her grandsons, from doing so. Such snubs would have gravely offended the Maharaja and Kharak yet the Rani exacerbated a worsening situation by going on to complain that Kharak was being showered with *jagirs* while her grandsons received none. The breaking point came once Sher Singh had attained the age of responsibility and Ranjit Singh pressed Sada Kaur to bequeath the administration of her estates to him. Knowing that he was out to sideline her permanently, Sada Kaur refused and even threatened to seek the protection of the British in the Cis-Sutlej and to hand over to them the town of Vadhni which Ranjit had conquered and transferred to her in 1808. Ranjit then lured Sada Kaur to Lahore on the pretext of discussing *jagirs* for Sher and Tara. Strangely unsuspecting, she accepted the invitation, only to find herself being coldly told by him that he had transferred her territories to the boys and that she should retire. The outmanoeuvred Rani spiritedly threw the suggestion back in his face but he remained implacable. She tried to escape from Lahore where she had no influence, but her absence was soon detected and she was brought back. Her territory was sequestered and the forts, the munitions and the wealth of the Kanhaya *misl* were confiscated. Batala was granted as a *jagir* to Sher Singh while the rest of his grandmother's estates were placed under the governorship of Sardar Desa Singh Majithia. Broken-hearted but not destroyed, Sada Kaur lived on under a form of house arrest until her death in December 1832.

6

AT THE MIDPOINT:
THE FLOURISHING STATE

By 1819, Ranjit Singh was midway through his reign, and he now had about half of the territory that he would eventually acquire. He could only have achieved even this much by ensuring that his civil and military institutions could support the expansion, and that they and the country as a whole were supported by an economy that brought in sufficient material prosperity through trade and industry, and by social and judicial arrangements that did not undermine the Maharaja's popular support. Though comprehensive records are absent, it seems reasonable at this stage to review the Punjab's evolution into a unified political entity.

In his early years, Ranjit had been able to count on one really first-class civil aide, Aziz-ud-din. This extraordinarily able man was still very much at his side at the midpoint. He had been a crucial adviser on any number of occasions, most notably in cooling tempers over relations with the British. It is not too much to say that without him Ranjit would not have survived. Aziz-ud-din complemented Ranjit through his education and fluency and had total loyalty to both country and ruler. Yet he was never afraid to air his moderating opinions, nor was Ranjit ever reluctant to hear them, for he knew they were underpinned by a far-sighted assessment of the country's best interests.

Two other notable aides early on were Devi Das and Kirpa Ram in financial affairs. In 1808, however, Diwan Bhawani Das became the head of a unit which organised financial arrangements in newly conquered territories.[1] He impressed Ranjit Singh sufficiently to become finance minister in 1811. Bhawani Das had handled financial matters under Shah Zaman and so had extensive experience in fiscal administration which he put to good use in establishing a proper system of national accounting. He created separate streams for land revenue (the main source of state income), customs and excise duties, tributes and presents, property reversions and forfeitures, and registration fees.[2] In all, he built up 15 *daftars* (offices) in which members of staff laboriously scrutinised and stamped pay orders before and after the Maharaja approved them – orally, for a courtier to transcribe into Persian – for payment. Unfortunately, Bhawani Das was not wholly honest and, given his high position and area of work, he was bound to fall foul of the Maharaja. He finally did so after the capture of Multan when, following reports, Ranjit concluded that he had been bribed by Muzaffar Khan to call off the siege, and dismissed him.[3] Bhawani Das's system of examining and stamping and rechecking eventually had to be streamlined as the Punjab expanded, though it was a useful arrangement to have early on when the state's administrative affairs were being established.

Another high-ranking courtier who suffered a similar fate at about the same time was Khushal Singh. A Brahmin before converting to Sikhism, he had come to Ranjit's attention as an ordinary soldier. The Maharaja made him a royal bodyguard; he clearly went on to impress his master a great deal more, ending up as keeper of the royal palace and royal chamberlain. These posts gave him quasi-prime ministerial powers, perhaps the most important of which was acting as gateway to Ranjit Singh. No one obtained a personal appointment without going through Khushal Singh. Like Bhawani Das, however, he had serious weaknesses. These were shown when he secured court postings for two relatives, Bhai Ram Singh and Tej Singh. The first proved troublesome within Ranjit's lifetime, and the second embarked upon treachery after his death. Khushal Singh himself was dismissed after a nervous breakdown rendered him too difficult to manage. However, he later returned to royal favour.

Khushal Singh was replaced, in 1818, by Dhian Singh Dogra as gatekeeper to the Maharaja and rose steadily to the highest political office. He had been presented to Ranjit Singh as a 16-year-old by his elder brother Gulab in 1812 and the Maharaja had inducted him into the army. Dhian Singh's polish and fine bearing remained in Ranjit's mind and his adroit instincts heightened the Maharaja's opinion of him yet further. As with Aziz-ud-din, Dhian Singh was assigned military roles from time to time, but his capacity in civil affairs was stronger and took him ever higher in Lahore.

We have already met Aziz-ud-din's brother Nur-ud-din. His home ministerial duties were wide-ranging. They included being apothecary-general, almoner, director of the royal palaces, custodian – one of three – of the keys to the Treasury and commandant of the arsenal at Lahore Fort. The third Fakir brother, Imam-ud-din, was a familiar figure in the provinces as well as at court.

A further key person at court was Lehna Singh Majithia. He hailed from a set of three related families of Sikhs from Majithia, a town ten miles north of Amritsar. This clan had thrown in its lot with Ranjit Singh during the late 1700s. As he began to establish his empire around the turn of the nineteenth century, so the Majithias gained in prominence. They became very influential in the army, with no fewer than ten different Majithia generals serving between 1800 and 1849. The best known of these were Generals Lehna Singh, Surat Singh and Amar Singh; each represented one of the three branches of the family.

Lehna Singh was also important in the civil sphere. Indeed, the historian Dr Kirpal Singh assessed him as the ablest and most ingenious of all the Maharaja's courtiers.[4] He was certainly multi-talented. As governor of Kangra, he was both efficient and liked by the people. He had a scientific and mechanical turn of mind which helped him to produce armaments. He fought in the Multan campaign of 1818. He had a responsibility for the Golden Temple at Amritsar, where he installed a marble structure inlaid with precious stones – carnelian, serpentine and lapis lazuli. And he sometimes acted as a special emissary,[5] in particular when he was deputed to receive Alexander Burnes in 1831 and to escort Governor-General Lord Auckland during part of the British mission of 1838.

Of course, many invaluable support staff operated beneath these attentive and hard-working men. However, while the latter could direct them at the centre, and oversee subordinate managers and clerical workers there, they could not do the same in the provinces. Broadly, at the midway stage of Ranjit Singh's reign there were three types of provincial area.[6] First, there was a core zone, closest to the capital, between the Sutlej and the Jhelum rivers. This area had come under the Maharaja's control by about 1810. His later conquests of territories between the Indus and the Jhelum, and south to Multan and north to Kashmir, constituted the second or intermediate tier. Some of this diverse area was only just beginning to come under effective control from the centre by 1820. The third zone, on or near to the country's long border around the west, north and east, was the one where control from the centre was necessarily at its loosest and, consequently, where there was a greater reliance on local rulers.

The central zone was divided into districts each headed by a *nazim*. Communications between them and the Darbar were quick, not least because the Maharaja himself travelled a great deal within the zone and could suddenly appear in the midst of anxious officials and assess how they were doing. He ordered punishment where matters were amiss. But he did not keep such a tight grip in the second zone. Here, the *nazims* were of higher rank than those in the first area. They were more likely to be able to influence the appointment of *kardars* in the zone, and they were much less likely to encounter their king there. His visits to Multan were rare and he never visited Kashmir at all. On the other hand, he exercised some oversight through regular reports from the *nazims*, plus information from local intelligence officials appointed from the centre.

The third zone was only in the process of formation by the end of the second decade. Up until then it was mostly a patchwork of self-administering units on the periphery. However, Ranjit's success in Peshawar opened up the area to Lahore's influence, and Hazara in the mountainous north was brought under direct control. A maladroit attempt to suppress a revolt in Hazara led to Ranjit Singh severely disciplining the man he deemed responsible, Hukma Singh. Hukma had taken part in the Kasur expedition of 1807 and had won the Maharaja's further approval for his part in an attack on the Kanhaya citadel of Pathankot in 1808, in the seizure of Sialkot the same year and in the battles for Attock. Ranjit affectionately called him 'Chimni', meaning a man of small stature whose swiftness resembled that of a little bird. Hukma Singh became governor of Ramnagar and Controller of Customs, including salt mine duties. In 1818, Ranjit rewarded him with the governorships of Attock and Hazara. However, Hukma's fame did not prevent the Maharaja from dismissing him for mishandling the Hazara revolt.

Kohat (south of Peshawar), the south-western towns of Dera Ismail Khan and Dera Ghazi Khan (neither of which had been conquered by 1820) and Peshawar itself were not taken under direct control until the 1830s. These and other far-flung areas were under the lightest influence from Lahore and they were the most difficult places to manage, being exposed to Afghan agitation and containing the least civic-minded subjects. Troops were sometimes called in to enforce payment of taxes. Ranjit knew he could not afford to ignore them totally. Precisely because they were exposed to constant danger, he kept his eye on what went on even in the most remote corners of his extending country, and occasionally intervened in their civil affairs by countermanding decisions.

It should be noted that traditional Sikh thinking and practice over the raising of money exerted a baleful effect upon enterprise. On land tax, the state's share was assumed to be at least half of the gross product, though demands for more than half were not supposed to occur.[7] The system bore down on the poor no less than it did on the rich. Not all of the sums collected ended up in the state's coffers, a fact of which everyone was aware. When a farmer had to hand over half or more of his income to an untrustworthy and disrespectful *kardar*, it discouraged him from investing in his land and tending it.

In customs and excise arrangements no distinction was drawn between essential goods and luxuries. Nor did it make any difference whether the items were home-made or foreign (though under Ranjit Singh attempts were made to charge Punjabi merchants less than foreign merchants).[8] It was virtually impossible to evade payments to customs men, for the Punjab was covered with their offices. However, some observers have argued that these arrangements were ameliorated by the state returning with one hand what it took with the other.[9] There was abundant opportunity for employment in state service, so, for example, soldiers both remitted money back to their families and were consumers of manufactured goods. The state also channelled much land revenue to religious groups, Sikh and non-Sikh alike, though the Sikh groups had the main share, particularly the Udasi, Sodhi and Bedis sub-groups. Under Ranjit Singh artists and writers were also patronised.[10]

Land cultivation provided the main source of Punjabi people's income.[11] Most cultivated land – about one-quarter of the country – was held by peasant proprietors of whom there were twice as many as land tenants. Both proprietor and tenant paid land revenue, but the tenant also paid *malikana*, an allowance, to the proprietor. Farmers used a wooden plough. They sowed by scattering, drilling and dibbling (placing seed in a hole made with a stick). Their fields were harrowed to remove clods, smooth the top and cover the seed. Weeds were removed by hand-hoeing. Thorny branches were used for fencing in order to prevent animals from getting at the crop, and scarecrows or other platforms were erected to keep birds away. Reaping was done by hand, threshing by *phallas* of sticks and straw, and winnowing by shaking the threshed crop to separate grain from the straw. Although most tools were still wooden, some implements – sickles, spades, a few hoes – were made of iron imported from Kangra and Kulu in the northern hills and from north of Peshawar.

Notwithstanding agriculture's dominance, urbanisation continued to grow during Ranjit Singh's era, as it had in the eighteenth century, when old urban centres such as Gujranwala, Gujrat, Sialkot and Wazirabad underwent something of a rebirth. These and other growing places expanded further under Ranjit's reign – for instance, Wazirabad under the Italian Paolo Avitabile – while still others such as Amritsar and Multan continued to thrive. There was no significant structural change in human terms[12] – no mass movement or major dilution of the ethnic, religious and caste groups – but the increased interaction between state institutions and society allowed for more social mobility, mostly upward, aided by the Sikh rejection of caste restrictions, which removed some of the formal barriers to advancement.

Important changes occurred in the top ranks of society.[13] Sikh rule displaced Mughals and Afghans, with the majority of new rulers being Jats (the main ethnic group in the Punjab). However, in keeping with the tolerance of Sikh tradition, non-Jats and non-Sikhs were also represented, along with some non-Punjabis, including Europeans.

In the justice system, there was little of the modern practice that sets the law apart from the executive. The judicial system ranked alongside other components of executive activity – defence, acquisition of new territory, taxation, maintaining order – and the area *kardar* was a judicial officer, revenue collector and general supervisor for the *nazim* and ultimately the government. Promoting individual and family welfare and encouraging trade and industry were seen as desirable rather than essential elements of good government.

Punjabi judicial concepts and court procedures were simple and straightforward. There were no written laws, justice was done on the basis of custom and there was no distinction between matters that would in later times be classed as civil or as criminal. *Kardars* were to a degree supported by *panchayats*, who dealt with village disputes, and by a set of officials known as *adaltis*, but the *kardar* handled land, inheritance and revenue disputes directly. Lack of evidence could result in a complainant being fined. Fining was also the normal consequence of a judgement of guilt (thus, state income was constantly replenished following guilty verdicts). At the same time, more drastic sentences were imposed for offences such as violence. These could be caning or lashing, or in the most serious cases the amputation of a limb, ear or nose. Imprisonment of ordinary citizens was virtually unknown – incarceration tended to be reserved for important people who were deemed a threat to the state.

In sum, although the nature of civil rule, revenue assessing, individual livelihoods, social mobility and judicial administration had remained much the same since the eighteenth century, some of the Maharaja's dynamism had inevitably begun to impact on them by the end of the second decade of his reign. To a degree this was due to his economic policies relating to trade and industry, and to his influence on cultural developments.

✧

Since this section contains some statistics, it should be emphasised that there is some dispute over the reliability of the figures. For example, among the most basic statistics in any society are those relating to the population. But in the case of the Punjab in the early 1800s the figures conflict. One source claimed that Muslims comprised 80 per cent of the population, Hindus 10 per cent and Sikhs 10 per cent;[14] another that the proportions were Muslims 45 per cent, Hindus 45 per cent and Sikhs 10 per cent.[15] There is no hard evidence from Ranjit's reign. A British-run census for the Punjab excluding Kashmir of 1881 – long after Ranjit Singh's time – suggests the likely population in his era: 11,662,434 Muslims, 9,232,295 Hindus and 1,716,114 Sikhs (giving proportions of 51 per cent, 41 per cent and 7.5 per cent). One can speak only in probabilities and generalities: that Sikhs were a minority, that Muslims were almost certainly the majority, with Hindus being a sizeable number in between.

Nearly 90 per cent of Sikhs lived in the core region of the Punjab (in the Bist Jullunder and the upper portions of the Rachna and Bari Doabs), along with 74 per cent of the Hindus and 38–39 per cent of the Muslims, which still meant that Sikhs were in a minority in the area of their greatest settlement. In this area, some 65 per cent of those living in these areas were town dwellers, against 12 per cent overall.

In terms of occupation, almost half of the people were landowners and agriculturalists (with about 28 per cent in the services sector, 12 per cent in mercantile communities and 8 per cent in religious and professional groups). Agricultural workers sowed a wide range of crops, mainly cereals, which took up 90 per cent of cultivated land, wheat being the single most important of them. (Cash crops, making up 10 per cent of cultivated land, were important in terms of foreign trade with Afghanistan, India, Turkistan and elsewhere.) Rain and river-waters were unreliable, so farmers used wells and canals – predominantly in the south-west – some permanent, some made in the rainy periods. Since rainfall was mostly unpredictable and unevenly distributed, Ranjit Singh showed a particular concern to improve irrigation.[16] State authorities provided vital help by managing the existing canals and supporting construction of the others. *Nazims* and *kard-ars* were told to develop agriculture by offering loans to build and maintain wells and to buy seeds, tools and bullocks. Cultivators were exempt from the grazing tax. The state also encouraged the founding of new villages to extend cultivation. The reduced like-lihood of invasion encouraged proprietors to remain where they were, or to return if circumstances had caused them to leave. The state itself was a major buyer and seller of farm produce.

The kingdom of Lahore became a veritable hive of trade and industry.[17] Thriving regional and local trading centres developed alongside the main trading centres such as Amritsar, Lahore and Multan.[18] The centres naturally developed connections with one another. Ranjit Singh ensured that the caravans of traders and merchants were afforded maximum facilities and protec-tion against attacks within and from outside the country. Partic-ular communities tended to monopolise trade: Khatris, Aroras, Bhatias and Suds among Hindus, and Khojas and Parachas among Muslims. Credit and banking facilities existed, with interest or shares in profits being allowed. The rupee was the main medium of exchange, though barter also applied in some areas such as Hazara and Kashmir.

Under Ranjit Singh industries thrived, particularly textiles, metal work and leather work. Textiles (mainly woollens, silks and cottons) made up the single biggest industry, dominated by shawls, carpets, blankets and rugs made mainly for the wealthier echelons of society. Ranjit Singh himself liked to provide woollen gifts, especially Kashmiri shawls which were famed internation-ally. The quality of silks and cottons was equally superb: cotton chintz, coarse cloth, bed-covers, turbans and muslin.

Kashmir as a whole presented a picture of wealth and progress mixed with the very opposites.[19] The shawl industry had flour-ished under the Mughals, and Ranjit Singh's efforts to assist trade and industry helped Kashmir, for instance, in making highway robbery a thing of the past. On the other hand, partly because of Kashmir's relative industrial wealth, taxation was seen as burden-some, and banking and currency arrangements as complex and confusing. In addition, the nine provincial governors appointed between 1819 and 1846 were often corrupt, taking advantage of the fact that Ranjit Singh never visited Kashmir. Their failings kept many Kashmiris impoverished. The province also suffered from earthquakes and famines. A great famine in 1833 killed many thousands of people, which had an inevitable knock-on effect upon Kashmiri trade and industry. The Maharaja displayed characteristic energy and humanity by despatching thousands of mules laden with wheat, corn and blankets to the stricken province.[20]

Metal work was second to textiles in importance, with armaments making up the main part. Weapons and other military materials from Amritsar, Multan, Shujabad and Lahore were always in demand, with the state as the major client.[21] The industry paid well, providing for painters, carpenters, blacksmiths, armourers and turners who produced cannons, matchlocks, carbines, pistols and other guns, steel caps and helmets, daggers, spears and lances. By the midpoint of the reign, most of the army's fighting equipment was home-produced.

Other industries crucial to the arms business were also well supported by the government. It appointed boatmen, controlled ferries and ran several iron and salt mines, salt being crucial for health and preserving food. Private entrepreneurs were encouraged in other spheres of the economy: textiles, the paper and woodwork industries, brass and copper concerns making kitchenware.

The army, so vital to the steady establishment of a strong civil state, had continued to improve in number, organisation and quality during the second decade, providing the essential basis for conquest. Dr Shiv Kumar Gupta, Professor of History at the Punjabi University, Patiala, has noted that the period from 1809 to 1821 showed considerable changes in almost every aspect of the military system.[22] Training and drilling of cavalrymen was very much an innovation of this period. The infantry also underwent a metamorphosis, with Sikhs joining the ranks in greater numbers.[23] In 1810 a specialist artillery unit, the Artillery-Topkhana, was raised; by 1812 it was the main artillery unit and commanded by a Muslim, Mian Ghaus Khan. Recruitment remained voluntary, a high intake being assured by martial tradition (among the Jats, Dogras, Awans, Tiwans and others), by the social cachet attached to army service and by Ranjit Singh's fighting reputation and exemplary support of his men – and women (the 150-strong Zenana, or Amazon Corps was all-female). Ranjit made the army inclusive, an outstanding instance of which concerned Mazhabis, members of the Harijans or the 'Untouchables' of Hindu society. For the first time in the history of the subcontinent, Mazhabis became a formal component of an army.

There remained a problem in the relationship between administration and the army that was never entirely overcome during Ranjit's reign: payment. The traditional scorn felt by soldiers towards cash payments had died away, but the state had chronic difficulty providing cash punctually. Ranjit Singh tried to adopt the system of monthly pay used by the British, but this was such a major innovation in Punjabi terms that it rarely worked. Men were often paid five or six months in arrears. In time, this failing caused resentment and even feelings of mutiny in some detachments. Generally, Ranjit Singh chose good subordinates and left them to get on with their jobs, holding them on a long leash. But he was never able to overcome the irregularity of payment to servicemen, a problem that after his death would become a grave threat to the stable authority of his heirs, with fatal consequences for the long-term security of his kingdom.

Notwithstanding the problems caused by irregular payments, the military expanded in Ranjit Singh's second decade, laying a foundation as a disciplined, feared fighting force on which European, mainly French, fighting men could build after their arrival in 1822. Ranjit had been powerfully influenced by European military discipline in the early 1800s when he had contact with the forces of George Thomas and Lord Lake.[24] He applied some of what he saw in their forces to reforming the army. However, the arrival of high-level Europeans in the Punjab itself and their subsequent impact upon life at many levels in the country count as a significant feature of the Maharaja's era.

Early in March 1822 Ranjit Singh, having been informed that two white *feringhees* (foreigners) were making their way to Lahore, had agents track their movements. The foreigners were two French adventurers, Jean Baptiste Ventura and Jean François Allard. Ventura, who was born in 1785, had fought in the major battles of Moscow and Waterloo, rising to the rank of colonel.[25] However, after Napoleon's fall his regiment was disbanded and he travelled to the East (some say along with Allard). He found no worthwhile opportunities in Egypt or Persia, but he and Allard heard of lucrative possibilities in the Punjab. Allard, also born in 1785, became a soldier earlier than Ventura but he too lost his post following Waterloo and left for the East. Charming and gentle, Allard found work in Persia in 1820 where he might have met Ventura for the first time. With Britain pressing the Persians to dismiss their French employees, the Frenchmen needed little encouragement to go further east. Dressed as Persian traders while passing through Afghanistan, they arrived in Peshawar and stayed in a mosque. Both had long beards, which aided their disguises among Muslims. Allard had also taken the trouble to learn Persian.

The two ex-soldiers travelled on to Lahore and in March were received there with characteristic courtesy by the Maharaja. Always inquisitive, he plied them with questions about their knowledge of foreign armies, including the British, and how they rated the latter *vis-à-vis* the French. He even asked them for their opinions on his own army and showed them his troops. He apparently invited his guests to put the men through some movements but with great discretion they refused on the grounds that they had nothing to teach these trained soldiers.[26] The Frenchmen offered the imaginative analogy that 'a shawl once woven, cannot be woven in another fashion'. Ranjit Singh would have warmed to such respectful charm, the more so when the guests offered to train a battalion free of charge. They also indicated – tactfully and by inference – that they would accept employment in his service.

Ventura and Allard were clearly well briefed on how to conduct themselves in the legendary warrior-leader's presence. Aziz-ud-din would almost certainly have prepared them, judging by their felicitous language. For his part, the Maharaja would, of course, also have been pre-advised. However, his welcoming demeanour concealed some suspicions. After all, he had enemies, and Ventura and Allard had just travelled through some of their countries. Having gained a measure of confidence in the visitors, he went on to invite them to apply for service – having the offer made in French to make sure that they were not really from elsewhere, such as England. He also probed their honesty by getting them to respond to a spoof letter, supposedly from an Englishman. Ventura and Allard passed these little tests with flying colours. Finally, after they were cleared for appointment they had to agree to five conditions relating to loyalty, personal conduct and families.

Although a few Europeans had been employed in the Punjab since 1809, when a British deserter had joined up, these two Frenchmen were much more eminent. Moreover, the French army had trained them in a wide range of military matters, including tactics, engineering and warfare, and they had fought in extremely testing conditions. By the end of May 1822 Ranjit Singh had placed a battalion under Ventura and Allard and promised them 500 horsemen under Misr Diwan Chand. Initially, the French discipline was too much for some men, but with Ranjit's backing the new commanders prevailed. However, the Maharaja made sure to give each of them distinct duties rather than have them constantly working in harness, which might have encouraged homesickness and distracted them from state business. Put in charge of training Sikh infantry on European lines, Ventura made them the equal of the best European soldiers. He also reorganised the army brilliantly; improvements after he arrived were mostly due to his initiative and skill. Similarly, Allard shone after Ranjit ordered him to produce a cavalry corps on European lines. All in all, Ventura and Allard were of crucial importance to Ranjit Singh and this led to the employment of more Europeans.

᪥

7

SECULARISM AND TALES

OF THE HERO

anjit Singh's willingness to employ Europeans at senior
levels was a bold and unusual example of his secularism. The Darbar already comprised people from different ethnic and religious groups, which risked the creation or
even explosion of negative feelings. To inject an alien element
increased the risk. Only a very strong and admired leader could
have got away with it.

Ranjit Singh's secularism was the central feature of his
approach to building a state. Secularism in the sense in which he
practised it was not of an irreligious or anti-religious kind. On
the contrary, religious worship was very much an aspect of Ranjit
Singh's secularism. But what he wanted was a balance of faiths
and ethnic groups, with people free to worship the God of their
choice or, indeed, to have no spiritual faith at all if that was their
wish. G.S. Dhillon among others highlighted Ranjit's secularism to
counter a perceived over-emphasis upon his military and political
achievements.[1] Dhillon noted how Ranjit Singh was moulded by
the Sikhism in which he was born and brought up, and stressed
the nature of Sikhism as a way of life – its fusion of spiritual discipline, social order and egalitarianism. Yet, once he was ruler, he
did not proclaim Sikhism as the Punjab's main religion or even
propagate it as a religion. This was in line with Sikhism itself as
taught by the Gurus, for whom pluralism was not just desirable
but the very essence of the Sikh code. This was what underpinned
Ranjit's enlightened humanitarianism.

His moderation contrasted with the Mughals' destruction of non-Muslim religious sites and institutions. Sikhism as

incorporated by Ranjit Singh also differed from Hinduism in pre-Muslim India, which had been looked upon as divinely ordained. Brahmins had enjoyed a special status with exemptions from some of the laws plus the right to obtain income from the people under the Brahmin Avimasti tax. Those at the lower end of the caste system suffered accordingly, and one group, the Buddhists, were almost eliminated from the subcontinent. Ranjit Singh's respect for all faiths was like a light set against this dark historical background. He opened up career prospects for men of merit irrespective of their religion or social origin. He tried to favour evenly all those who had pleased him.

He knew the value of favouring individuals. He heard of a Muslim calligraphist who had spent years transcribing the Qur'an beautifully by hand and was about to leave the Punjab to sell his exceptional product because no one there would buy it. Touched by this report, the Maharaja summoned him to an audience. Ranjit respectfully pressed the calligrapher's fine piece of work against his forehead and then purchased it, giving the man more than he had asked for. Ranjit later presented the book to Aziz-ud-din and asked him to recite something from it. He did so and Ranjit observed that the reference was similar to something in the Granth. Aziz-ud-din agreed and said that the ultimate ideal of both the Qur'an and the Granth was the same. Gratified by that response, the Maharaja then asked his faithful adviser to keep the calligrapher's excellent work as a mark of their mutual respect and friendship.

Ranjit Singh treated all religions with consideration. Although Sikhs and their institutions were allocated the lion's share of endowments and charities, they did not receive vastly more than other religions. After the conquest of Multan in 1818, Ranjit Singh authorised a huge annual grant for the mausoleum of Bahawal Haq. Also in that year he had a dam constructed near Lahore to prevent a Muslim tomb from being washed away. He was similarly concerned for the Hindus. Darbar records show grants to Purohits (priests who minister to royalty) and Brahmins. Pandits Brij Raj and Madhusudan were awarded extensive lands. State-supported plots were set aside for cows. Ranjit Singh had the roof of the Jawalamukhi temple in Kangra gilded as a thanksgiving.

Courtiers came from the whole spectrum of races and religions. Two other Muslim brothers, Sarafraz Khan and Zulfakar Khan, were prominent at court.[2] These were the sons of Muzaffar Khan, who had given Ranjit Singh trouble over acquiring Multan, and were quite likely kept at Lahore as hostages to ensure their father's continued loyalty. Numerous talented Hindu courtiers held high bureaucratic positions connected to the Lahore Darbar, not least the Diwans Bhawani Das, Ganga Ram (accountant general) and Dina Nath (comptroller-general), but also the notorious Tej Singh (general) and Lal Singh (treasurer and later *wazir* to Rani Jind Kaur). Sikhs of course were present in large numbers, appointed equally to posts within the capital and on its frontiers. Thus Khushal Singh was head chamberlain and an important political figure at the Darbar; whilst Hari Singh Nalwa fought like a pioneer on the Northwest Frontier of India, expanding Punjabi rule deeper into Afghan territory over time. Jean Baptiste Ventura, Jean François Allard, Paolo Avitabile and Claude August Court were the most prominent of the small band of Europeans. Balwant Singh has written that the army was 'officered by Europeans, Hindus, Sikhs, Mohammadans, Rajputs – on a cosmopolitan basis'.[3]

The basis of Ranjit's secularism was compromise, a policy that coexisted harmoniously with his ruthlessness and warrior spirit,[4] and one that made him exceptional among indigenous southern Asian rulers. It worked well: during his reign there were no major outbreaks of communal infighting or of repression and punishments of people or groups simply because they came from a particular ethnic background or religion. The Maharaja's secularist style was never entirely popular in all quarters though and he did at times face some unsettling challenges from the more fundamentalist sections of the population, especially the insurgent activity of the Wahabis. Although Ranjit Singh was able to curtail the threat posed by this movement, the troublesome group would later exploit the political turmoil after the Maharaja's death by attempting to carve a niche for themselves out of the territory of the Lahore kingdom.

There were also occasional outbursts of religiously fuelled upset and protest by Akali Nihangs, even led by the general Phula

Singh, whom the Maharaja sometimes struggled to rein in. The Akali Nihangs were particularly antagonistic towards Europeans, who unwittingly transgressed Sikh religious mores and were met with violence and even threats of murder as a consequence. This group was consistently uneasy with the idea of serving under a Maharaja, since they adhered to a strain of Sikhism that espoused a republican ideal, but the quality of Ranjit Singh's leadership seems to have kept them quiescent for at least the duration of his reign.

Probably because it was unprecedented in ruling circles, Ranjit Singh's concern with equality led to many tales being spun about him. His bravery, sincerity and modest bearing touched people and made him a hero in folktales as well as real life. It seems that the burdens of ordinary men and women were lessened by a leader who appealed to their imagination.

ⴵ

Among the many books which were produced in 2001 to commemorate the bicentenary of his coronation was one containing almost six dozen items of folklore.[5] This testifies both to Ranjit Singh's impact on the popular imagination and the importance of tales in magnifying his stature. No history of his life would be complete without mentioning at least some of those that attached to him.

One dramatised Ranjit Singh's emphasis upon equality between rival traditions. Once, when the Sikh *misls* were at the height of their power and feelings towards non-Sikhs could be overly suspicious, two Punjabis, one a Sikh Nihang, one a Muslim, were travelling separately from Lahore towards Amritsar on foot. The Sikh came across the Muslim walking ahead of him, which offended him because Sikhs, not Muslims, were associated with ruling the Punjab. He bade the Muslim to walk behind him. The Muslim agreed to do so but then the Sikh grew worried that onlookers would suppose that the Muslim was driving the Sikh ahead of him. He then asked the Muslim to walk alongside him. The Muslim, who clearly had great patience, did so, only for the Sikh to then fret that that, too, would look inappropriate. By now he had run out of options. The Nihang then put his arm round the Muslim so that the latter would appear to be carrying him.

Another tale concerns the way Ranjit Singh dispensed justice. A man came before the Darbar to complain that a third party to whom he had lent money had not repaid it. Ranjit asked him to return the next day. Meanwhile, he arranged for the third party to be brought before the court, where he denied ever receiving the money. When the complainant returned, Ranjit asked him whether anyone had witnessed the transaction. On hearing that no one had done so the Maharaja asked him where it had occurred. Beneath a tree in a forest, the man replied. Ranjit then asked him to go and fetch the tree as his witness. Flummoxed, the man left for the forest. Meanwhile, Ranjit busied himself on other matters but intermittently asked the third party, now sitting in a corner, how far the man could be from the forest. Overawed by the circumstances, the man answered in such detail that it became obvious that he had been at the location. Ranjit Singh ordered his arrest, at which point the man broke down and admitted that he had indeed borrowed the money. He begged for forgiveness. When the somewhat naive lender returned and said that the tree had not accompanied him, the Maharaja gently chided him for his foolishness, said that the tree had, in effect, given evidence anyway and told him to depart when he had got his money back from the borrower. The situation between the two men was promptly resolved and they quickly left.

This story illustrates the Maharaja's willingness to go to extraordinary lengths to ensure justice for an aggrieved citizen, his refusal to allow another party to get away with lying and his humanity in not punishing the liar. The humiliation of being caught out and the fear that Ranjit Singh would not forget the episode would have exerted their own salutary effects upon the transgressor.

On another occasion, Ranjit had to live up to a myth to ensure its survival. One of his informal titles was 'Paras Maharaja', which alluded to a legend that anything he touched turned to gold.[6] A woman thought she could get rich by having him touch something of hers. One day the Maharaja visited her town and she placed herself not far from where he would be passing. When he was sufficiently near she rushed forward and pressed a soot-encrusted iron *tawa* (cooking grill) against his feet. Fearful soldiers

arrested her amid an outraged crowd. An astonished Ranjit asked
her why she had damaged his clothes. She protested that she had
not spoiled his clothes but had transformed her *tawa* into gold.
Realising the innocence of her action, Ranjit Singh ordering his
servants to give her gold that weighed as much as the *tawa*, showing the high premium that Ranjit placed upon myths and how far
he was prepared to go to embellish them.

In the next story, he is similarly indulgent when hit by a clod
of earth while astride his elephant in Lahore. His escort rounded
up the boys who had hurled the earth and brought them before
the Maharaja. Shaking with trepidation, they said they had been
trying to hit a fruit tree in order to knock some sweet fruits from
it. Satisfied that the boys had meant no harm, he laughed and said
that if a tree provided sweet fruit when hit by a clod of earth a
king must provide something more. He then gave them some gold
coins and they returned home overjoyed. This tale emphasises his
generosity and lack of pomposity.

The moral of another tale is that even Ranjit's generosity could
not solve all problems. He came across a little boy who was crying
loudly and his mother who was not responding. The youngster's
shrill noise caused Ranjit to ask why she was not doing anything
to stop it. The woman said that the child would cry no matter what
she did. The persistent Maharaja asked the child what he wanted
and, on being told that it was a small pot, he had one brought for
the boy. The youngster continued to cry. His mother asked him
why he was still upset and he said he wanted an elephant. Game
for any situation, the Maharaja promptly gave him his elephant
but *still* the child cried. Nonplussed, Ranjit wanted to know why,
only to learn that he wanted the elephant placed in the small pot.
Even Ranjit could not make that happen. He told the woman that
all children occasionally behaved like hers, and handed her a
present before leaving.

A story with a similar moral tells of how Ranjit Singh went
to pay obeisance at the Golden Temple and heard a *ragi* singing
the Kirtan (a hymn involving call-and-response chanting) in a
particularly melodious voice. The Maharaja asked about the singer
and was told that he was poor, lived alone and prepared his own
meals. His poverty was such that even his *tawa* was made from

hard mud. Ranjit felt a surge of pity that this talented singer should be eking out a living in straitened circumstances. He returned to Lahore and gathered together some gifts for when he next visited Amritsar. He then rode as far as he could on his elephant until the streets of Amritsar became too narrow to negotiate. He then went on foot the rest of the way to the man's abode. However, far from being pleased that Maharaja Ranjit Singh wanted to visit him, the man first hid and then climbed onto his roof. Of course, that scarcely concealed him and so when the Maharaja came into view the man was reduced to bellowing at him to 'Go away!' Perplexed, Ranjit did as he was asked, muttering, 'Look, I am trying to give him something but he refuses. There are people who run after me to whom I don't want to give anything.'

So the tales were not designed to show that the Maharaja always succeeded in whatever he set out to do. The deep strain of humility in the Sikh psyche meant that people admired him no less if he sometimes failed in his endeavours, after having done his utmost to succeed.

The tales also placed a premium upon wisdom gained through imagination. The Maharaja's ingenuity was tested to extreme limits with two women (so it is said) who were disputing the ownership of a pail of milk. One said that she had filled it from her herd of cows and buffalos, the other that she had filled it from her one goat. Superficially, the matter seemed to fall in the first woman's favour. She could have formed a well-filled pail from her superior number of beasts. But the second woman stuck to her complaint. Ranjit hit on a solution. He ordered each woman to be given a container full of water and asked them to go and wash their hands and faces. When they returned he noticed that the first woman had used up her water but had failed to properly clean her face and hands. By contrast, the other woman had done so without using up all her water. Ranjit Singh rewarded her sense of economy by deciding in her favour.

The Maharaja, it seems, was willing to base decisions on intuition. Once he appointed a servant who had been dismissed from royal service elsewhere. He told Ranjit Singh that he had a hundred failings but the employer who had sacked him had decided not to overlook even one of them. Noting this admission of fault, and sensing that actually the man was worth employing, Ranjit engaged him at four times the pay of other servants. Not surprisingly, this apparently inexplicable favouritism triggered objections among the servants. Ranjit Singh tried to reason with them but they remained unimpressed, so during an expedition he tested the new man and the other servants by getting them all to make enquiries about a group of businessmen who had established a camp nearby. One by one the servants returned with bits of information. Then their new colleague spoke with the businessmen and returned with all manner of useful information about where they had come from, when and where they were going, what they were selling and what they envisaged making as a profit. He also discovered how many animals they had with them, and even found out whether the men were married or single. Delighted, the Maharaja asked the other servants whether they now understood why the diligent newcomer was being paid so much more than normal. The story goes that they not only understood but were in awe of Ranjit's sagacity in recognising his qualities.

Many more tales arose from events later in his career. All served to enhance his renown among his people. It would be fascinating to know how and when they were propagated and by whom, but we can be certain that the Darbar did nothing to discourage their transmission across the country and their absorption into the national consciousness.

THE THIRD DECADE

By 1822 Ranjit Singh had made most of his territorial conquests, almost entirely by his own efforts. But later that year further disputes between ruling Afghan brothers came to a head and once again posed a threat to the Punjab. Ten and twenty years or so before, the troublemakers were Shahs Zaman and Mahmud. Now the problem was ill-feeling between Yar Mohammad Khan and his elder brother, Mohammad Azim Khan. This had broken out following a visit to Peshawar by Aziz-ud-din, whose respectful reception there by Yar Mohammad had angered the Pathans. Azim Khan championed their cause. Ranjit's conquest of Peshawar had aroused much anger in Afghanistan and over 25,000 warriors volunteered for service. Azim Khan marched his mixed band of regulars and irregulars from Kabul. When he arrived in Peshawar on 27 January 1823 Yar Mohammad Khan hurriedly left for the safety of Yusafzai territory.

The Lahore Darbar was naturally shaken by this turn of events. Ranjit Singh had no alternative but to assemble a large force to quell the revolt. Once again Misr Diwan Chand, Hari Singh Nalwa and Phula Singh were the top commanders, but this time they were joined by three other generals leading battalions they themselves had trained. The Frenchmen Allard and Ventura were two of them. The third was the Gurkha, Balbhadra Kunwar. Balbhadra had commanded the Nepalese army against the British in 1814 and outfought them until, accepting that the odds were hopelessly against him, had fled into the hills. The British honoured him and his Gurkhas with a plaque at Dhera Dunmut. He was an impressive addition to the army.

Prince Sher Singh (then only 15 years old) and Hari Singh Nalwa were picked to spearhead the attack. They crossed the Attock via a pontoon bridge and reached the fort of Jahangiria. Following a light skirmish, the Afghans darted from the fort and fled. In a counter-measure, Azim Khan invoked the cry of Jihad, upon which many Yusafzais and Khattaks flocked to the banner. Oblivious to this renewed threat, the Maharaja had been staying in the rear, even taking time out to hunt along the way. When the Darbar's forces reached the eastern bank of the Attock they found that the enemy had destroyed their bridge. Worse, Sher Singh was besieged in the fort at Jahangiria. As Ranjit Singh was in imminent danger of defeat, Azim Khan was now being assisted by his brothers Dost Mohammad and Jabbar Khan.

Ranjit caught up with the action and realised he had to make a swift do-or-die decision. There was no bridge across the Attock and the hills were surrounded by hostile forces, leaving the Punjabis with no way out. Believing he had no other fighting choice, he ordered his troops to cross the river. Knowing they must be inspired into such drastic, possibly suicidal, action he positioned himself for all to see, recited a prayer and plunged with his mount into the river. The loyal troops followed him. Inevitably, many men drowned in the cold, treacherous currents, along with camels, elephants, horses and mules, while many valuable items of war equipment were also lost. But Ranjit's action afforded a priceless degree of surprise and most of the troops were able to cross and seize the western banks before the Afghans could respond. Ranjit's forces then entrenched themselves and the demoralised Afghans retreated. At the gates of Jahangiria, Prince Sher Singh welcomed his father with joy and relief. The army had added another legendary success to its already impressive tally.

However, the Punjabis remained in extreme danger. Not only had the downcast but numerous Afghans gathered in open fields near the town of Naushera but other Afghan forces had taken up positions to the west of the Landai, a stream which ran between Naushera and Peshawar. The Maharaja consulted his generals. An impassioned Ventura urged him to exploit again his advantage with sharp action before the opposition had time to coalesce and outflank them. Ranjit Singh could see the sense of that. He quickly ordered the army to surround Naushera and encamp on the available bank of the Landai. He then instructed the infantry to open fire. Although their guns were superior to the Afghans' equipment, the latter's numerical advantage plus what they regarded as their holy duty to fight like men possessed enabled them to hold out for some time. Ranjit Singh ordered a cavalry attack. Successive waves of horsemen rode up to the enemy, fired and then turned back. The defenders tried to overcome this tactic by charging at another point but the alert Punjabi forces got on top of them there too. The Punjabis corralled them within range of the Khalsa guns. Even then the defenders held out. Realising that they could only be beaten by equally determined holy fighters, Ranjit played his trump card, the Nihangs. Phula Singh now had his finest hour – literally – as for a whole hour he led his desperadoes in a whirl of hand-to-hand engagements. When his horse was killed beneath him he clambered on to an elephant and dashed back into the fray. Leading from the front in this way was, of course, ultra-risky and he paid the ultimate price. The hero of Multan and Kashmir fell in a hail of Afghan bullets. For all the occasional difficulties his impulsive behaviour had sometimes caused Ranjit, the Maharaja felt the loss of Phula Singh deeply and he ordered a shrine to be constructed at the place where he had fallen in battle. The Gurkha leader Balbhadra also died in action.

Other Sikh troops under Prince Kharak Singh now attacked. Even though half the Afghans had been slain, the remainder still held out on high ground. The attackers were reinforced and the Afghan defenders at last dislodged. The remaining Ghazis fought their way out and into the hills. Azim Khan belatedly rushed to the scene from Peshawar but was pinned to his side of the Landai while men under Hari Singh Nalwa rained artillery fire on his forces and drove them back. Meanwhile the cavalry again rode into action. Mortified, Azim Khan could only watch the slaughter from a distance. He returned to Afghanistan a broken man.

Once again a victorious Ranjit Singh entered Peshawar to a rousing reception. However, in a further sign of how difficult it was to enforce control in far-flung possessions, the occupiers soon found themselves under hit-and-run attacks at night. These were obviously inspired or at least condoned by the vanquished leaders. As he had done before over Peshawar, Ranjit felt he had to compromise with Yar Mohammad and Dost Mohammad (Azim Khan did not show his face). He received the humbled, apologising pair in a friendly fashion and was magnanimous with them. Yar Mohammad was reinstated at Peshawar in return for his offer of tribute. Ranjit Singh then rode home to Lahore where men and women of all traditions greeted him with acclaim and were showered with gold and silver coins in return. He publicly thanked the Almighty for the victory.

The Punjabis' triumph at Naushera was of the utmost importance in extending and securing their north-west territory towards Afghanistan. Although it was hard to believe the historic threat to their entire country from that quarter had truly passed for good, in fact it had, though troubles would still flare intermittently. In military terms, Ranjit Singh's liquidation of Afghan rule between the Indus and Peshawar was his single greatest achievement. The Afghans had always been the Punjab's worst threat. True, the region had been attacked from the north-east and the east, too, but not as savagely or as repeatedly as from the north-west. And in any case, Ranjit Singh had already made satisfactory arrangements with the Gurkha and British authorities who ruled Nepal and India. Gurkhas had fought with the Punjabis at Naushera and British observers had attended at Ranjit Singh's invitation. Neither the Gurkhas nor the British had any love for the Afghans, so the latter could not count on them to acquiesce in any future designs that they might make upon the Punjab. Politically, for the first time Ranjit Singh's Punjab really was the land of the five rivers. He controlled all that lay between them.

But he was not prepared to declare himself satisfied, with the result that one aspect of his foreign policy caused consternation among the British to the east. This was the idea of expanding Punjabi territory yet further to the south-west, into the province of Sindh. This land was ruled by three amirs who were located in Hyderabad, Khairpur and Mirpur. Members of the dynasty of Talpur, which had ruled Sindh for a century, they owed allegiance to Kabul but had stopped paying tribute and so were to all intents and purposes independent. But they were also very weak and thus tried to pursue a policy of isolation. Therefore, they had made no threats whatsoever to the Punjab.

Ranjit Singh's designs on Sindh appear as extraterritorial thinking of a kind he had not previously entertained. His ambition could not be compared with that over the Cis-Sutlej. There were Sikh *misls* in the Cis-Sutlej, and the political aspirations of many people there lay in the direction of the Punjab. But in Sindh most of the populace was Muslim, there was a sizeable Hindu minority and Sikhs were merely one of several other small minorities. The province also had its own native language, Sindhi. Although the Sindh peasantry were oppressed by a combination of the political establishment in Kabul and the local rulers, there was no significant yearning among the people to be ruled by Ranjit Singh. That said, the 1809 Treaty of Amritsar had worried the Talpurian amirs who put out their own feelers to the Maharaja of Lahore in the hope of his being their ally, too, in case the British proved troublesome.

British activity in Sindh gave Ranjit Singh some justification for considering extending the Lahore Darbar's authority over it. British relations with the province stretched back to 1758 when the ruler Ghulam Ali Khan Kalhora had allowed some Britons to establish trading bases there. Although Ghulam's successor Sarfraz Ali Khan Kalhora made the British leave in 1775, in 1798 India's governor-general, Lord Mornington, approved a plan for an official, Nathan Crowe, to negotiate new trade rights with the Talpurias who had overthrown the Kalhoras. Crowe succeeded, only to be expelled from Sindh in 1800. But the British did not give up. In 1809 they secured Sindhian agreement to keep French people out of the province. In 1820 that was supplemented by a treaty under which the amirs would halt their tribesmen's incursions into Cutch, near the eastern banks of the Indus, which the British had taken over the year before. The incursions continued and in 1825 British troops laid on a border demonstration of their military prowess to try and overawe the amirs.

A second reason for the Punjabis to take an interest in Sindh lay in their continued fear of Afghanistan. Following the comprehensive defeat at Naushera, the possibility arose of Afghanistan posing a threat to the Punjab's underbelly from Sindh. The Darbar was duty bound to take this prospect seriously. Possessing Sindh would also afford access to the sea: Sindh stretched right down to the Indian Ocean. Although there is no evidence that Ranjit Singh wanted to move into Sindh for that reason, it cannot be ruled out.

By 1825, when the British troops were firing their guns to impress the amirs, both the East India Company and the Darbar well understood that each entertained a close interest in Sindh. Ranjit Singh's expression of it had been just as noisy as that of the British. His conquest of Multan in 1818 had brought the Darbar's rule down as far as Sindh and so induced a degree of tension there. Border disputes erupted, resulting in Sindhi representatives going to Lahore to try to reach a settlement, but to no avail. In 1823 Ranjit led an expedition to subdue the Sindh tribes and demand tribute from the Talpurian amirs. The mission encouraged Ranjit. By now he fully appreciated just how feeble the amirs were, and so the north Sindh commercial city of Shikarpur appeared all the more attainable.

The British disliked the notion of Ranjit Singh acquiring Sindh, in part because that would close off the possibility of *their* doing so. British control of Sindh would afford easier access to some parts of British-ruled India and so made a certain economic and commercial sense. In 1822 British worries about Ranjit's interest caused them somewhat impertinently to ask him to explain his intentions over Sindh. Affronted, in October that year the Maharaja replied, advising them in a diplomatic phrase to beware of gossip: 'Let the mirror of friendship be kept clear and polished.' He must have known that his put-down was disingenuous, given his own interest.

Sindh would return as an issue between the British and the Darbar, but for the time being it disappeared beneath the surface. In any case, the written exchanges of 1822 preceded the Darbar army's great victory at Naushera in the north-west where the British had no concerns over Ranjit Singh's ambitions. That landmark success had come at a heavy price. First, the mental and physical strain probably contributed to Ranjit's first attack of bodily paralysis. For any human being, not least a busy and active man, no event is more worrying than being overtaken by a sudden collapse. His indisposition naturally affected the smooth running of state affairs, which were already disrupted by the financial cost of Naushera. When he had recovered from this severe setback he embarked on a tour of his domains in order to raise money from dues and tributes.

Although his efforts resulted in the Treasury being fuller than it had been for a long time,[1] monetary concerns continued to plague the Darbar. An indication of their stressful effect arose in dramatic fashion in January 1825 after the Maharaja asked the two French officers to pay two months of their salary to help refill the Punjab's coffers. There are times when a request is in effect an order, rejection of which risks retribution. And it was not the done thing for anyone to turn down an obviously important request from the Maharaja, who would in any case have been aware of the tinge of resentment that his employment of Europeans had created among some of his officials. He also knew that Allard and Ventura had plenty of money left over from their service under Bonaparte, so they could easily have afforded to release some of their new pay, which in any case was perfectly adequate. They refused.

Ranjit Singh could not let pass a rebuff such as this, and from foreign subjects into the bargain. He felt the snub so acutely that he lashed out at them in the open Darbar, drawing his dagger and screaming abuse at them until calmed down by other officers. By 1825 both men had proved themselves as valuable employees, but that counted for nothing against the honour of the head of state. Nonetheless, he was, as we know, inclined to forgive those who repented. The shaken Frenchmen apologised, and once again became the recipients of Ranjit's favours.

That same year, 1825, Ventura obtained Ranjit's permission to marry an Armenian Christian and Ranjit was among those who offered wedding presents. The marriage produced a daughter, Victoria, though Ventura's wife later left her husband as she could not abide him keeping a *zenana*. Allard, too, married a Punjabi girl and raised a family of five children. He did not force his wife to change her Hindu religion, though he later had their children baptised in France.

Professionally, both men continued to shine. In July 1825, six months after Ranjit had blazed at them in the open Darbar, Misr Diwan Chand died. This was another hard personal blow for both Ranjit and the Punjab, but Ventura helped to restore morale when he undertook a successful campaign at Gandhgarh in 1826. By 1829, the cavalry under Allard had increased fourfold and it remained at this strength until near the end of Ranjit's reign, efficient, smart and admired by all.

On the other hand, the strain of the financial situation might have contributed towards two swift and ill-judged decisions. The first occurred when Fateh Singh Ahluwalia fled to the Cis-Sutlej and sought British protection. Ranjit was in part to blame for this and he knew it. His liquidation of the *misls* had been ruthless and only Fateh's remained. Fateh thought he saw the writing on the wall. His flight enabled Ranjit Singh to take the simple step of taking over his *misl* without ejecting him from it, but at the same time Fateh's evident distrust hurt Ranjit considerably.

The second instance of poor judgement was wholly Ranjit's. In January 1826 he again toured outside Lahore and this time he appointed Sher Singh to act in his stead while he was away. Given that Prince Sher was still only 18 and Kharak was 23, their father's very public decision left Kharak feeling put out. Ranjit appears to have failed to speak with him before his decision. Although Prince Sher's leadership qualities were already superior to Kharak's, it was nonetheless tactless to show favouritism quite so blatantly. The Maharaja's surprising behaviour offers a further example of the strain he was under. Later in 1826 he had a second major attack of paralysis. He felt the end must be near and asked to be taken to Amritsar so that if he died at least he would be in the Sikhs' holy city.[2] However, Imam-ud-din obtained the services of a British doctor called Murray, part of whose treatment included rest in relaxed conditions outside the bustling city centre. His ministrations worked. The Maharaja's condition improved and he returned to duty. Meanwhile, during his father's illness, Prince Kharak had been so worried about the future that he put out feelers to the British in the hope of securing their support for his claim to the succession.

Ranjit's recovery was crowned by Fateh Singh Ahluwalia's decision to return. The British had not welcomed him, for his presence fitted badly with their policy of showing friendship towards Ranjit. That, plus repeated urgings by Darbar emissaries, drew

Fateh home. He humbled himself before the Maharaja and the pair tearfully embraced. Ranjit had the sense to restore Fateh's *misl* to him as part of their settlement.

There was a certain listlessness about Ranjit's rule in the mid-1820s, exemplified by his reluctance to enforce his claim to Sindh, despite a chance to do so. In 1823 the British had turned their attention eastwards, when in 1823 the Burmese occupied an island, Shahpuri, which placed them at odds with the East India Company. In February 1824 the British declared war on Burma. Burma's thick forests made the war difficult and it took two years to ensure victory. In 1826, Ranjit Singh had an opportunity to go for Sindh. If he had done so, the overstretched British would have been hard put to stop him. But he didn't. It is not clear why – caution, perhaps, or lack of energy as a result of his illness, or simply a desire to adhere to his long-established policy of keeping in with the British.

ɛ⁄ɔ

As well as the happy return of Fateh Singh Ahluwalia, 1827 saw the arrival of another two foreigners who would go on to give fine service to the Punjab: an Italian, Paolo Avitabile and another Frenchman, Claude August Court.

Born in 1791 near Naples, Avitabile served in local militia and in the artillery of the regular army during the Napoleonic Wars. Following Napoleon's final defeat in 1815, Naples was reunited with Sicily, and Avitabile joined the new, merged army. He was wounded in service, overlooked for promotion and resigned his commission in disgust. Like Allard and Ventura, Avitabile went to Persia, where his ability and bravery were properly recognised by the Shah: he rose to the rank of colonel. From 1820 he also gained administrative experience in Kurdish districts for which he was honoured by the state and which proved useful later under Ranjit Singh. But the pay was poor, and when he heard from his compatriot, Ventura, of possible prospects under Ranjit Singh he jumped at the chance. He took employment in the Punjab in 1826. His initial duties are somewhat vague – some say artillery, some infantry – but this impressively tall and extrovert man went on to be best remembered for his time as governor of Wazirabad.

While in Persia, Avitabile had met Court who would be the fourth significant European to throw in his lot with Ranjit Singh during this decade. Born in France in 1793, Court had fought courageously in Napoleon's last major campaigns. In 1818 a dearth of prospects at home caused him, too, to put European soldiering behind him and to go and serve in Persia. Eight years later he rode with Avitabile to seek fortune in the Punjab. They arrived in Lahore together, like Allard and Ventura before them. Thereafter, however, their career paths diverged. Court, like Ranjit Singh, was short and bore disfiguring marks of smallpox. Wise, courteous, though rather stiff, he appealed to Ranjit, who employed him to improve his army's artillery, which he did conspicuously well. He was also given infantry battalions and responsibility for the ordnance. In 1829 he married a Muslim girl whom he loved deeply but who died in 1837. He then married a Kashmiri girl who later converted to Christianity. Notwithstanding these marriages, he maintained a harem, as did Avitabile.

Only one of these four highly placed Europeans went on to earn much local affection. That was Allard. Good-looking and benevolent by nature, his humility appealed to Punjabis, not least Ranjit Singh. When Allard died early in 1839 the courtiers were reluctant to inform Ranjit, whose own health was then in its final state of fragility. Meanwhile, all four provided excellent service at a time of increasing danger presented by an outsider of a completely different sort.

Early in the 1800s a young *madrassa* graduate called Syed Ahmed had joined a Pathan military force to operate mainly as a fighter but with the added duty of leading the soldiers in prayer. During this time Syed Ahmed learnt about European weaponry, including the use of artillery. Shah Abdul Aziz, the Sunni Islamic scholar, greeted him warmly in Delhi and many of the graduates and students were instructed to become disciples of Syed Ahmed, who was more of a fighter and an agitator than scholar. The Shah declared that British rule rendered the subcontinent Dar-ul-Harb, or an area not under Islamic control. This implied that such rule should be resisted, which meant having a leader who would be willing to persuade men to fight and die in the cause. Syed Ahmed looked to be the man for the task. At the same time, while emphasising the need for Jihad, Syed Ahmed did not outline any immediate plans. Instead, in 1821 he left for Mecca on a pilgrimage. Rather than go direct, he travelled via Calcutta, adding about 2,000 miles to the journey and gathering almost 100,000 followers along the way. Now aged 37, he returned to Delhi in May 1823 with a vision of Jihad as a means of social and personal improvement as well as physical struggle.

The Lahore Darbar could draw no comfort from the Shah's vision. Syed Ahmed included Sikhism within his objections to non-Muslim control in the subcontinent and, in practice, he took aim at them rather than at the British, whom he doubtless perceived to be less vulnerable. Accordingly, he convinced his followers of the need to declare Jihad against the Sikhs, liberate the Punjab from the Sikhs and restore it to Muslim rule. As well as his followers, he had several highly placed supporters, including the Mughal king in Delhi (although Delhi was about all he now ruled). On 21 December 1826 Syed Ahmed officially announced the Jihad against Sikhs. Another top figure, Yar Mohammad, now joined his band of supporters. Satisfied that the Jihadists would prevail against Ranjit Singh, the untrustworthy Yar withdrew from Peshawar as proof of his belief.

The Punjab's north-west was once again exposed to extreme danger. Ranjit Singh called up a new general, Budh Singh Sandhanwalia, to take back Peshawar. Ventura and Allard were sent along with him. The disciplined Darbar forces overcame the wilder defenders and Peshawar was back in Darbar hands. The wretched Yar Mohammad was once again forced to seek Ranjit's forgiveness. Immediately thereafter, there occurred an incident in which historical truth is mixed with myth. Ranjit Singh determined to obtain from Yar Mohammad his striking white Persian horse, Leili, of rare beauty and fine breeding fit for a Maharaja. He would do so by using the Koh-i-Noor diamond.

The story goes that Ranjit had already heard of Leili before having to do battle with Syed Ahmed. He had dispatched Fakir Aziz-ud-din to Peshawar to persuade Yar to let him have the animal. At first Yar Mohammad offered a number of horses, but Leili was not one of them. When asked why he had excluded Leili, Yar Mohammad made matters worse for himself by saying that

the horse was dead. On being told that, Ranjit snorted with disbe-
lief. At this point the facts become more obscure. According to
some, the reason why Ranjit Singh sent Budh Singh Sandhanwalia
to Peshawar was not so much to fight a war as to obtain the horse.
Budh Singh Sandhanwalia was then killed and the Maharaja
sent Allard and Ventura to take over. They managed to bring Yar
Mohammad's brother and – some accounts say – 12-year-old son
as hostages to the Maharaja's court. Ranjit then demanded Leili
from Yar Mohammad. When the latter still refused, so the story
goes, Ranjit went to war again and finally took possession of his
legendary horse.

Leili was taken to Lahore – in October 1827 by several accounts
– and toured the capital majestically decorated with costly jewels,
including the Koh-i-Noor. The court poet, Qadir Yar, composed a
poem in praise of Leili. Baron Charles Hügel,[3] an Austrian army
officer, diplomat, botanist and explorer, who visited the Punjab,
claimed that Ranjit Singh told him that it cost 12,000 soldiers and
a vast sum in rupees to possess Leili. Being such a lover of horses
he naturally admired many others besides Leili. He had already
obtained an elegant steed, Gauharbar, from the Barakzai family
and also jealously guarded his rights to another mount, Dooloo.
On one occasion he admonished the wilful Sher Singh so angrily
for taking Dooloo without his permission that Nur-ud-din intervened to calm him down. But neither Dooloo nor Gauharbar nor
any other horse aroused his awe and affection as much as Leili. A
few years later when Leili died, the Maharaja wept inconsolably
and the horse was given a state burial which included a 21-gun
salute.[4]

Whatever the true sequence of events that led to Yar surrendering Leili, Syed Ahmed was not crushed by the Darbar forces'
recapture of Peshawar. Rather, he and groups of supporters took
refuge in the hills and from there made a series of quick, pinprick
attacks on their victors, showing far and wide that they were still
very much alive and kicking. On 6 June 1827 Charles Metcalfe
reported to Calcutta from Delhi that Syed Ahmed had helped
to establish 'a very extensive, if not universal, influence over the
minds of our Mohammedan subjects. During the period of their
recent attacks on Ranjit Singh's territories, the most fervent anxiety

for their success pervaded the Mohamedan population at Delhi. A number quitted their houses and marched to join them.'[5]

The situation in Ranjit's north-west domain turned into what we today would recognise as classic guerrilla warfare: unpredictable hit-and-run attacks repeated over many years, designed to wear down the much more powerful enemy. Syed's men had a draining effect on a Punjab that was still feeling the pinch from the more set-piece battles of that decade. Five more years would pass before this particular threat was reduced to a containable level.

In 1830 Prince Sher Singh led a successful counter-attack but even then, almost four years after announcing the Jihad of December 1826, the fighters defied defeat. Shortly afterwards, when Yar Mohammad was killed, Syed Ahmed marched into Peshawar. But what seemed like a most damaging setback for the Punjabis now turned to their advantage. Syed Ahmed had something of Ranjit Singh's fighting nature but none of his humility. He assumed the mantle of conqueror, introducing coins bearing his name and image. From far and wide, Muslims poured into Peshawar and its surrounding area. The influx proved to be the last straw for the war-weary populace. The Darbar forces had tried periodically to win over Syed's supporters with offers of money, and this stratagem now began to work. Syed Ahmed was forced out and Sher Singh took Peshawar back under Sikh control.

In May 1831 this soldier-prince crowned his success by trapping troops led by Syed Ahmed himself into a climactic battle at Balakot in which he split Syed's resources, thereby weakening them. Those that were divided from Syed's main force were left particularly exposed. However, his resolute men continued to fight, and Sher Singh had to call on his equally zealous Akalis to force the issue. A Briton, Alexander Gardner, who became colonel of artillery under Ranjit Singh, watched as the Darbar soldiers made their prize kill: 'I was literally within a few hundred yards of the Syed when he fell, but I did not see the angel descend and carry him off to paradise, although many of his followers remembered afterwards that they had seen it distinctly enough.'[6]

Although Syed had been a menace for many years, Sher Singh, who possessed his father's magnanimity, covered the slain Muslim with a shawl before he was buried with ceremonial honours. But even with Syed gone, his movement did not die completely. The Barakzai leader Dost Mohammad kept his name and spirit alive.

૭૭

Ranjit Singh's latent interest in Sindh was now rekindled by British activity in the Indus region. The Lahore Darbar would have been gravely concerned had it known what initially sparked this activity – policy change at the highest political level in London. Lord Ellenborough, the 'rash and overbearing' President of the Board of Control in the Duke of Wellington's government,[7] wanted Britain to invade the Punjab and Afghanistan.[8]

Ellenborough had ministerial responsibility for the East India Company, whose charter was due for review, and he was convinced Russia intended to invade India. 'The invasion of India [by Russia]', he had written, 'is not only practicable but easy, unless we determine to act as an Asiatic Power. We should occupy Lahore and Kabul.' But by January 1830 he accepted that this recommendation could not be taken forward at the snap of an imperial finger. He now decided that Russia's designs in Central Asia were to be feared not so much because Russia might directly attack India – a proposition for which there was no evidence – but because it might arouse anti-British feeling to India's north and west, including Sindh. To pre-empt such a threat, and to expand British influence and power, Ellenborough appointed a commissioner to explore Sindh.

The agent who was to spearhead Britain's new manifestation of its Sindhi interest was a Scottish soldier-traveller-explorer, Captain Alexander Burnes. Born in 1805, Burnes had joined the army in India in his mid-teens. He learnt Hindustani and Persian, in which he became an interpreter. Appointed political agent at Cutch, near to the east banks of the Indus, his exploring interests were aroused by being in an unsurveyed area. In 1829 he recommended that he should make a survey, which linked in neatly with London's political interests. Lest Burnes's proposal should upset the amirs of Sindh, the British decided to oil the way with a gift of five large horses from King William IV to Ranjit Singh, which they claimed would need to be transported up the River Indus.

Fortunately for relations all round, Wellington's government fell in November 1830 and Ellenborough with it.⁹ His departure meant that diplomacy could proceed on the ground without London taking a potentially wrecking interest in it. Lord (William) Bentinck, the British governor-general of India, now came into contact with the Punjab government more directly. Balancing his wish to keep in with the British and his suspicion of them as foreign players, Ranjit took the opportunity early in 1831 to approve a visit by Aziz-ud-din, Hari Singh Nalwa and Moti Ram to meet with Bentinck on his first tour of northern India. Bentinck, a former soldier, was proving an energetic governor-general, cutting costs and abolishing a number of Indian customs that the British found offensive, in particular *sati*.

The three Darbar dignitaries impressed Bentinck and his British support staff. They in effect continued smoothing the path towards a top-level meeting. Bentinck decided that the issues of Sindh and the Indus were so important that he must meet with Ranjit Singh himself. Accordingly, he sent Captain Claude Wade, Agent to the Governor-General for the Affairs of the Punjab and Northwest Frontier, to Lahore to sound out the Maharaja.

Wade was an auspicious choice. Indian-born, he became a cadet in the Bengal service of the East India Company in 1809 and mastered Persian. By 1823 he had switched to civilian service and become Calcutta's diplomatic agent at Ludhiana. He arrived at Ranjit Singh's camp on 22 May 1831 and mentioned Bentinck's desire to meet with him. However, he added that the governor-general wanted the Maharaja to invite him to a meeting rather than the other way round. Bentinck also desired that the Maharaja would call on him first rather than vice versa. Although Wade put all this as tactfully as he could, the proposal was inherently insensitive and could not fail to create suspicion. Ranjit Singh did not immediately respond to it. He did, however, express his goodwill, and he appears to have warmed to Wade, which was helpful because he would come across him again in July when Wade would once more urge an invitation upon him.

Meanwhile, Captain Burnes and his companions had travelled some way north up the Indus, having commenced their journey in March 1831. The party was weighed down with goods. In addition to their own equipment and the five horses, they had a huge coach which Bentinck had provided as another gift for the Maharaja. As with Charles Metcalfe's mission of over 20 years earlier to Lahore, Burnes had been ordered to use his time not just to survey but to make notes on Sindh's government, army and other institutions. However, Ranjit Singh soon drew the right conclusions about Burnes's mission from his own agents' reports. The government sent Lehna Singh Majithia, the scientifically qualified member of the Darbar, to greet Burnes and to discuss his team's findings. Lehna Singh's technical expertise and his handsome reception of the new arrivals impressed Burnes, who shed even more of his standard contemporary European prejudice against brown-skinned Asians when, wide-eyed, he observed some of the support staff kill a tiger that had attacked one of their fellows. Burnes went on to hail the bravery of Sikhs generally and of their country as containing 'the most rising people in modern India'.[10]

Since the newcomers bore gifts from their king, the Darbar treated them as VIPs. On 18 July Aziz-ud-din and Gulab Singh officially welcomed Burnes just outside Lahore. Next day he and his party were received by the Maharaja himself. Burnes was taken by surprise when, stooping to remove his shoes, he found himself being clasped tightly by what appeared to be an old-looking man of not more than 5 feet 3 inches in height. (Burnes's reference to Ranjit being old-looking is revealing: Ranjit was now 50 years of age, and his vigorous, dangerous life and career may have given his face a worn look.)

The Britons were seated and, following opening pleasantries, Burnes handed the Maharaja a letter from Bentinck on behalf of William IV. Fakir Aziz-ud-din read out the Persian text which included references to the great mutual friendship and to the present of horses. Ranjit was openly pleased when he saw the gigantic horses, which he said were the size of small elephants. Following a parade of some of his own horses, Ranjit pounded Burnes with questions about the Indus and its inhabitants. All this time Burnes was taking in the Darbar. As many others had done before him, he noted both the Maharaja's modesty and the rapt attention and respect the sardars paid him. The effect was to enhance his regard for the people among whom he found himself.

For his part, Ranjit evidently assessed Burnes as a man with whom he could do business. When they met again they breakfasted on horseback. On 25 July Burnes was accorded the privilege of a more private audience. Between displays by dancing girls, the Maharaja outlined his account of the Anglo-Punjabi relationship and his encounters with Metcalfe and Ochterlony and others over the preceding decades and emphasised that he had acted as a good friend and ally. Then he raised what for him was clearly the nub of the meeting: Sindh. He candidly explained his interest in the province and asked about that of Britain. Burnes, of course, was not empowered to comment, but Ranjit would have known that. Rather, on Sindh he simply wanted Burnes to be able to tell Calcutta what he had said and asked. The meeting then reverted to relaxation and watching dancing displays.

Incidentally, in his *Travels into Bokhara*, Burnes provided a fine description of one of Ranjit's hunts:

He rode a favourite bay horse, covered with an elegant saddle-cloth of the richest embroidery, ornamented, in its border, by almost every beast and bird which the sportsman calls his own. Runjeet was dressed in a tunic of green shawls, lined with fur; his dagger was studded with the richest brilliants; and a light metal shield, the gift of the ex-King of Cabool, completed his equipment. A train of elephants followed him; and a pack of dogs of motley breed, natives of Sinde, Bokhara, Iran and his own dominions, led the van. His falconers supported their noble birds on their fists. They fluttered at his side, and shook the bells suspended from their feet. A company of infantry in extended order, with two or three hundred horsemen, swept the ground; and we followed the foresters with their rude halberds, who soon disturbed the game. We were to encounter hogs instead of tigers. The swords of the Seiks glittered in the sun; and in the course of half an hour eight monsters had bitten the dust, and many more were entrapped by snares. Most of the animals had been slain by the horse-men with their swords; a few had been first wounded by the matchlock … The scene took place in a plain covered with high grass, in the open patches of which we could see from our elephants the brilliant display with great advantage. … The live hogs were then brought, tied by one leg to a stake, and baited with dogs. The sport is a cruel one, and does not afford any great amusement; the courage and fire of the animals are renewed by dashing water over them. After witnessing it for a short time, an order was given to set all the live hogs at liberty, as Runjeet said that they might praise his humanity; and the infuriated animals scampered through the crowded encampment, to the great delight of the assembled multitude.

Burnes's stamina – it was high summer in the Punjab – and his good sense and tact helped smooth the way for a top-level meeting between the Maharaja and the British governor-general. Ranjit Singh's respect for the young Briton was possibly of crucial importance, for according to one account he also received Claude Wade at the meeting where he was presented with the British gifts.[11] Wade had returned to Lahore specifically to remind Ranjit of Bentinck's wish to meet him. Since Ranjit had already warmed to Wade, it is fair to suppose that his positive feelings towards these two foreign emissaries was decisive in his agreement to meet Bentinck on the latter's terms. Notwithstanding the Darbar's superb reception for Burnes, several sardars rightly disliked both the British proposal for the Maharaja to make the invitation and the notion of him first calling on the governor-general, whose status, they believed, was inferior to that of Ranji Singh.

On this occasion, the Maharaja swallowed his pride with remarkably good grace. First, he gave Burnes a glittering send-off. Burnes was shown the Koh-i-Noor, given rings encrusted with a diamond and an emerald plus four other ornaments, a horse and a robe of honour. Ranjit's letter for William IV was sealed in a silk purse with two pearls tied to its string. Burnes was then escorted to Amritsar, where he paid his respects at the Golden Temple, and thence to a meeting with Fateh Singh Ahluwalia before his departure.

In addition, Ranjit invited Bentinck to meet him, without any comment about the impertinence of the British terms. He and Fakir Aziz-ud-din composed a rich greeting. He told the governor-general that he had always been 'watering this sapling of friendship to see it rise into a thickly foliaged tree'. Delighted and perhaps relieved, Bentinck replied in a similar vein.

Alexander Burnes's report on Sindh for Bentinck confirmed that the Indus was suitable for navigation and that it went through the territory of the amir of Khairpur, who could be depended upon to be friendly. Burnes's comments on the other amirs were also to the effect that they would be willing to allow the British to use Sindh for purposes of passage as the price of security against Ranjit Singh.

Beyond Burnes's report, broader political events were opening the way for Britain to further its interest in Sindh. Russia and Persia concluded a war (1826–28) by signing the Treaty of Turkmanchai, by which Russia's frontier in the Caucasus advanced to include present-day Georgia and Azerbaijan, much to Britain's alarm. Reporting to London, Lord Bentinck recommended formalising a scheme for navigating the Indus which would afford Britain commercial advantages, increase its influence in Sindh and stem that of Ranjit Singh. But the British could not risk acting in such a way as to offend him. They had at least to make an effort to secure his cooperation while sneakily continuing to negotiate directly with the amirs.

❧❧

A GRAND SUMMIT OF EQUALS
AND RANJIT'S NOBLES

The Punjabis and the British had agreed to the summit meeting taking place at Rupar (now Rupnagar) on the left bank of the Sutlej. The Darbar went to imaginative lengths to make it an occasion to remember. Workmen created a huge eight-acre park and built a mound offering spectacular views on which they erected a pavilion resembling (in a nod to the Hindu population on the other side of the Sutlej) a Hindu temple. Ranjit's tents were placed next to the pavilion, with marquees woven from yellow silk and satin. They were layered with striking embroidery, while the ground was covered in fabulous carpets. The Punjabis also made a garden containing plots in the shape of birds and other animals. An enormous variety of flowers were in bloom, enhancing the riot of rich colours. Finally, a bridge made of flat-bottomed boats lashed together led across the river. With the British side also having gone to great lengths to impress, the spectacle struck observers as the height of magnificence, a veritable 'field of cloth of gold'.

Thousands were drafted in to accompany one party or the other. No fewer than 22,000 Darbar cavalrymen and infantrymen attended, a reminder to the British of how strong the Punjabi forces now were. A little over 100 distinguished Punjabi civilians also attended, along with princes and nobles. On the British side, 60 civilian and military officers accompanied the governor-general, along with two squadrons of lancers, a mounted band, a regiment, two battalions of Native Infantry,[1] eight guns of horse-drawn artillery and two squadrons of cavalry under Lieutenant James Skinner, who took notes that later proved invaluable to historians.

Ranjit Singh arrived at the site on 25 October. After a good night's rest he carried out his religious observances and then climbed aboard his gold-bedecked elephant, followed by 1,000 horsemen dressed in silk coats. Some 3,000 soldiers plus a regiment commanded by Jean François Allard had already crossed the bridge as the advance party. After Ranjit, too, had crossed over, he and Bentinck dismounted from their elephants and embraced. The two parties then spent a whole hour in pleasantries, enquiring about each other's health and welfare, exchanging presents of robes, ornaments, guns, pistols, horses, elephants and jewellery, and finally watching dancing girls. The British showed they had done their homework on the Maharaja's interests by laying on a demonstration of English folk dancing. That pleased Ranjit and the Darbar no end. The official Lahore diarist Sohan Lal Suri wrote that the 'desert of ill-will changed to an orchard of goodwill and the rust of anxiety was erased from the hearts of the people' [2] – a flowery effusion that was typical of the officialese of the time, but which also hinted at the original response to British machinations.

The elaborate formalities and the relatively small number of people who spoke both Punjabi and English kept conversation down, leaving plenty of time for the leaders to get around to serious discussions about their respective political interests. On the 26th Bentinck, escorted by Prince Kharak, paid his return visit to Ranjit Singh on the left bank of the Sutlej. His official welcome was followed by more exchanges of presents and dancing displays, plus military parades, of which there would be many over the next three days. Characteristically, Ranjit Singh made the most of them by asking endless questions. He was particularly interested in the British soldiers' square formations which he astutely assessed offered them protection like a wall of iron. Lieutenant Skinner noted how the Maharaja 'proved himself to be a far superior soldier to any other native' and 'moved about as if he himself was in command of the [British army's] troops'.[3]

At some point in the proceedings, the conversation between the two principals turned to river navigation. The British were concerned not only with passage up the Indus but were also interested in using the other regional rivers in the Punjab in order to transfer goods between north-western areas of British-ruled India and the point where the Indus could be used cost-effectively. The British were again in contact with the amirs. Henry Pottinger, the British Resident in Cutch, had gone to Hyderabad earlier in October 1831. At first the amirs were unwilling to do Britain's bidding, so Pottinger deployed the iron fist within the velvet glove and cajoled them into agreeing to sign commercial treaties.

Concerned, Ranjit enquired whether the British proposed to extend their rule to Sindh. Claude Wade, who replied, happily reassured him that they had no intention of doing so. Their motives were purely commercial, he said, adding that the amirs had seen things that way, too. Though disingenuous, the latter remark would have placed Ranjit on the back foot. He tried to press for an advantage by referring to his influence over neighbouring Bahawalpur and his inclination to exert some sort of authority over Sindh. However, these were weak cards. Bahawalpur was strictly a separate issue, and Punjabi rule in Sindh could no more be morally justified than British rule could. Bentinck had no difficulty in resisting Ranjit, who was left with the impression that the British would certainly not support a Punjabi annexation of Sindh and, in view of their treaties with the amirs, would most probably oppose it.

The implications of the deftly delivered British response took some time to work their way fully into the Maharaja's consciousness. He was enjoying what amounted to exceedingly fulsome celebrations with the British, so his irritation over the fact that for a second time in 22 years they had blocked one of his strategic aims was slow to ignite. But ignite it did, beneath his continued admiration and respect for them. First, they had halted his moves in the south-east, on the right side of the Sutlej (by the Treaty of Amritsar, which had offered Ranjit Singh some advantages). Now they had blocked him in the south-west, in a region with which, unlike the Punjab, the British had no common border. He was bound to feel affronted.

Worse, the convivial proceedings with Bentinck and his party had become riotous as alcoholic drinks were consumed one after another, and some sardars disliked what they regarded as decadent and immoral behaviour. Sohan Lal Suri recorded an incident where an Akali lost control and lunged at Ranjit with his drawn

sword. He was intercepted before he could do any harm, but Ranjit
Singh would have known that other figures at the Darbar shared
his assailant's distaste for the lack of decorum during what was,
after all, an official visit by an acting head of state.

And this was a head of state who was determined to limit Sikh
ambitions. Politically, all that Bentinck had offered was perpetual
friendship, which amounted to nothing new. Even though Ranjit
Singh appreciated British support or acquiescence for his actions
within the Punjab, the fact was that they had penned him in –
and could in the last resort use their superior military strength
to keep him so. Even their very useful parting gift of two horse-
artillery guns was another reminder of that supremacy, for they
would hardly have given the Darbar such powerful weapons if
they thought they could be used decisively against them.

Ironically, the ostensible basis of the political dispute – navigation on the Indus – proved much less commercially advantageous
than the British thought it would. The envisaged inflow of traders
from Balakh, Bukhara, Kabul and Turkistan failed to materialise,
as did ideas for holding trade fairs on the Indus. Disputes arose
over supervising and collecting tolls. On the other hand, Britain
gained politically from the whole affair by checking Ranjit Singh
and establishing some tenuous influence in Sindh. And Ranjit
Singh soon renewed his expressions of goodwill towards Britons as individuals. Early in 1832, Alexander Burnes was tasked
with an investigative mission to Afghanistan which meant passing through the Punjab. He politely wrote to the Maharaja who
instantly offered him his country's full cooperation. Ranjit then
put aside a good deal of time to talk, drink and hunt with Burnes.
Ranjit also took him to Lahore to celebrate the religious festival of
Basant in which Sikhs, Hindus and Muslims alike all participated.
During his journey through the Punjab, Burnes passed through
many villages and observed how people looked well dressed and
happy and lived in well-kept, comfortable houses. He also came
across an incident of Sikh/Muslim accord. A Muslim veterinary
doctor had cured some Sikhs' horses of a mysterious disease, in
return for which the Sikhs repaired his place of worship.

At the same time, the British interruption of Ranjit's ambitions
in Sindh caused the Maharaja for the first time to act overtly in

defiance of them. He encouraged the amirs to have no truck with foreign activity in Sindh. Naturally, the amirs did not care for such advice from Ranjit Singh because they regarded his own interests there as foreign, but his action was nonetheless a departure from his previously pro-British policy. Ranjit Singh also urged Shah Shuja to take on the Barakzais, who were being wooed by the British; he tried to alarm the British by telling them that Russia was seeking his friendship, and he revived his claims to some territory to the east of the Sutlej. As an indication of their concern to maintain good relations, the British gave way regarding several towns and villages but they stood firm over Ferozepur. Instead, in 1835 they fortified it, an act which vitiated much of the existing goodwill.

Much else happened meanwhile. Several more Europeans followed the trail blazed by the French pioneers and joined the Darbar service. One was Transylvanian-born Dr John Martin Honigberger, who became Ranjit's court physician. He had left home in 1815 and travelled extensively, particularly in Asia, which he regarded as the cradle of humanity and the birthplace of religion and science. Having heard from Paolo Avitabile about opportunities under Ranjit Singh, he arrived in Lahore in 1829. Honigberger obtained experience as a physician and treated Raja Suchet Singh in Kashmir before Ranjit appointed him physician to the Darbar. Although Honigberger interrupted his service to return to Europe, he went back to the Punjab, where he became famous for bringing homoeopathy to the subcontinent. He was still court physician when the British annexed the country in 1849.

Another arrival was Josiah Harlan, an American. Harlan served as an army doctor in India before going to Afghanistan where he spied for Shah Shuja on Dost Mohammad Khan. However, he had also agreed to spy for the British and for the Sikhs, and even for Dost, too. Inevitably, his duplicity became known and he quietly left Kabul, reaching Lahore in 1829. Despite his dubious background, Harlan, like Honigberger, became popular with the sardars by treating them medically. He was governor of Nurpur and Jasrota until 1832, when the populace made complaints about him. After he proved a weak administrator in Gujrat as well, he was summoned to Lahore and admonished. These and other

Europeans continued in service, and more would follow in their tracks.

ℰℛ

Whatever Ranjit Singh's difficulties, he was sustained by his extensive interests away from the dangerous and exhausting world of politics and its endless civil and military byways. In addition to his religious faith and horse-riding skills, Ranjit was regarded as a patron of the arts. His indulgence and understanding of the finer sensibilities went far beyond dancing girls. The famous twentieth-century Indian writer Mulk Raj Anand wrote in his journal *Marg* that Ranjit Singh released the creative energies of people to construct buildings worthy of the new empire, to develop the arts as part of enjoying life and to appreciate the beauty of artistic creations.[4] Painters and musicians became recognised as national assets, not just as talented private artists, contributing to the Punjab's brief flowering as a confident and respected country.

To a degree, Ranjit Singh's Punjab was introduced to the finer arts through his conquests. For instance, that of Kangra brought people into close touch with Pahari art (sometimes known as hill painting). Darbar courtiers patronised Pahari artists, who drew miniatures with lyrical themes and made religious and mythical wall-paintings. Sikhism's forbiddance of image worship did not mean that there was no scope for portraying gods and goddesses. Ranjit Singh's artistic inclinations were also enhanced by his recognition that portraiture was liked and expected by foreigners with whom he came into contact. He came to understand that artistic works made for constructive conversation which oiled the wheels of political discourse.

By then Ranjit had long been allowing artists to portray his own image. Initially, his modesty and his unprepossessing appearance meant he disliked the idea of being sketched. Gradually, however, he grew to appreciate the fact that artists were not concerned with bringing out his less appealing features but were emphasising his alertness, self-possession and majesty. In time, Ranjit even allowed painters to sketch him from his left side, thereby taking in his blind eye. Towards the end of his life, the British painter Emily Eden, sister of Governor-General Lord Auckland, for whom she acted as hostess, was one who did so. The British took Jiwan Ram, a Delhi artist, along to the Rupar summit to paint him. As a result of all this, Ranjit Singh's era became distinguished in the art of portraiture.

Ranjit also encouraged other arts, reflecting his secularism. A Muslim craftsman was chosen to fulfil the Darbar's decision to build an impregnable wall around Amritsar. He liked to have the sitarist Attar Khan play for him during the rainy season, and would suspend court proceedings to go with his advisers to admire the beauty of gathering monsoon clouds.

Perhaps because he had not been taught to read and write as a boy, the Maharaja revered the written word and had a significant influence on Punjabi literature. Martial terms entered the spoken and written language. Although Persian continued to be the most common tongue, Ranjit's confirmation of Lahore as the country's capital meant that Lahori came to be the accepted dialect. The city formed a contrast with Amritsar which grew into a centre of Sikh learning and philosophy. During his reign, Punjabi began to be used to propagate Sikh teachings, and Urdu verse-forms – *ghazal* (rhyming couplets on the subject of loss and separation) and *masnavi* (long poetic romances) – also entered the language.

Ranjit Singh had a particular interest in medals, in the design of which he became innovative. He instituted an Order of Merit known as the Star of the Prosperity of the Punjab (Kaukab-i-Iqbal-i-Panjab) on the occasion of the marriage of Prince Nau Nihal Singh in March 1837. This decoration was a star-shaped gold medal measuring two-and-a-quarter inches across, with five large and five small pointed branches issuing outwards alternately from a round centre. The centre bore an effigy of the Maharaja seated on a carpet on one side, with his name amid a floral pattern on the other. The medal was to be worn round the neck suspended on a gold and scarlet ribbon. The order was in three classes, the medal for each being distinguished by the size and quality of the inset precious stones. The star of the first class, ornamented with a single large diamond, was for members of the royal family and a very few distinguished chiefs and nobles. The intermediate award, with a diamond of smaller size and an emerald, was for courtiers, provincial governors, army generals and ambassadors in recognition of proven service in their fields. The star of the third class, which had a single emerald, was presented to army colonels, majors and captains, civil servants and other citizens who had earned the sovereign's confidence. The first recipient of the first-class award was actually a foreigner, Sir Henry Fane, commander-in-chief of the British army in India, in 1837. Ranjit also honoured Paolo Avitabile with it.

⁊

As Ranjit Singh consolidated his rule and expanded his empire, he appointed men with a special administrative, military and political status to take forward civil and military administration. The position of these nobles demands special attention. In a country such as Britain, aristocrats from the House of Lords historically provided the bulk of the country's rulers, but were gradually being supplanted by elected men from the House of Commons. The British aristocracy, a hereditary system, was complex, with a rigidly defined pecking order. The Punjabi arrangements were more straightforward. The system was intended to help resolve the apparent contradiction between the Sikh tradition of equality and the notion of kingship. The Punjabi nobles ranked immediately below the Maharaja and were the instruments of his authority. Although in theory all powers were vested in the Maharaja, in practice they were exercised by the nobles who, therefore, provided much of the source of his strength. Of course, as in any powerful body there had to be *some* rankings. Princes, ministers, courtiers, provincial governors and army commanders belonged to the primary level. *Thanadars*, *kardars* and army officers made up the secondary level. But with the exception of the regular army officers, there was a less noticeable differentiation between and within these two levels than in the British system.

The Punjab's nobles were prominent in social life, which was inextricably related to their jobs. A key requirement both socially and professionally was that they live up to the grandeur of the court. They happily indulged the Maharaja's wish for them to attend sessions richly dressed. They were well paid and so could afford to do so. Indeed, they spent a sizeable proportion of their income on conspicuous consumption. As well as covering themselves in fabulous silks and jewels, they lived in fort-like mansions and constructed other buildings and gardens. They threw themselves into expensive 'manly' pastimes such as hunting, that joy of aristocracies everywhere. They spent freely, even recklessly, on social ceremonies and festivals, and patronised painters, musicians and dancers.

The rest of this section draws on a dissertation which mentioned just under 1,100 names of nobles who served the kingdom of Lahore.[5] (Its author was careful to note that this was not necessarily the number at any given point in time – such an assessment had proved impossible to make in view of the constantly changing boundaries.) Of this number, 530 were Sikhs, 310 were Hindus, 179 were Muslims and 65 were Christians. These four groups made up almost all of the nobility. The Sikhs' share of just under half did not reflect their very small share of the Punjab's population. By the same token, the Muslims who were the single largest group of people in the Punjab made up rather less than one-fifth of the nobles. The Christians were almost all Europeans who had come to work in the kingdom of Lahore.

These putative figures prove an important point: Ranjit Singh's appointments to the nobility were not made *purely* on grounds of secularism and merit, the two principles at the heart of Ranjit's system of appointments to the Punjab's nobility. The statistics imply that he regarded Sikhs as more worthy and talented than the other groups, and Muslims as being the least deserving. But nothing that Ranjit Singh ever said or did indicates that he held such discriminatory opinions. So the imbalanced composition of the nobility requires some other explanation.

The nobles were not drawn from any particular community, race or region, except in the sense that the Maharaja would not allow any one group to predominate. This is proved by the fact that the Sikh proportion was just under the 50 per cent that would have given them a controlling majority and undermined the claim that secularism was paramount. The second major principle – that appointment should be on merit – was vital in view of the need for each noble to exercise authority. Ranjit could not afford to appoint incompetents in an expanding country that faced threats on so many fronts.

Religion and competence were not the only matters of which the Maharaja took account. Another factor was racial or ethnic background. Jats made up 30 per cent of the nobles, which was appropriate in that they were the country's majority ethnic group. Khatris (17 per cent), Rajputs (11), Brahmins (7), Pathans (4) and Sayyads (2) comprised just over 40 per cent of the rest of the nobility. (Unfortunately, information is too scanty about the remaining 29 per cent to say which groups they came from.) It is certainly the case that most Jat nobles were Sikhs. However, almost 20 other Jat clans were represented and they included significant numbers of Hindus and Muslims. The Muslim element was drawn largely from the Kharal, Awan, Tiwana, Sial, Trun and, in particular, the Sayyad tribes. The three Fakir brothers were Sayyads. The wide range of groups and sub-groups reflects Ranjit Singh's concern to choose from all points on the ethnic spectrum. Even the few Europeans originated from different lands.

The Maharaja also took account of regional distribution in his appointments and, once again, emphasised diversity. As would be expected, Punjabi people from within the five *doabs* made up the majority, though they came to only slightly more than half the total. The significantly densely populated Bari Doab had the single highest share among the five. Almost 60 per cent of the country's Sikhs lived there. The numbers of people from elsewhere were much smaller. For instance, Hindus made up only just over 4 per cent and all other groups were even smaller. As with religious faith and ethnic origin, the regional component in the nobility was strongly but not overwhelmingly Sikh.

The social status of appointees was also varied, but here there is an additional reason why Sikhs were prominent. Almost half of the nobility was made up of people from the existing aristocracy for whom Ranjit had to have regard when he became ruler and as his kingdom expanded. He sometimes had to choose nobles for reasons of political accommodation and conciliation. Most of the ruling families whom he dispossessed remained in or joined the ranks of the nobility. He inherited Rajputs and Afghans and others as well as Sikhs. In addition, many of their officers and other retainers were recruited. So of necessity a large proportion of nobles were people who might not have been appointed for

reasons of secularism, merit, ethnic background, regional distribution and social origin. *Not* to have appointed them would have
encouraged ill-feeling which would have detracted from Ranjit
Singh's desire for a unified state. The surest way to obtain the
dispossessed dignitaries' cooperation was to keep them on in an
important capacity.

Appointing people for pragmatic reasons takes us into the
subject of a long-existing custom which Ranjit Singh never
entirely abandoned, that of vassalage. The contractual relationship between Maharaja and vassal was not entirely the same as
that between him and his nobles. Although the vassal had some
right to be heard, his status was less exalted than that of many of
the nobles.[6] As the nobility expanded, the Maharaja showed less
inclination towards vassalage and slowly but surely squeezed the
system until little was left of it. While it lasted, however, those
chiefs who were made vassals were left to run their local affairs so
long as they accepted a number of stipulations. The most fundamental of these was Ranjit's suzerainty. Vassals also had to pay
an annual *nazrana* to the Maharaja, provide fighting men if called
upon to do so and be subordinate to the Maharaja's control of relations between vassals. An erring vassal could be disciplined or
have his status removed, a sanction that became more common as
the Maharaja saw vassalage as an anachronism within a centrally
governed state.

Generally Ranjit made a point of choosing many people from
hitherto much less prominent positions in society. Many of the
Jat Sikhs who constituted the majority in the nobility were from
peasant and professional backgrounds. Of the identified nobles, 30
per cent were agriculturalists, 17 per cent came from the mercantile class and 2 per cent were from other professional groups. The
differences between Ranjit's appointees produced some interesting
results. Khatris and Brahmins turned out to be the best admin-
istrators, being appointed disproportionately to the Royal Secre-
tariat and other key areas, such as overseeing land revenue. The
presence of Muslims increased significantly as Ranjit Singh's territorial expansions mopped up strongly Muslim areas, and many
of the Muslim nobles rose to influential military positions, especially in the artillery, half of the officers of which were Muslim.[7] In

addition, some Muslim officers hailed from across the river Sutlej: Sheikh Basawan, Aziz Khan and Bakhtawar Khan were from Hindustan.

Some European nobles were prominent in civil as well as military life. Jean Baptiste Ventura so won Ranjit Singh's confidence that he was made not only commander-in-chief of the Sikh army (a colossal honour in itself) but also governor of Derajat, and then, having performed so well, governor of Kashmir. Ventura was also technically gifted. He had a state-of-the-art paddle-boat built for Ranjit Singh and he found a way of obtaining cool water from a well in summer which allowed Ranjit to dispense with ice. Jean François Allard, too, was multi-talented. He introduced the carbine – a short-barrelled, easily handled form of musket – to the army, and built a steamboat which improved navigation on the Indus (though the river's silt and currents always made this inherently difficult).[8] Paolo Avitabile became a general, governor of Wazirabad and commander of Peshawar. He improved the place considerably, partly because he had no scruples about being cruel. By Avitabile's own account he cut down on criminality by dangling from posts 50 of the worst criminals every day until he had made a scarcity of them. He also cut out the tongues of liars and tale-bearers, and even did likewise to a surgeon who claimed to be able to restore their speech.[9] There is no record of the Maharaja upbraiding Avitabile for his actions despite their being a blatant breach of his anti-capital punishment policy – perhaps because he saw that the alternative to brutally severe rule in Peshawar was anarchy and carnage.

The position of the Europeans was always questionable. The indigenous nobles were reluctant to embrace what they saw as an undesirable intrusion, and resented the Europeans being granted land and other favours. Prince Kharak, too, disliked their presence, and the Maharaja would ruthlessly disregard their contracts should they offend him or prove unsuitable.[10] Generally, the Europeans felt reasonably sure of their security under Ranjit Singh. Few of them ever asked for leave but even when they did go home on leave they often made the arduous journey thousands of miles back to Asia. In 1837 Ranjit Singh granted Ventura two years' leave but early in 1839, having heard of the Maharaja's illness, he returned to the Punjab, remaining there until 1843, despite the chaos that ensued after Ranjit's death. As the Europeans had anticipated, Ranjit's successors were far less welcoming. By 1844 only two of them remained.

Jagirs continued to provide the principal mode of payment to nobles in both the civil and the military spheres. Assignment of land was looked upon as a special favour that was more prestigious and lucrative than any other form of remuneration. *Jagirs* also cushioned the downward mobility of the dispossessed families while providing a base for the upward mobility of the newer nobles. Respectability and authority largely rested upon the nature of the *jagir* the noble enjoyed. Military ones differed from the civil in that the military *jagirdars* maintained troops and were paid for doing so. The Maharaja took a close interest in how they performed. He punished those who failed to maintain a fixed quota of horsemen. This was an important aspect of his control. He did not tolerate negligence among his nobles, and he made no exceptions. Even the illustrious Hari Singh Nalwa was fined and imprisoned for a few days in 1826 for breaching the horsemen rule. Ventura, too, was ordered to compensate some Khatris in Peshawar and to rebuild their houses which he had knocked down. A *jagirdar* had to seek the Maharaja's permission to leave his territory. Punishments varied from the mild (a fine or brief confinement) to the harsh (confiscation of possessions) to the brutal (Sukh Dial was beaten so severely that he died). *Jagirdars* were also switched around so that a given *jagirdar* could not become over-powerful in one area. On the other hand, those who served well were duly recognised through honours, promotions, medals and certificates. The Maharaja's practice of having spies positioned around his kingdom enabled him to know what was going on, and this had a salutary effect upon the nobles.

In conclusion, the nobility exemplified Ranjit's aim to build up a kingdom in which secularism and merit were enshrined above all else, and his simultaneous concern with the nature of his kingdom as an essentially Sikh state, not in numbers of people but rather in culture and character, especially in the central region. The region's people felt a strong need to assert their distinctiveness from India to the east and Afghanistan to the west. Invasions or rule by self-seekers from one or the other had never served the Punjab well. In contrast, Ranjit Singh had from the start been determined to create a state between them in which Punjabis could live as happily and as prosperously as their time and circumstances allowed. All this was directly relevant to the composition of the nobility in Ranjit's time. After all, the nobles were absolutely crucial to the very existence of the state itself. A disgruntled, divided nobility spelt decay and disaster. But a well-ordered, disciplined, industrious and emblematic cadre of great and good officers would produce just the opposite effect. The evidence is that the nobles under Ranjit Singh served him, their people and their country very well.

10

AFGHAN AND BRITISH PROVOCATION

Ranjit Singh had had periodic trouble with Dost Mohammad Khan, the Barakzai ruler. The dauntless Afghan had
not allowed Ranjit to sleep in peace over Peshawar, forcing
him to compromise over its governance after his conquest in 1818.
Dost chalked up another mini-success with the Battle of Naushera
in 1823. Then in the early 1830s Dost had lent his support to the
movement founded by Syed Ahmed, until the latter's defeat and
death in 1831. Meanwhile, Dost had been expanding his power
in Afghanistan. In 1826 he had extended it from the south-east
portion bordering the kingdom of Lahore to Kabul itself, making
himself a formidable regional player.

Ranjit's efforts to woo Shah Shuja in the wake of the bitter-
sweet summit with Bentinck had failed when he overplayed his
hand, seeking not only Shuja's renunciation of his titles to key
places including Multan and Peshawar but also tribute of various
kinds, plus conditions relating to the ruling of Afghanistan. The
Shah decided that he could not risk appearing to rule as Ranjit
Singh's puppet and so made no response to his offer. However,
Shuja's attempt to recapture the throne without his aid failed.
This left Ranjit in what he regarded as an unpalatable situation.
His north-west frontier might be secure but it was not invulner-
able and he was ruling there to an extent on sufferance, having
allowed Dost Mohammad to retain influence through his brother
Yar's administration of Peshawar. A defeat of Shah Shuja by Dost
Mohammad would allow Dost again to rub in the fact of his pres-
ence. Ranjit Singh decided to pre-empt such a prospect with sharp
action, and he chose a tough character for the job. In 1834 Hari

Singh Nalwa was appointed governor of Peshawar, the first non-Muslim to hold the position. This estimable character, who had already been awarded important military honours plus a civil assignment, appeared to be just the man to hold down a major post in exposed conditions.

However, the scale of Hari Singh Nalwa's assignment might have been too much even for him. He left day-to-day responsibility for governing Peshawar in the hands of Prince Nau Nihal Singh while he set out to subdue the Pathans outside the city itself. As he anticipated, Pathans were attacking Khalsa columns in the sort of hit-and-run manner that Sikhs themselves had employed with striking success against Afghans in earlier times. Hari Singh Nalwa determined on extreme measures to enforce his rule. Defensively, he built a series of forts. Offensively, he countered guerrilla raids by razing villages to the ground.[1] Later that year Dost Mohammad endeavoured to win back Afghan supremacy in and around Peshawar. He tried to enlist British support but once again they refused to betray Ranjit Singh. In January 1835 the Afghan ruler, in desperation, resorted to calling a Jihad. Tribesmen from the Yusafzai, Mohmand and Khatak tribes answered the call. Yet again the Punjabis faced a threatening situation in the north-west.

Another slice of the good fortune that often attended Ranjit Singh now came his way. The Maharaja dispatched foreign minister Aziz-ud-din and Josiah Harlan as envoys to try to persuade Dost to accept Punjabi possession of Peshawar. He apparently thought the smooth-talking Harlan's former service with Dost would help win the Afghan ruler over. Initially, Dost behaved as brazenly as Ranjit himself might have done. He took the two envoys hostage. Outraged by this gross breach of protocol, Aziz-ud-din objected strongly but Harlan used subtler tactics to deadly effect. He actually managed to rework his old double-dealing within the Barakzai ranks and sowed such suspicion among the brothers that they withdrew from Peshawar as if under a spell. The Punjabis had gained a notable victory without firing a shot. This extraordinary outcome did not mean that Dost Mohammad was finished, but it did halt the threat and allowed a most welcome respite to Ranjit Singh.

As often happened, Ranjit had more than one matter to handle beyond his borders. In 1834 an important issue arose to the north-east involving General Zorawar Singh Kalhuria, the governor of Kishtwar, over 5,000 feet up in the foothills of the Himalayas. Born in 1786, Zorawar Singh joined the army in 1817. His zeal and enterprise earned him various appointments before he became governor of Kishtwar. This little territory near to the source of the River Chenab was under the Hindus until the 1600s when it fell into Muslim hands. Some of its people had also converted but many remained true to their ancestral faith. Even though it was recently conquered, Zorawar Singh had little difficulty keeping the peace. He even expanded the area in 1835 when nearby Paddar was taken in battle.

However, this was of secondary importance to the general's other aggressive activities. Several small principalities to the east of Kishtwar paid tribute to the Gyalpo (King) of Ladakh. When in 1834 the Raja of Timbus sought Zorawar's help against the Gyalpo, Zorawar saw a chance to expand the Punjab's frontiers even further, up to the borders of China, and also earn drought-stricken Kishtwar some badly needed revenue. The general needed little encouragement to come to the Raja's aid. With some 5,000 eager and experienced mountain fighters to hand, Zorawar had no trouble in crossing the mountain ranges and entering Ladakh. In the spring of 1835 he defeated the large Ladakhi army of Banko Kahlon and marched his victorious troops towards Leh, near to the Punjab's far north-eastern frontier. The ruler then agreed to pay him a war indemnity and an annual tribute.

Flushed with this success, in the winter of 1835–36 Zorawar Singh asked the Maharaja for permission to exploit the situation by winning still more northern territory and obtaining a lengthy border with China. Ranjit Singh might well have been tempted to agree. The Darbar had won its bloodless victory in the north-west and had now also done well at little human cost in the north and north-east. However, Ranjit's cautious side prevailed, at least for the moment, for two possible reasons.

First, on 17 August 1835 he had suffered his third stroke, which paralysed his face and his right side. After the previous strokes of 1823 and 1826 and all the other stresses of rule, the attack severely restricted his ability to administer. When Baron von Hügel saw him in 1836 he wrote that the Maharaja was so affected that he could no longer easily be understood.[2]

Secondly, Zorawar's success risked provoking the British. Claude Wade, who by now was in charge of their relations with Ranjit Singh, strongly protested over Zorawar's actions because they involved what for the British was the unwelcome prospect of the kingdom of Lahore sharing a frontier with China. Ranjit Singh countered by pointing out that all of the territory concerned was to the west and north of the Sutlej, whereas the British had long determined to limit the Maharaja's authority to the east of the river. But the British simply invoked the upper reaches of the Indus as the preferred limit of Ranjit Singh's western and northern borders. They had no wish to see his state extend further north. As a symbolic show of their annoyance, the British offered asylum to the deposed Ladakhi family.

They made a still more powerful objection to Ranjit's political moves in and towards Sindh. Ranjit had used the period following Dost Mohammad's capitulation to try to persuade the amirs to resist British pressure for commercial favours and, therefore, political influence in the province. But the amirs had scorned his approaches and enticed Mazari people who lived at the confluence of the Indus and the Sutlej to attack Punjabi posts and plunder their villages. The Maharaja appointed Prince Kharak to subdue the Mazaris. The heir to the throne acquitted himself well, capturing several towns in the summer of 1836, including an outpost called Rojhan. It was these advances that attracted British disapproval.

Kharak then sought his father's approval to take Shikarpur, an import commercial centre and a place of vociferous anti-Sikh activity. Ranjit hesitated, rightly wary of British opinion. In August Claude Wade was granted an audience and pressed the Maharaja not to extend the reach of his army. Ranjit Singh reasoned with him that the Mazaris had behaved intolerably, Shah Shuja had transferred his title to Shikarpur to the Maharaja, and the area was far from the east bank of the Sutlej, beyond which he accepted that the British had a strong imperial interest. Wade tried to argue that Ranjit should acknowledge British interest in Sindh, but could provide no good reason. Not surprisingly, Ranjit's aides were furious, feeling strongly that their government should stand its ground and be prepared to fight the British. After all, the army was now very formidable indeed. And, in any case, if the British were prepared to be obstructive over something that (in the Darbar's opinion) was none of Britain's business, then they were quite capable of invading the Punjab. Thus, if a war was likely, let it occur at the Punjab's timing rather than that of the British.

The Maharaja was in an unenviable position. Dhian Singh Dogra, his increasingly influential prime minister, was among those who urged strong action. And at heart Ranjit fully shared Dhian's and the other courtiers' spirited opinions. Everything they said was rooted in justice and good sense. But, mindful of both the value of past British indulgence and of their immense firepower, he set aside his anger. Having pondered, he asked the emollient Aziz-ud-din to try to persuade Wade to look upon the Sindh border area as neutral territory. When that failed, Ranjit asked Wade if the whole matter could be deferred until he had had an opportunity to discuss it with Lord Auckland, the new governor-general, whom he had not met. But Wade had been given plenty of scope to resist Ranjit Singh's arguments, and did so with superior references to British concerns with 'welfare and prosperity' and 'respect and consideration'. Exasperated, Ranjit asked sarcastically what the phrases meant. Wade thought he was being serious and attempted a reply, only to be sharply interrupted by Ranjit telling him that he knew only too well what they meant. Their series of meetings ended in angry deadlock. Ranjit refused to sign any further agreements relating to Sindh or to withdraw from Rojhan. Yet even now Ranjit could not bring himself to abandon his long-established policy of accommodation with the British. It sometimes strained his patience – as in the recent negotiations with Wade – but he decided he could not risk the Punjab's independence.

A new factor – Afghan diplomatic assertiveness – might have influenced him. Dost Mohammad decided to build his own bilateral relationship with Lord Auckland. On 31 May 1836 he wrote to Auckland congratulating him on his appointment and seeking his advice on a settlement with the 'reckless and misguided'

Sikhs, as he called them.[3] Dost's message of friendship included an expression that must later have haunted him: he hoped 'that your Lordship will consider me and my country as your own'. Neither Dost nor Auckland could have imagined that within a few years this would come to pass. But in 1836 the British were cautious over Afghanistan. Afghan diplomatic initiatives were rare, and Dost's were somewhat unsubtle, so they still held as fast to their alliance with Ranjit Singh as he did with them. On 22 August, therefore, Auckland replied, gently batting away Dost's request: 'My friend, you are aware that it is not the practice of the British Government to interfere with the affairs of independent states.' He was careful, however, to include something positive, proposing a commercial mission, which he placed in the hands of Alexander Burnes.

Lord Auckland stressed the commercial nature of Burnes's visit in an extremely friendly letter to Ranjit Singh, saying 'the English and the Sikh nation will be united to the end of time', so Ranjit was fully aware of what the British were trying to do, or at least what they *said* they were trying to do, for rarely do states reveal all to third parties.[4] Ranjit also knew that the British wanted agreements with the amirs of Sindh. Against this background of continued British interest to his south-west and their new interest to his traditionally more dangerous north-west, Ranjit Singh decided to give the British pride of place at the wedding of his adored grandson, Nau Nihal Singh, near Amritsar. Early in 1837 he wrote to Sir Henry Fane, the commander-in-chief of the British army, in characteristically fulsome terms:

> Friendly and kind Sir, in consideration of the friendship which promotes unity and sincerity, in these auspicious days marked by a thousand happy omens we wish to complete the picture of our desires by arranging the marriage of our son, Prince Nau Nihal Singh, who is fortune's favourite child, the lustre on the forehead of felicity, the apple of the eye of our dominions, the lord of the glorious garden of sovereignty and the solace of our soul, with the pen of friendship we write to request your Excellency, who is replete with amiable and friendly qualities, to grace this occasion with your presence and so make our joy and happiness limitless.[5]

With Lord Auckland's approval, the commander-in-chief accepted. Fane and his party were officially welcomed to the Punjab by Prince Sher Singh on the west bank of the Sutlej. To begin with, the British party stayed with Sher Singh and were impressed not only by his strong physical appearance but also by his attachment to all things European. Sher's residence was filled with French wines, phials of French scents and other such luxuries. When the British arrived in Amritsar they were met by Prince Kharak and Raja Dhian Singh. This time their admiration was for the Raja, though, as with Sher, the memoirs of Fane's accompanying nephew (who was also called Henry) indicate that Dhian impressed them through his physical bearing and accoutrements rather than his character and personality.[6]

Nau Nihal's marriage took place on 6 March 1837. That morning the British called on the Maharaja. Young Henry Fane's note of Ranjit's appearance was indicative of the way the years had ravaged his appearance. He looked infirm and ten years older than he actually was (56); his good eye was bleary and blood-shot. However he appeared to British eyes, the Maharaja, now in the 38th year of his rule, remained full of life. He showered them with questions of all sorts, the transparent sincerity behind them once again winning the British over. The guests were even more impressed when, after the ceremony of handing presents to the groom, they were at the head of a massive crowd which followed the Maharaja's party on its way to the wedding place. An incredulous Fane junior thought that between 500,000 and 600,000 people were there, struggling to obtain a glimpse of the revered Maharaja. Fane was less impressed with the bridegroom, who looked thin, unhealthy and riddled with smallpox, though he discerned intelligence and good manners too.

After the marriage that evening, Ranjit entertained the British and, generous as always, shared his alcoholic drinks liberally with them. Fane noted their potency and how Ranjit consumed one tumbler after another. The British were left utterly fatigued. They remained as guests for several days and went to an exhibition of the bride's dowry and to a grand soirée in the Maharaja's pavilion, at which he once again plied them with questions and liquor. He also inspected their troops and asked even more questions, this time about Persia's relationship with Russia which, being a sensitive subject, the British were hard put to answer. He was just as inquisitive with ordinary members of the party. When he examined the presents of military materiel that the British had brought him, he spoke with the gunners about their equipment.

The British relaxed their natural stiffness a little during the festival of Holi, which is celebrated at springtime all over India and in Asian communities around the world. The first main event of burning the demoness Holika's sister Hiranjakashipu on a bonfire at night was no problem for the jaded guests, but they were caught up in the second day's celebration more directly. This involves people hurling coloured powder and water at each other, the rationale being that, as the winter weather changes, fevers and colds are more likely to break out. The playful lobbing of the coloured powders is held to have a beneficial effect because they contain medicinal herbs.

The Maharaja joined in with gusto, making several throws at the senior Afghan guest who was soon covered in splashes of colour. The British, including Sir Henry Fane, joined in the fun and ended up as powder-encrusted as everyone else. They departed eastwards with their admiration for the Maharaja fully replenished.

Probably because the occasion was not ostensibly political and the senior British guest was neither a politician nor his constitutional equal, Ranjit Singh raised no important negotiating points with Sir Henry Fane. But hardly had the celebrations ended before another military – and therefore political – menace arose in the north-west, in the form of Dost Mohammad, who was proving himself to be the kingdom's single most persistent adversary.

❧

Though Henry Fane did not say so, there was no doubt that Ranjit Singh was ill – three strokes, von Hügel's comments on his reduced capacity for speech, and then in 1837 a fourth attack which paralysed his right side for several months. It was as well that Ranjit was able to leave the next round of warfare with the Afghans to another man.

It was Dost Mohammad – again – who started it. He found

the forts put in place by Peshawar's governor, Hari Singh Nalwa, too much of a provocation. In April 1837 he took advantage of two circumstances to attack them. The first was that Nalwa himself was sick. The second was the absence locally of many of the Punjabi troops, recalled to Amritsar for Nau Nihal Singh's wedding. Dost seized his chance, leading some 25,000 men to attack the most prominent forts at Shabqadr and Jamrud, both strategically placed near the Khyber Pass. Afghan forces pounded the less well-defended fort at Jamrud while other units besieged Shabqadr to ensure that its 1,500 men could not go to the aid of the 600 at Jamrud. With Afghan artillery destroying Jamrud's walls and the defenders sheltering in ditches, a brave Sikh woman disguised as an Afghan breached the Afghan lines to deliver to Hari Singh Nalwa a message from the fort's commander, Maha Singh Mirpura, that he could hold out no longer. The indisposed Hari Singh rose from his bed to lead a rescue mission, reinforced by troops sent with all speed from Amritsar, 250 miles away. The news created panic among the Afghans, who withdrew from Jamrud and took up a defensive position.

Despite his reinforcements, Nalwa was outnumbered three to one. So he did not hasten to attack but stood ready in battle formation, waiting for Dost to make a move. To his surprise none came. The opposing groups faced each other in a state of phoney war for a whole week. Hari Singh gradually realised why the Afghans were not taking him on: they were too frightened to do so. Accordingly he decided to take the fight to them and on 30 April attacked with typical ferocity. However, not fully recovered from his illness, the weakened general was less careful than usual of his personal safety and rode too far in front of his supporting troops. Mohammad Akbar Khan, Dost's son, leapt into action, catching the attackers unawares, fatally wounding Nalwa and capturing some of his guns and men.

Nalwa knew he was dying, but used his precious few remaining minutes to order his commanders not to mention his death but to rally the men into forcing the Afghans back. This they did with a vengeance. The Punjabis killed some 11,000 of them, almost twice the attackers' fatalities. It was another great victory and a further example of the superlative morale and discipline of the army. Ranjit Singh was not present and his deputy had been killed, yet still the Punjabis had prevailed.

To begin with, the retreating Afghans tried not to see it that way. Dost Mohammad hailed their killing of Nalwa as a victory in itself and pronounced his son the winner. However, the Afghans had been forced out of the territory they had attacked and lost a great many men in the process. On 11 September Dost tried reaching out again to Ranjit Singh. In a maladroit letter he told the Maharaja that if he would let him have Peshawar he would create no further trouble and would not seek British help. But if Ranjit turned him down, he would fight and seek their support. Ranjit Singh did not take him seriously. It was he, not Dost, who had won this important battle. He dismissed Dost's comments about seeking British help: the British were *his* allies, he said, and would not betray him.

Ranjit, however, was unaware that the British, in response to an approach from Dost Mohammad, were about to woo him in Kabul: Alexander Burnes arrived there on 20 September. The jousting between the two Asian leaders now became part of a wider affair, the Great Game of European imperialism in central and southern Asia. The British had become the major power in the Indian subcontinent after the Treaty of Paris of 1763. As part of building up control of India, they had worked to keep France at bay in Afghanistan and Persia, as exemplified by the 1809 treaties with those countries. But by the 1830s the British believed that the major European threat to their interests in India came from Russia. The Russians, for their part, disliked the northern expansion of Britain in – and then beyond – India, which they believed threatened their own ambitions in central Asia. At this point, in the 1830s, British and Russian spheres of influence were moving steadily closer to one another and were about to meet in Afghanistan.

Burnes's arrival in Kabul in September 1837 brought the Game more into the open. That was because Russia was simultaneously exerting its own influence through its representative, Captain P. Vitkevich, who, like Burnes, was ostensibly in Kabul for commercial discussions. The Russians were also quietly supporting Persia in its attempt to retrieve the key city of Herat in western

Afghanistan. In 1837 Persia advanced on Herat along with Russian advisers. The British disliked the prospect of Persia obtaining Herat because they feared it would mean a heightened threat to India from the north-west.

Time usually allowed the British to work the Great Game subtly, but they had no such luxury available in 1837. Afghanistan was suddenly a pivotal player. The British found themselves up against the harsh reality that they were unable to offer much to Dost Mohammad without abandoning Ranjit Singh. They wanted Dost to sever all contact with the Russians (and so expel Vitkevich) and to desist from claiming Peshawar. In return, the British government could try and persuade Ranjit Singh to be more amenable with Afghanistan. However, the British refused to put such an agreement in writing and, in any case, Dost insisted on keeping his claim to Peshawar alive. The resultant impasse meant that Dost in effect terminated the British mission – ironic, given that Dost himself had made the initial approach. Notwithstanding his admiration for Ranjit Singh, Burnes had wanted Calcutta to take Dost Mohammad more seriously; he thought him 'commendable'. [7]

In British officialdom, confusion reigned, with conflicting attitudes and policies. Burnes backed Dost, who was an enemy of Ranjit, who was officially supported by the government which was being urged to back Dost by its agent in Kabul, who was now (in April 1838) being thrown out. The only fixed point in all this was Ranjit Singh. Forced to choose between Ranjit Singh and Dost Mohammad, the British plumped for the Maharaja, 'the most powerful and valuable of our friends' as the governor-general remarked on 12 May.[8] These two – the most eminent people in British-ruled India and the Punjab – had not yet met, and decided to make good the lack. Preliminary meetings between officials happened in Calcutta and Adinanagar (now Dinanagar) in the far northern state of Gurdaspur. The Maharaja liked to retreat to the cool of Adinanagar in the early summer, where he had a modest palace set amid a large well-watered garden bisected by a canal. The British visitors noted how, soon after dark, the Maharaja retired to rest in his gold-embroidered tent, which was open at the front and guarded by just a few men. His sword and shield were laid out by his pillow and a saddled horse stood ready at the entrance. In this quiet resort, the hosts and their guests spent some days making complimentary speeches, inspecting troops and watching dancing girls, while Ranjit distributed his usual alcoholic brews. W.G. Osborne, the military secretary to the governor-general, made detailed notes about Ranjit Singh. He noted nothing about the Maharaja appearing gravely ill. On the contrary, he seemed to be as animated as ever, his good eye roving from face to face as he threw question after question at the guests about wine, army horses, the relative merits of cavalry and infantry and about British army soldiers and equipment. Osborne observed that, although the main courtiers squatted on the floor around the royal chair, Prime Minister Dhian Singh Dogra remained standing behind it.

Sir William Macnaghten, the mission leader, read to the Darbar Lord Auckland's message, the main point of which was his proposal to restore Shah Shuja to the throne of Kabul. Auckland suggested two ways to make this happen. One envisaged the army taking military action in Afghanistan with British financial and military support; as part of this offer the British would be content to see the Sikhs take Shikarpur in Sindh. The second proposal was for the Darbar to act independently without British support, which the British thought the less favourable option because, they said, of the risk of combined Afghan and Persian retaliation. Neither proposal allowed for Darbar forces to actually occupy Kabul following Shuja's reinstatement.

The Darbar ministers quickly warmed to the idea of restoring Shah Shuja, with whom they had had fewer problems than with Dost Mohammad. However, the Darbar was not to be easily persuaded about the best way to take the objective forward. At least one scholar has argued that Ranjit Singh made no objections to Macnaghten's proposal, while most of his ministers did.[9] But Britain's records indicate that, while the Maharaja *and* the senior courtiers were content with the idea of reinstating Shuja, they raised many questions over the practicalities, including the number of British officers involved and what forces Britain would offer generally. The next day, Ranjit asked through two close aides, Aziz-ud-din and Rai Gobind Jas, what Britain would do to help if the Darbar accepted the second proposal (that the Punjabis take independent action) and the army then found itself faced with joint Afghan and Persian opposition that the British had warned about.[10] Macnaghten airily said that Britain would not countenance the prospect of defeat, but Ranjit was not convinced.

It should be said that, if the negotiations seemed tense, relations were always good. Ranjit found the British good company socially, which helped when their political and military behaviour was tiresome. Even on 3 June, the day on which Macnaghten unfolded the controversial proposals to an intent Darbar, Ranjit Singh showed great humour during an artillery practice. When a shell exploded with perfect accuracy just where it was intended, he turned, beaming, and said, 'I think that will do for Dost Mohammad'.

Concerned to get a firm commitment from the British, Ranjit sent Aziz-ud-din and Rai Gobind Jas back to Macnaghten on 6 June, asking for a guarantee of Shuja's conduct after his restoration, a share in the levy from the Sindhian amirs and the ceding to the Punjab of the major eastern Afghan town of Jalalabad. The British agreed to the first two (despite the difficulty of controlling Shuja), but rejected Ranjit's request for Jalalabad. On 18 June talks resumed, this time at Lahore, cholera having broken out in Adinanagar.[11]

The number of Darbar aides whom Ranjit had asked to consider the British position had risen from two to five, a good indication of how the Maharaja sought agreement on major issues.[12] The fifth was Dhian Singh, who had grimaced and shaken his head when listening to the British proposals on 3 June. The British team included Alexander Burnes, whom the Punjabis tried to use as a mediator. Burnes now appears to have played a double game. On the one hand, his presence served to cause or deepen a rift between Ranjit Singh and Dhian Singh and maybe some other senior aides. Burnes had apparently shed his liking for Dost and provoked Ranjit by saying that Dost had called him a brute and would continue to torment him. That incensed Ranjit, who now agreed strongly to what the British had proposed, but this in turn upset the doubtful Darbar ministers. Led by Dhian Singh, several aides pleaded with Ranjit to pull back.[13] A British diary entry suggests they succeeded: W.G. Osborne noted on 19 June that the 'old lion has turned sulky, and refuses to sign the treaty, wishing to stipulate all sorts of concessions which cannot be granted, and thus reference to headquarters is rendered necessary'.[14] Was this opposition or caution? The evidence is unclear. Like all canny negotiators, Ranjit Singh did not reveal his hand prematurely.

But if Burnes created something of a cleavage among his hosts he also caused one within his own side, because Macnaghten felt he was too ready to do the Darbar's bidding.[15] As a result, tensions heightened so much that a second intermediary proved necessary, Lieutenant Frederick Mackeson. However, the Punjabis might not have realised that there was another twist to the internal British ill-feeling. Part of Macnaghten's irritation with Burnes spilled over from his annoyance at what he regarded as vacillation by Lord Auckland, who was not willing to push the Maharaja too hard. Macnaghten thought all this contributed to Ranjit Singh's questioning of the British proposals, which Macnaghten viewed as delaying tactics. In an attempt to bring matters to a head, Macnaghten tried to intimidate the Darbar by warning that the British would proceed unilaterally in the absence of an agreement.

On the Punjabi side, whatever the truth of his outlook between 2 and 19 June, Ranjit Singh had indeed been holding out for more assurances but, military assistance apart, these amounted to more than the British were prepared to offer. Fundamentally the Darbar's reservations were justified. Any proposal by one country for another to carry out that proposal is surely suspect, for it must predominantly be in the proposer's interests. Not surprisingly, therefore, most of the courtiers were unenthusiastic about the British recommendation, and none more so than Dhian Singh. However, Macnaghten's threat paid off: Aziz-ud-din and Bhai Ram Singh urged Dhian Singh and the Maharaja to see the danger if the Punjab refused to cooperate with the British and the British took their plan forward.[16] If that happened, Afghanistan would have a leader who owed some obligation to them but not to the Punjab. But these arguments held no water. The British army had to traverse the Punjab to invade Afghanistan; it could hardly do so against Punjabi wishes. Also, the British had not been acquainted with Afghanistan for anything like as long as the Punjabis had. No Afghan ruler had been naturally friendly to the Punjab, and many had been the opposite. No Punjabi would welcome the prospect of shedding yet more blood in the north-west corridor, this time in the *cause* of an Afghan.

Yet Ranjit Singh agreed to a tripartite agreement between himself, Shah Shuja and Lord Auckland to help Shuja regain the throne he had briefly occupied in 1809. The British got busy drafting a treaty which purported to be an accord between Ranjit Singh and Shuja in which the British were not directly involved. Under its terms the Shah was to be restored at Kabul, would disclaim titles to Shikarpur and to those areas of Afghanistan that the Punjabis had previously captured, would pay for the Punjabi military help in reinstating him and would not negotiate with a foreign power without Punjabi and British consent. He and the Punjabis would treat each other with consideration and as equals. Ranjit Singh signed the treaty on 26 June.

The tension dissipated. Britons and Punjabis celebrated their agreement with lavish entertainment. So gratified were the two sides over having resolved the bilateral differences that they momentarily overlooked the need for Shah Shuja also to accept the terms. It was not until 9 July that, with Ranjit's agreement, the British took the text to Ludhiana for that purpose.[17] Shuja demanded some changes before he signed. In effect, he wanted nothing on paper that could be construed as his having agreed to pay tribute to Ranjit Singh, else he would be hopelessly compromised in the eyes of his own people. The British managed to satisfy him without altering the wording in such a way as to upset Ranjit Singh. On 17 July the British mission left Ludhiana with the signed treaty and Shah Shuja began raising his agreed military contribution of 6,000 men.

In an internal dispatch of 14 August, Lord Auckland showed that he was living in a dream world over Shah Shuja and Afghanistan. He wrote:

> Of the justice of the course to be pursued there can exist no reasonable doubt. We owe it to our safety to assist the lawful sovereign of Afghanistan in the recovery of his throne ... we should have an ally who is interested in resisting aggression and establishing tranquillity in place of a chief seeking to identify

himself with those whose schemes of aggrandizement and conquest are not to be disguised.[18]

The governor-general's assumptions were based on sand. He and his advisers had no reason whatsoever to suppose that Shah Shuja was the saviour they portrayed him to be, and they exhibited no understanding of a country's natural disinclination to accept a ruler imposed by outsiders of any kind, especially Europeans. The British also seemed determined to underestimate Dost Mohammad, whom – in a stunning reversal – they would in due course restore to power in Kabul, where he would turn out to be a far better bet from Britain's point of view.

On 1 October, Auckland went public and announced what became known as the Simla Manifesto which outlined the reasons for *British* intervention in Afghanistan: to ensure the welfare of India, the British must have a trustworthy ally on India's western frontier (so the decision was not being made primarily in the interests of the Punjab, or of Afghanistan for that matter). Troops would be withdrawn as soon as Shuja was reinstalled in Kabul. The British denied that they would be invading Afghanistan; they were merely supporting its legitimate government.

Just three weeks later, on 22 October, the chief supporting argument in favour of dethroning Dost Mohammad collapsed. Persian forces lifted their siege of Herat and thereby ended any need for Russian backing for the Afghan government. This major event offered the Lahore court a clear opportunity to seek a reconsideration of policy but, inexplicably, the sardars did not pursue it. Should they have done so? Indeed, should they ever have had any truck whatsoever with the British scheme? The British had placed the Maharaja in the most complicated diplomatic circumstances he would ever know. They, a third party, had proposed that he should intervene in Afghanistan, the powerful neighbouring country which had posed, and continued to pose, a threat to peace in the Punjab. The plan meant the Punjabis would be helping to restore an ex-ruler who could then only be seen as someone who had regained power not through his own efforts but through those of scheming outsiders, primarily for their own ends. Thus the ex-ruler would be in a situation where not only he but his backers faced resentment, which undermined the stated purpose of intervention – to produce stability.

The British themselves realised the enormity of what they were proposing to Ranjit. Calcutta decided that the governor-general should meet with the Maharaja to ensure a signed deal.

11

FATEFUL CONCLUSION WITH THE BRITISH

Ranjit Singh had wanted to meet Lord Auckland in 1836 to resolve the diplomatic dispute over Sindh, but had been deflected by Claude Wade. Two years on and with war approaching, Ranjit Singh was again looking forward to meeting Auckland. The two sides agreed to meet at Ferozepur in the Cis-Sutlej, which was to a degree a goodwill gesture on the part of the British in view of their refusal in 1835 to yield control of it to Ranjit. The first meeting took place there on 29 November 1838, the start of what turned out to be the Maharaja's last top-level foreign venture.

Travel to the venue exposed the British party to the positive feelings among people in this easterly part of the Punjab towards the Maharaja.[1] When Aziz-ud-din received Auckland he once again deployed his flowery brand of diplomatic charm by remarking that, 'The lustre of one sun has long shone with splendour over our horizon; but when two suns come together, the refulgence will be overpowering.' This set the scene for a happy series of meetings between the two principals. Henry Fane, who had a grandstand view, describes the first Darbar session convening to the sounds of cannons firing and chaotic crowds intermingling with elephants. After three-quarters of an hour largely taken up with Ranjit Singh's questions, presents were given. One, an oil-painting of Britain's new monarch, Queen Victoria, by Emily Eden pleased the Darbar so much that a royal salute was fired from 100 guns. Another gift, a horse, also took Ranjit's fancy and he dashed outside to examine it, going on later to inspect two howitzer guns, pronouncing them to be the most valuable of the gifts for the

Punjab as a whole. Clearly, Ranjit's faculties were in sound working order, even though he was physically diminished. Emily Eden described him as resembling 'an old mouse, with grey whiskers and one eye'. A touching aspect of Darbar proceedings caught Miss Eden's eye: as was usual at such events, children of dead soldiers were allowed the freedom of the court, crawling around the legs of the Maharaja and the governor-general.

On 30 November, Ranjit Singh made his return visit to Auckland, presenting gifts to everyone in the British party. That evening was supposedly a business occasion, but with everything agreed for the invasion of Afghanistan there was little to discuss and much of the time was devoted to watching dancing girls and drinking. Since William Macnaghten had mischievously assured Ranjit that Auckland was a good drinker – when, in fact, he was abstemious – the governor-general had to down his share of Ranjit's drinks. Emily Eden was also handed one but evaded the ordeal of swallowing the substance – 'one drop of which actually burnt the outside of my lips' – by being on Ranjit's blind side and pouring it onto the carpet unnoticed. Amid all the revelry, however, on one serious point the Maharaja was properly alert: he flatly rejected the British suggestion for a resident to be stationed at his court. Any such appointment would have been seen as an intrusive British presence.

Further meetings followed, in Amritsar and finally in Lahore. Each consisted of a mix of formality and informal revelry. But tragically the exertions proved too much for the Maharaja.

Emily Eden noted on 24 December in Amritsar that all scheduled events had been deferred owing to Ranjit having a cold and a fever. By the next day his condition had deteriorated and the British feared that another stroke was on the way. Nonetheless, he gamely received them in Lahore on the 28th and dispensed more presents. They had thoughtfully and astutely brought some gifts in return: emeralds in the form of a bunch of grapes and a ring with a large diamond. Ranjit sat up in his bed to study the ring on his finger and was impressed. The governor-general said he hoped the Maharaja would occasionally wear it.

At that point their rapid and happy sequence of encounters abruptly ended. To Ranjit Singh's credit, he acted throughout with the dignity and mental resilience of a natural leader at the highest level. Even during the final week when he was practically crippled by a stroke he behaved with admirable decorum, as befitted the matter which had led up to the summit: the Punjabis' agreement to Britain's proposal to restore Shah Shuja to the throne at Kabul with Punjabi and British military backing.[2]

It is not surprising that, to a degree, the Maharaja and his ministers should have been attracted to the proposal. The British and the Punjabis possessed enormous firepower, individually let alone as a combination. By the late 1830s the army comprised about 75,000 men, at least half of whom were regularly trained and equipped.[3] The infantry was the best organised branch, though the cavalry still attracted many recruits and remained a skilled body. The artillerymen had at their disposal some 700 pieces of artillery. This powerful army had gained victory after victory, often over Afghanistan.

That country remained an unstable menace and in 1838 was led by a man who, like Afghans before him, had double-crossed the Punjab. By contrast, the British on the other side had made no overt trouble during Ranjit Singh's four decades in power. Even though they had highhandedly set limits to his territorial aims, they had been far more trustworthy than any other leaders. Why not, therefore, pursue a major aim, guaranteed by them, which could settle the Punjab's problem with Afghanistan and thereby produce a more orderly, peaceful situation on both sides – with the offer of involvement in Sindh thrown in as a sweetener? Especially as Britain was now a major world power.

Politically and militarily, therefore, there was good reason to suppose that intervening in Afghanistan made sense. Yet, with hindsight, the case against clearly outweighs the arguments in favour. In particular, the Darbar's failure to call for a policy rethink following the Persian withdrawal from Herat was an obvious failing. The British plan went ahead as though nothing had happened.

The Ranjit Singh/Lord Auckland summit was still in progress when a two-pronged army under the overall command of Sir John Keane set out from the Punjab in December to invade Afghanistan. With them was William Macnaghten, who had been appointed

Britain's chief representative to Kabul. Difficulties soon arose. A dispute between the invading factions began even before the long march commenced. The sub-army under Colonel Sheikh Basawan gathered in the central region, tasked with forcing the Khyber Pass. For two reasons he had an exacting task planning his assault. The first was the sheer difficulty presented by the route. The Khyber Pass opened up about ten miles west of Peshawar and then wound its way for over 30 miles to a point west of Torkham in Afghanistan. At one point the pass was a mere 15 metres wide between steep canyon walls. The route was extremely hilly as well as twisty. At this time there was no purpose-built road there, let alone a railway. (The first roadway was not built until 1879; and the railway took six years to construct before its completion in 1925.)

His second problem was more human. As the Darbar should have expected, many of the Afghans who were loyal to Shah Shuja were acutely suspicious of Sikh participation in his restoration. This ill-feeling flared in the central region because Shuja's son, Prince Taimur, was there with a mixed force of Afghans and Pathans to accompany the Punjabis. Fortunately for the mission, a third party, Claude Wade, was also present and acted as a conciliator. He had his work cut out to effect a joint effort.

The second part of the invading force was also faced with a daunting task. Its journey was through the southern passes via Kandahar and Ghazni. That was because it was very largely a British army, and Ranjit Singh did not want white imperialists marching in high profile through his country. But the southern route meant marching westward to Kandahar and then doing a sharp three-quarter turn towards Ghazni which lay some way to the north-east. This journey was three times the distance of the more direct route via the Khyber Pass, and that caused considerable problems. Supplies became exhausted and some were lost owing to attacks by tribesmen in Baluchistan. This in turn led to many soldiers starving, plus horses dying because the scanty water was reserved for the men. Normally Ranjit Singh took fully into account the need to preserve as many men and animals as possible in warlike adventures. This time he was less able to do so and they fell victim to the joint decision to go into Afghanistan using a roundabout route.

Problems of cooperation arose again once the marches commenced. The invasion leaders, already anxious over the Maharaja's health, became more so when he appeared laggardly over providing reinforcements.[4] On 27 February Wade sent a worried letter to Ranjit reminding him of his promise to furnish a Muslim contingent of 5,000 men. On 21 March Ranjit wrote with details of the 5,000 men, but the British were vexed that their arrival was so delayed, blaming the courtiers who they believed now ruled the Darbar. Their mood improved later that month when they encountered the European generals Avitabile and Court, who gave what aid they could in and around Peshawar, but that apparently annoyed the Maharaja, who reproached Avitabile for helping them. The British also felt uncomfortable in Peshawar itself. They sensed inter-tribal enmity, tension between Muslims and Hindus, and Muslim and Yusufzai dislike of Sikh rule. The heat, too, they found oppressive.

However, Keane's men stolidly pressed on with their advance. On 13 April, their spirits rose again when Ventura arrived and was as supportive as the other Europeans had been. Then, after marching 147 miles, the mainly British force reached Kandahar on 4 May 1839. Its next objective, Ghazni, proved harder to crack as it commanded the trade routes and roads leading into Kabul, and so was better defended. Ghazni was finally overcome on 23 July. Sheikh Basawan, too, had done a terrific job breaking through the treacherous Khyber Pass with the other army. He was given the honour of leading the men through Kabul in the victory parade. By then Dost Mohammad had left Afghanistan with his followers. On 7 August, Shah Shuja was enthroned again at Kabul, 30 years after his first spell there.

This appeared to be a successful fulfilment of the joint Punjabi/ British policy, but it proved only a temporary solution, and the prelude to disaster. The British, their Indian troops and Punjabi allies subsequently left Afghanistan in defeat, a catastrophe accentuated by Shah Shuja's assassination. Admittedly we cannot be sure that matters would have turned out any more satisfactorily if the agreement had not been signed. This part of the world was as much of a cauldron of tension and bloodshed in the 1840s as it was before that time or as it is in the twenty-first century. Whatever the Lahore Darbar had agreed or not agreed to might not have prevented the outbreak of further fighting. But, even if more trouble had occurred, that does not justify the decision to support the British proposal to intervene in another country with no guarantee of a positive outcome and which the turbulent history of the region suggested would not last.

In signing up in effect to do Britain's bidding, Ranjit Singh made his only serious mistake in three decades of dealing with European imperialists. They served his interests but were playing with fire in making far-reaching proposals involving Afghanistan. In his youth, he might have realised that. But by 1838 he was ailing and lacked his previous, almost superhuman strength. Increasingly wracked by ill-health, his razor-sharp mental faculties had receded and his legendary decisiveness had been blunted. His apparent periodic attempts at obstruction in 1838–39 suggest a half-heartedness he had never displayed before his decline. The Maharaja's illness goes a long way to explaining why he made his fateful decision to commit the Punjab to a badly formulated British idea.

⌘

By the time Shah Shuja had been reinstalled in Kabul, Ranjit Singh had been dead for almost six weeks. The days leading up to his demise had been full of apprehension, like the period before some looming catastrophe: people knew it was going to happen and awaited the event with a numb foreboding, their concern for their prostrate Maharaja mingling with a rising anxiety over the future without him.

Ranjit Singh possessed an iron constitution, which over the years he honed through daily exercise outdoors and a fairly fixed personal routine, but he never had been supremely fit, and his habits served to undermine him as much as strengthen him. The Maharaja's first major illness was recorded in 1806 and was attributed to his indulgence in drinking toxic concoctions that might well have floored a Churchill. However, he did not fall seriously ill again until the 1820s when he suffered his first two strokes, which were followed by a third in 1835 and a fourth in 1837. The cumulative wear and tear of paralysis followed by a reversion to the strain of official activity made recovery increasingly difficult.

Doctors could do little. Dr Josiah Harlan had at some point not later than 1836 boasted that he could cure the stricken Maharaja, but he behaved arrogantly by demanding a high fee and Ranjit Singh dismissed him from his post as governor of Wazirabad. He was allowed back after a military success, but Ranjit Singh still despised him and even one of the European officers, Honigberger, regarded him as a cheat and a money-grabber. At the same time, Harlan recognised the dangerous state Ranjit was in, and he rendered him a signal service by asking the British to appoint a suitable doctor to tend to him. As a result, a Dr W.L. McGregor was assigned to the Maharaja's service. He arrived in Lahore towards the end of 1836, along with electrical equipment for shocking Ranjit's body back into life when necessary. Such treatment was, of course, not without danger and, like many great men, the proud Ranjit Singh could be strongly averse to medical treatment, particularly of an invasive kind. Anguished over his condition, top aides including Dhian Singh and Khushal Singh put themselves through the electrical treatment by way of encouragement, but the sceptical Maharaja would not cooperate and this particular treatment had to be stopped.

Ranjit's seizure in December 1838 almost killed him there and then. He became dependent not only upon European clinicians, of whom he now had several, but also a few confidants with whom he could communicate through sign language. Fakir Aziz-ud-din, truly the Lahore Darbar's man for all seasons, proved indispensable in this role. Acting as Ranjit's most diligent medium, the Fakir would place an ear close to Ranjit's mouth to catch his whispered stammer; when that method sometimes failed, the frail Maharaja would be forced to communicate by turning his head or his stronger hand to the left or right. The faithful Aziz-ud-din tended him as closely as a parent would an ailing child. Bhai Ram Singh also gave invaluable help with interpreting Ranjit's sign language.

The bitter January weather kept Ranjit largely indoors. That month, Jean François Allard died, and Ranjit's grief could well have exacerbated his declining mental health. February brought longer days and brighter weather, and Ranjit got out more. He recovered sufficiently to be able to travel to Amritsar to pray for his health and to distribute animals and jewellery. But the improvement was relative; he was still extremely unwell. His living conditions made matters worse. A British doctor named Steele noted that, in addition to being airless, the Maharaja's property was damp and smelly from surrounding swampy ground. These poor conditions for recuperation were worsened by his followers being, as always, afforded easy access to their monarch even in his parlous state. Steele insisted that his patient be moved to a better environment, though he knew that that could not be more than a palliative. Ranjit was still virtually speechless in May, though he had regained a little of his old animation. Fifty Brahmins were called up to pray for his recovery, but by the end of the month he was facing up to the fact that he would not survive.

By June Ranjit had six doctors plus other medical staff in attendance but he continued to be an awkward patient. For instance, he naturally took more positively to a prescription by Dr Honigberger which combined drops of nightshade with sugar and brandy than he did to the more strictly medicinal solutions of the British physicians. However, despite Honigberger's rich potions he did not accept his advice to be removed to better conditions that were available at the fort; apparently, his astrologers cautioned against any move before 13 June. When Ranjit at last went there on the evening of the 13th he found the fresher air congenial to his spirits. But it was too late. On 20 June he suffered a relapse, and began to bleed from his nose and experience pain in his knees. Always realistic rather than foolishly optimistic, he told Prince Kharak that being better one day and then ill again the next meant he was fundamentally unwell. Ranjit had been confiding in his eldest son, and he now accepted Aziz-ud-din's advice to entrust the affairs of state to him, with Raja Dhian Singh continuing as chief minister, a decision officially proclaimed on the 21st, midsummer's day. His officials hoped that vesting supreme authority in the official heir and the tough-minded top minister would see the country through what would at the very least be a considerable change.

The next day, Ranjit fell further into deep illness. The sardars instructed that forts were to be reinforced and their guards made extra vigilant and – this order must have aroused their deepest despair – that a bier should be procured. Although Ranjit pulled back from the brink a little, he relapsed again so badly that by the evening of 24 June he was constantly surrounded by ministers both as a mark of respect and in case they were urgently needed.

That day saw the first disturbance of what became a torrent, which over the next seven years translated into crimes and bloody deeds that culminated in the British seizure of the Punjab. Prince Sher Singh was at Batala, but on hearing of the gravity of his father's condition he hastened to Amritsar to take possession of the Fort of Gobindgarh and the State Treasury. He returned whence he came after finding that they were already heavily guarded. In addition, Kharak had directed him to come to Lahore, but Sher feared that the elder Prince and Dhian Singh Dogra might have him confined and thus not only refused to obey Kharak's order but would not attend his father's funeral either. Prince Sher did not get to Lahore until 9 July.

Meanwhile Ranjit fell into a coma. He recovered from it on the 26th in time to complete his own personal last wishes: the presentation of his weapons to his courtiers (inevitably accompanied by tears on the part of all present); orders to distribute his animals – even his prized horses – to all corners of the subcontinent; and a direction for the Koh-i-Noor to be removed to the Temple of Jagannath in Puri in the state of Orissa in eastern India, which was believed by some to be its original home but which was a long way from the Punjab. The decision seemed to flummox the courtiers. The fact that the Maharaja wanted the priceless stone placed in a Hindu shrine was not in itself surprising in view of his secularism, but disposing of the hitherto well-guarded gem to such a far-off site outside Punjabi control suggests he had not made the order with a clear mind. Surely, having gone to so much trouble to obtain it, he would have been loath to risk its complete loss? At any rate, the wish seemed to put his aides into a state of rudderless confusion. Bhai Gobind Ram said that the Maharaja had ordered Dhian Singh to dispose of the gem; Dhian said that Kharak Singh should do the disposing; the heir to the throne said the gem was with Misser Beli Ram; and Misser Beli Ram replied that the stone was in Amritsar. Apparently some of this irresponsible discussion was overheard by Ranjit, who frowned, as if worried about the future of his kingdom.

The Maharaja fell again into unconsciousness and, on the evening of the next day, 27 June, he died. The *Lahore Akhbar* newspaper subsequently reported that:

> The death of the Maharaja being known, the Ranees, Koonwer Khurruck Singh, Raja Dhian Singh, Jumadar Khooshal Singh and others raised their voices in lamentation, tearing their hair, casting earth on their heads, throwing themselves on the ground and striking their heads against bricks and stone. This continued during the night by the side of the corpse. Every now and then looking towards the corpse their shrieks were shriller.

And we may be certain that such displays of grief were repeated a thousand-fold and more as the news spread throughout the land.

During the night of 27/28 June Ranjit's body lay in state on the floor surrounded by oil lamps. Brahmins and Bahais constantly recited mantras and the Granth. In the world outside, further security measures were ordered. More ominously, during a meeting without Kharak's presence the sardars unanimously agreed that he could not be automatically trusted to maintain their *jagirs*. Therefore they decided to draft a deed to the effect that the *jagirs* would remain in place and take such action as appeared appropriate should Kharak refuse to approve it. This was the first overt sign that the edifice of unity that Ranjit had laboured so long to build was cracking. The sardars took their action despite having agreed at a meeting convened by Kharak the day before that they would all act in mutual concord. Their secret agreement looked even more shoddy when early on the 28th Dhian Singh broke down and declared that he would burn himself alive on Ranjit's funeral pyre. Kharak led the horrified ministers in beseeching him not to do so, to which he finally agreed. However, four of Ranjit Singh's ranis (and seven of their slave-girls) stuck to their decision to carry out the old tradition of self-immolation.

At court later that morning, all the ministers approached the new Maharaja and pledged their loyalty to him. They had apparently already made clear to him their apprehensions over his intentions, for he assured them that their *jagirs* would remain in place, though he did so only after they had made their pledges. By then

Ranjit's body had been prepared for his funeral by being bathed in fragrances and dressed with ornaments. His wooden bier, shaped like a ship with sails of embroidered silk, was wrought with gold and silver.[5] Henry Steinbach, a Prussian who had entered Khalsa service in 1836, later wrote an account of what happened next:

> The corpse of the late Maharaja, placed upon a splendid gilt car, constructed in the form of [a] ship, with sails of gilt cloth to waft him (according to native superstition) into paradise, was borne upon the shoulders of soldiers, preceded by native musicians, playing their wild and melancholy airs. His four queens, dressed in the most sumptuous apparel, then followed, each in a separate chair, borne upon the shoulders of the attendants; the female slaves followed on foot. Before each of the queen[s] was carried a large mirror … After them came the successor to the throne, the Maharaja Kurruck Singh, attended by the whole of the Sikh Sardars, bare-footed, and clothed in white; none but persons of noble rank being permitted to join the procession. To the last moment of this terrible sacrifice, the queens exhibited the most perfect equanimity; far from evincing any dread of the terrible death which awaited them, they appeared in a high state of excitement, and ascended the funeral pyre with alacrity. The slaves appeared perfectly resigned, but less enthusiastic. The body of the Maharaja having been placed upon the pile, the queens seated themselves around it, when the whole were covered with a canopy of the most costly Kashmir Shawls. The Maharaja Kurruck Singh then taking a lighted torch, pronounced a short prayer, set fire to the pile, and in an instant the whole mass, being composed of very ignitable material, was in flames. The noise from the [drums] and the shouts of the spectators immediately drowned any exclamation from the wretched victims. It was with some difficulty that the Raja Dhyan Singh … under strong excitement, was prevented from throwing himself into the flames. Considerable doubt has been thrown over the sincerity of this intended act of self-devotion; but the general opinion was that he fully intended it from the apparent absence of any motive for hypocrisy.[6]

Apart from his revealing indication of the mistrust that surrounded Dhian Singh Dogra, Steinbach's account accorded with less detailed reports. Despite the weather being very hot and the high sun beating down fiercely, the Lahore diarist picturesquely noted that, 'A small cloud appeared in the sky over the burning pile, and having shed a few tears, cleared away.'

Another report of what happened comes from the pen of an eminent German, Captain Leopold von Orlich, who had joined the British army, as he wrote in his preface, 'for the purpose of acquiring ... that military experience, which a long peace had prevented him from obtaining in his own country'. He put his experiences in letter form to two of the greatest German scholars of the day, the geographer Carl Ritter and the explorer-scientist Alexander von Humboldt. This account of Ranjit's funeral was addressed to von Humboldt:

Four of the wives and seven of his female slaves committed themselves to the flames with his body. An eye-witness told me that nothing had made so deep and lasting an impression on him as the moment when these female figures issued, in solemn procession, from the palace gate, amid the sound of music and the thunder of the artillery. Almost all the inhabitants of Lahore were present at this fearful solemnity. The corpse was placed in a sitting posture, between high piles of wood; and as soon as the flames were at their height, the unhappy victims prepared for death.

Two of the wives, who were only sixteen years of age, and possessed of extraordinary beauty, looked as if they were happy in being able, for the first time, to show their charms to the multitude; they took off their most precious jewels, gave them to their relations and friends, asked for a looking-glass, and with a slow and measured step walked towards the pile, sometimes gazing at the glass in their hand, then at the assembly, and anxiously asking if any change were observable in their countenance. They entered the glowing furnace, and in an instant were caught by the flames, and suffocated by the heat and smoke.

The other women seemed less resigned and cheerful; and, when they caught sight of the fearful element, horror was depicted on their countenances; but they knew that escape was impossible, and patiently submitted to their cruel fate.[7]

Ranjit's pyre burned for two days. After three days his and his consorts' ashes were placed in urns and the citizens of Lahore came in their tens of thousands to throw flowers upon them as they were carried by bearers on a *palanquin* (an enclosed litter) through the city's streets. The ashes were then conveyed to Hardwar 300 miles away on the Ganges, with crowds of people paying homage along the entire route. They all knew they were witnessing the passing of an era.

VICIOUS AFTERMATH

Ranjit Singh's death ushered in a long period of disruption which created grave instability. Seven changes of government took place between 1839 and 1845, six of them accompanied by bloodshed. The first fault line through which feuding erupted was the character of the new Maharaja. Kharak Singh was invested on 1 September 1839, yet by then he had already been largely ousted from administrative affairs. Kharak's unworldly piety and dissolute behaviour combined disastrously with his weak intellect and inattention to state business.

Kharak's best hope would have been to work closely with Dhian Singh Dogra, whose standing was high in the aftermath of Ranjit's death. Dhian Singh's son Hira Singh, with whom Ranjit Singh had been very close, now also counted in the political arena. Instead, Kharak turned to a childhood mentor and friend, Chet Singh. Chet rashly attempted to reduce Dhian's powers, and those of his brothers, Gulab Singh and Suchet Singh. On 8 October he threatened the prime minister in the Darbar, saying, 'See what will become of you in twenty-four hours.' Dhian Singh calmly replied, 'Your humble servant, sir; we *shall* see.' [1] Dhian and his brothers allegedly made good this defiance by murdering Chet Singh early the next morning in the Maharaja's presence. That showed how completely disrespected Kharak was, as well as the brutality of the Dogras.

By now much royal authority had devolved to Nau Nihal Singh, Kharak's son; he decided to work with Dhian, whose murder of Chet Singh seems not to have lessened his standing. For over a year the political situation was stable. Then two further deaths occurred. On 5 November 1840, Kharak, who had been under virtual house arrest, died, allegedly from food poisoning, triggering a succession crisis. The obvious contender was Nau Nihal but he died the very next day in an accident. Returning from his father's funeral, he was one of a party passing under a gateway of the Fort of Lahore when part of the arch fell on them all. Gulab Singh's son, Mian Udham Singh, also died then or shortly afterwards. Dhian Singh, two Bhais and Comptroller-General Dina Nath, who were slightly behind, were also hit but not seriously hurt. Dhian Singh quickly had Nau Nihal placed on a *palki* (canopy) and rushed inside. But dark rumours of a plot quickly spread about the incident, claiming that Nau Nihal's original injuries had been slight, that his courtiers were kept away from him for two days and that he had then died with his head somehow shattered. Some viewed the matter as a part of what they saw as the Dogra brothers' deep-laid plot to acquire total power. Others distanced themselves from the rumour, for no conspirator could have been certain of killing or even injuring Nau Nihal by such a hit-and-miss method. The whole truth will never be known.

The redoubtable Maharani Chand Kaur, Nau Nihal's mother and Kharak's widow, now came into her own. Although her 'brother-in-law' Sher Singh had claimed the throne with Dhian Singh's support, she encouraged Gulab Singh Dogra to counteract his brother's influence. She also asserted that Nau Nihal Singh's widow was pregnant and could give birth to a rightful successor. As a result, she was declared regent for her expected grandchild, with Sher Singh as vice-regent and Dhian remaining as prime minister. However, the triumvirate failed to work in unison. Two powerful Sandhanwalia sardars, Atar Singh and Ajit Singh, took advantage of this, gaining support from local elements of the army who took over Lahore. Chand Kaur was proclaimed Maharani on 2 December, and Sher Singh left for his estate. In January 1841 even Dhian Singh, too, was forced out of Lahore. Gulab Singh Dogra was given responsibility for defending the city.

Sher Singh quickly plotted revenge and, with much of the Punjabi forces supporting him, he proved more than a match for his sister-in-law. Later that January, he returned to Lahore at the head of a large force. The upheavals had disrupted army pay, which as we have seen was often not delivered punctually even under Ranjit Singh, much to the anger of many soldiers. In the increasingly unstable atmosphere after his death, their ill-feeling was even fiercer. Desperate to calm the soldiers' wrath, Chand Kaur paid them their arrears and lavished presents upon the officers. She also forbade the city's banks from lending money to Sher Singh. But the situation turned in his favour when regiments outside Lahore joined his revolt and thereby gave him an advantage. Sher forced his way into Lahore where he assured the citizens that they would remain unharmed. Some leading courtiers responded favourably and appealed to Chand Kaur and Gulab Singh to submit. But the tough-minded Maharani resolved to fight. For two days, Sher Singh's artillery shelled the fort but without achieving a decisive result. Then on the 17th the opportunistic Dhian Singh arrived and secured a ceasefire. Chand Kaur was persuaded to relinquish the regency and accept a *jagir*, Atar Singh and Ajit Singh were exiled, and Gulab Singh's force withdrew from the fort. However, Gulab apparently spirited away with him the state's gold and other jewels.

Sher Singh ascended the throne on 20 January and Dhian Singh was reinstated as wazir. Sher treated generously even people who had opposed him. The troops were warned not to molest the citizens, and commanders were told to ensure they didn't. However Sher Singh was unable to pay the troops – due to Gulab Singh's theft – and this led to mayhem. The aggrieved men killed regimental accountants and officers whom they suspected of embezzling their wages or of having dealings with the British; they also plundered the city. The ordinary soldiers then demanded the right to a voice in state affairs. They achieved their aim in part by incorporating the Panchayat into the army. Regiments began to elect their own *panches* who deliberated on the orders of the commanding officer and then made recommendations to the men – rather like twentieth-century Bolshevik 'soviets' without the theoretical context or political controls. Military discipline was severely undermined.

Sher Singh left state business largely in the hands of Dhian Singh. The two men worked in harness for over two years and they even strengthened the Punjab in a way from which Ranjit

Singh had recoiled: they conquered the strategically important Ladakh valley which secured the northern border against China. The two countries signed a peace treaty in September 1842 under which trade would continue to pass through Ladakh.

Relations with the British swung between amicable and tense, as catastrophe – one of the greatest military disasters in British imperial history – struck in Afghanistan. Following the 1839 victory, some British troops had returned to India, but it soon became clear that Shah Shuja's rule could be maintained only through the continued presence of British forces. Afghans resented both Shuja and the British, and resentment heightened when William Macnaghten tried to improve his troops' morale by allowing in their families, thus giving Afghans the impression that the British were occupiers. Dost Mohammad Khan failed in an attempted coup and was exiled to India in late 1840. By October 1841 Afghans were flocking to support Dost's son, Mohammad Akbar Khan. In November Sir Alexander Burnes, as he had become, and his aides were killed in Kabul and the remaining British forces were unable to restore their authority. Macnaghten offered to make Mohammad Akbar Afghanistan's vizier in exchange for allowing the British to stay. It was a disastrous mistake, for Akbar promptly ordered Macnaghten to be imprisoned. As he was being taken to his cell, a mob killed him and paraded his dismembered corpse through Kabul.

Clearly the only possible option now was retreat. In January 1842 Major-General William Elphinstone, commander of the British garrison in Kabul, secured an agreement providing for the safe departure of the British garrison and its dependants. Related to Mountstuart Elphinstone who had spearheaded Britain's fleeting diplomatic coup in 1809, he would now become the second Elphinstone to suffer a reverse over Shah Shuja. His effective surrender was never going to be allowed to end in a gentlemanly withdrawal. Struggling through snowbound passes, the retreating British were attacked again and again. Their numbers were reduced to fewer than 40 and in freezing conditions they had no shelter, little food and few weapons. On 13 January one of them, a surgeon named William Brydon, struggled into a British sentry post at Jalalabad and told the horrified detachment of how the Afghans had given the defeated Anglo-Indian force and their dependants no quarter. Some 4,500 soldiers and 12,000 civilians had been killed. Brydon was not the sole survivor, as was often claimed, but there were very few others. Elphinstone perished in Afghanistan some months later.

Amid this disastrous regional situation, which Britain had largely created, the British commissioners from Ludhiana now interceded, successfully, on behalf of the exiled Atar Singh and Ajit Singh, who wanted to return to the Punjab. Two other Sandhanwalias were released from confinement. As well as agreeing to accept the Sandhanwalias back with assurances that they would not disrupt his reign (assurances that were uncertain at best), Sher Singh was also persuaded to allow the British to escort Dost Mohammad Khan through the Punjab to be reinstalled in Kabul. All this was part of Britain's scheming to recover influence there. Without a British presence, Shah Shuja had remained in power only briefly, and he was assassinated in April 1842.

The Darbar signed a treaty with Dost, Lahore's former enemy. The beneficiary of Britain's reverses in Afghanistan, he was subsequently received in triumph at Kabul, despite being accompanied by British forces who came to rescue the few remaining British prisoners, burning Kabul's citadel and Great Bazaar in so doing. This additional destruction exacerbated local resentment of foreign influence, of which Dost was able to take advantage.

In March 1842 a British mission from Ludhiana had gone to Amritsar and offered condolences to Sher on the death of his predecessor and congratulated him upon his accession. Yet a year later, in March 1843, they turned against him. Demonstrations against Britain had broken out in Sindh following the humiliating end of the First Anglo-Afghan War. Sensitive to their loss of face in Afghanistan, the British decided to suppress the demonstrations, sending in a veteran general Sir Charles Napier. Finding little resistance, he decided to exceed his orders and annexed the province, which was placed under administration from Bombay, which further antagonised Sindhians.

Sher Singh and Dhian Singh's good working relations now came to an end, with distrust turning to outright hatred. The return of the Sandhanwalia relatives increased the tension.

Although Sher had shown magnanimity in allowing them back, they were not reconciled to him. Chand Kaur, whose cause they continued to champion from the safety of British territory, had died in June 1842 (murdered on Sher Singh's orders, some said), which did not lessen their hostility towards Sher. The spreading sourness was channelled into a murder plot of which the ruthless Dhian must have at least implicitly approved. It culminated on the morning of 15 September 1843, when the Maharaja went to inspect some Sandhanwalia troops with his 12-year-old son, Prince Pratap Singh.[2] He arrived late and Lehna Singh Sandhanwalia and Ajit Singh Sandhanwalia reproached him light-heartedly for the delay. They apparently sat down with him and asked him straight out for *jagirs*. Sher Singh hedged in response and asked to look at Ajit Singh's carbine which he had obtained from an Englishman. As Sher leant forward to take the rifle, Ajit Singh shot him with it and then decapitated him. Almost simultaneously, Lehna Singh hacked off the head of Sher's son. The European, Honigberger, claimed to have witnessed the death of Sher Singh and to have only just avoided losing his own life.

What transpired after Ajit Singh returned to Lahore Fort to report to Dhian Singh is uncertain. The accepted version is that he informed Dhian that Sher Singh had been killed, and that shortly after their meeting Ajit Singh killed Dhian, too. The details and rationale for this bloodletting are obscure. The Sandhanwalia relatives' ultimate plan was allegedly to install five-year-old Prince Duleep Singh as Maharaja with his mother, Rani Jindan, as regent and the Sandhanwalias wielding the real power. Things worked out rather differently.

༄

During the killings on 15 September, Dhian Singh's 25-year-old son Hira Singh happened to be outside Lahore with his uncle, Suchet Singh. Uncle and nephew acted quickly to quell the revolt. They rounded up enough troops to bombard the fort throughout the night and capture it. Ajit Singh and Lehna Singh Sandhanwalia received no mercy for their crimes.

Nonetheless, Hira Singh adopted their alleged plan to make Duleep Singh Maharaja – Duleep was crowned on 2 February

1844 – and Rani Jindan regent, while he himself became prime minister. He continued to eliminate the Sandhanwalias, seizing and executing those who did not escape from the country in time. He allocated most administrative matters to his childhood mentor, Pandit Jalla, while he himself concentrated on managing the army. This allowed Rani Jindan to assume an influence in court that undermined Hira. By the end of 1844 she had obtained support from army officers who agreed to overthrow him and Pandit Jalla. Isolated, the two men tried to escape from the country in December, but they were captured and killed.

The Rani took control of the government with her brother, Jawahar Singh, who became wazir. In an attempt to restore discipline, Jindan Kaur reconstituted the supreme Khalsa Council by giving representation to the principal sardars and restoring a working balance between the army *panchayats* and the civil administration. However, the army remained unpredictable. A segment encouraged another of Ranjit Singh's surviving sons, Peshaura Singh, to claim the throne, but he became yet another of Ranjit's children to be killed, along with Kashmira Singh. Another element turned against Gulab Singh and, early in 1845, took him hostage. Then Jawahar Singh became a target of criticism. To counteract the disaffection, Jindan Kaur betrothed Duleep Singh in the powerful Attariwala family and promised higher pay for the soldiers. But Jawahar Singh remained exposed. The Khalsa Council decided he had been party to the murders of Peshaura and Kashmira and was too pro-British. He was summoned before the army on 21 September 1845. Although accompanied by Rani Jindan and Duleep Singh, he was publicly killed. In November, the Maharani, having apparently recovered from this ordeal, appointed Misr Lal Singh as Jawahar's successor with the approval of the Khalsa Council.

The situation was now aggravated by the first of two wars with the British. The East India Company had been increasing its military strength. British accounts tend to stress that this was in response to their belief that the army had become unrestrained and represented a threat to British territory along the border. British attitudes were hardened by reports from Major George Broadfoot, a political agent who reported on the disorder in the Punjab. As Britain was keen to recover influence in Afghanistan, there was

in any case some desire to expand British influence in the country
in between, too.

Sikh and Indian historians have argued that the British military activity was not just defensive but offensive in nature, pointing to the preparation of offensive equipment such as bridging
trains and siege batteries. They also viewed Broadfoot's conduct
as hostile. The Punjabis attacked the British in December 1845. It
was a disastrous misjudgement. After a vigorous show of strength
they were beaten in February 1846 and forced to sign the Treaty
of Lahore. The complex loyalties in the Darbar were revealed by
this peace settlement. The army commander Tej Singh accepted
a reward from the British, while Gulab Singh, who had negoti-
ated the peace, accepted an appointment as Maharaja of Kashmir,
which was separated from the kingdom of Lahore.[3] These developments fanned rumours that Tej Singh had embarked on the war
to break the powerful but undisciplined army and to maintain a
hold on power. Also, Lal Singh was alleged to have corresponded
with a British political officer and betrayed state secrets.

Other parts of the treaty were more intrusive. The British
imposed a resident on Lahore, which gave them a sway over the
Punjabi government. The Punjabis ceded the Jalandhar Doab,
which gave the British a buffer zone between the Kingdom of
Lahore and the Cis-Sutlej. The British took over administration
of the five great rivers and forbade the Darbar to employ white
foreigners without permission. Although Duleep Singh would
remain Maharaja and Rani Jindan regent, the establishment of
a British resident and supporting garrison enabled the British to
begin dismantling the Punjab as a separate entity.

British control was tightened under the Treaty of Bhyrowal
in December 1846. Maharani Jindan Kaur had believed that the
British military force in Lahore was merely a temporary measure, but history shows repeatedly that once governments move
soldiers into disrupted regions they can be most reluctant to take
them out again. This proved true in the Punjab in 1846. Far from
quitting, during the year the British strengthened their authority. As a result, the Darbar ceased to exist as a sovereign political
body. Jindan Kaur surrendered power to the Council of Ministers
which had been appointed by the British, who would control the

regency until the Maharaja came of age in 1854. The Maharani was pensioned off with an annuity, but she was moved away from Lahore to neighbouring Sheikhupura where her allowance was reduced.

Shortly afterwards, the Second Anglo-Sikh War broke out following a revolt in Multan. A British political agent, Lieutenant Patrick Vans Agnew, sent to Multan to ensure control in April 1848, was murdered. Unrest increased as large numbers of Punjabi soldiers deserted to join the rebels. The British avoided fighting during the high summer and monsoon seasons, but in March 1849 they won a hard-fought conflict in which the two sides had gained a mutual respect for each other's fighting prowess. At the outbreak of the rebellion, Maharani Jindan Kaur was swiftly removed from the Punjab (a controversial act which some historians argue was a catalyst for the spread of anti-British feeling across the region) and was moved first to Benaras and then incarcerated in the high-security fort of Chunar. Despite even tighter conditions of confinement, the resilient ex-Maharani escaped to Nepal disguised as a maidservant. Her flight from jail came too late, however, as the Punjabi rebellion had by that time already been quashed by East India Company troops. On 30 March 1849, 150 years after the introduction of the Khalsa, Duleep Singh held his last court and signed away all rights to rule. A proclamation by Governor-General Lord Dalhousie annexing the Punjab was then read out.

Jindan Kaur arrived in Kathmandu shortly after the war ended. Her presence there was unwelcome because it risked arousing British anger against Nepal. However, Prime Minister Jung Bahadur granted her asylum and an allowance, mainly as a mark of respect to the memory of Ranjit Singh. Naturally, she was unhappy in her alien surroundings, especially as the British persuaded the Nepalese Darbar to impose restrictions on her.[4] The ex-Maharani protested against them, which led to Jung Bahadur expelling one of her attendants. Jindan Kaur then dismissed all her Nepalese staff and rebuffed an order to appear in the Darbar to acknowledge Nepalese hospitality. But a total and possibly dangerous breach was prevented when, late in 1860, she was told that Duleep was about to return to India and she could visit him in Calcutta. After she had done so he took her with him to England.

֍

CONCLUSION

The welter of events that overcame the Punjab after the summer of 1839 proved that maintaining Ranjit Singh's realm was beyond the blood relatives and politicians who followed him. None of them was able to rise above circumstances and self-interest. After just a decade, the Punjab was absorbed into British India. Many Asian observers have seen this as an inevitable consequence of British imperial ambitions. But this argument is largely contradicted by the history of the earlier 1800s. Then, although Britain was established in India and concerned to protect its interests there, the British sought agreements with Afghanistan and Persia, not conquest, in order to protect themselves from the threat (as they saw it) of French and Russian expansion.

Far from wanting to annex the Punjab, in 1808 they tried to win it over to their side as an accompaniment to their Afghan/Persian policy. Punjabi support for Britain – or at least acquiescence – was essential for the policy to succeed, so as to block off any attacks from the north-west. Initially the British had not wanted much in the form of agreement, seeing no need to bother with a formal treaty. But through patience, stamina and sheer political skill (and some daring provocation), Ranjit Singh got his way, winning solid British respect for him which lasted to the end of his days. This was important for the realisation of his own ambitions. From 1809 onwards, the British fended off attempts by third parties to take sides against Ranjit, and let him to do much as he pleased to their west. For the Punjab, whose history was littered with instances of betrayal by outsiders, trust in the British was of inestimable value.

Mindful of both British might and their reliability, Ranjit Singh stuck by the British from the Treaty of Amritsar of 1809 to the decision of 1838 to cooperate with their plan for regime change in Afghanistan. The friendship occasionally came under strain, most notably over Britain's blocking of Ranjit Singh's designs on Sindh province in the early 1830s, but Ranjit held tight to the Treaty of Amritsar, and was right to do so for his country's sake, because from the beginning almost to the end of his long reign he was menaced by Afghanistan. Although the Afghan threat to the Punjab as a political entity ended with the Punjabis' victory in the Battle of Naushera in 1823, it did not close the book on Afghan aggression, which continued to 1837. Britain's moral and material support was very important in the Darbar's endeavours to keep out successive Afghan rulers.

However, Ranjit Singh was wrong in 1838 to support Britain's new aggressive stance towards Afghanistan. British policy was given a veneer of respectability by their stated wish to reinstall Shah Shuja and to bring stability to the country. But Ranjit should have foreseen that neither intention could succeed for long. Afghanistan was inherently unstable, and a man who had already failed as a ruler and depended upon foreign support could not guarantee to re-establish himself in power.

At the same time, Britain's changed policy helped prevent the Afghans from attacking the Punjab after Ranjit Singh's death. In a humiliating about-turn, the British withdrew from Afghanistan in 1842 and reinstalled their *bête-noire* Dost Mohammad Khan in power. The Punjabis, whose cooperation with this move was obtained, made their own settlement with Dost. Thereafter the Afghans left the Punjab alone, even when the Punjab disintegrated, as Dost realised that Britain could well seek to control an unstable Punjab and it would be dangerous to make any moves which might provoke the British into action.

The Punjab being geographically at the centre of Britain's foreign policy concerns in south-central Asia enhanced Ranjit Singh's ability to make a powerful impact on international politics. Britain appreciated both his toughness and his essential straightforwardness and as a result respected him highly. Afghanistan's rulers did not accord him as much recognition as the British, but they did fear him, and fear kept its leaders in check.

Even if Ranjit Singh had inherited an established country and governed it well enough only to earn respect and fear, that would have been a major achievement in an age when the world was dominated by European power. Other nations and peoples could survive only through guile, goodwill, good luck and occasional aggression. Ranjit Singh, despite not inheriting a stable country, displayed all of these and so not only survived but prospered. His was a state unstable by definition because it was in transition, in the process of formation for most of his rule. Only a supremely powerful leader could have remained on top of such an entity.

Ranjit Singh was at all times concerned for everyone to know he was in charge and that the Punjab would unfold in his image. He transmitted this fundamental message not through bluster or arrogance but through example. The most important of his traits was physical bravery. Ranjit Singh had already acquired a reputation for valour before capturing Lahore and becoming Maharaja, but he consolidated it mainly through leading his men in battle situations. None of his other political aims would have been realised if he had not burnished this reputation. The Punjabis' cultural stress on boldness, their history of being invaded, their location between aggressive Afghanistan and powerful British India, the assertive manner in which the Sikhs had taken control under the *misl* system – all this presupposed a leader who was brave and seen to be so.

But bravery is not enough. Afghan leaders, too, were brave men but they tended to lack the other essential political talents – wisdom, far-sightedness, cunning and caution, for the last trait can be as important as any other when the life of a nation and its people are at stake. Ranjit applied one or more of these precious skills in almost all his political actions, whether fashioning the civil state, reforming the army or appointing people to influential positions. He also did so when deciding to go to war, though once militarily engaged he cast caution aside and went all out, not just to win but to exploit success by going for more than the original aim wherever possible.

Long before Winston Churchill proclaimed it, Ranjit Singh practised the guiding political doctrine that the great British war leader made famous: in war, resolution; in defeat, defiance;

in victory, magnanimity; and in peace, goodwill. Perhaps, given his times, the most unusual of his qualities were magnanimity in victory and goodwill towards those whose opinions differed from his own. He looked to end the bitterness once he had obtained what he had set out to win. Always practically minded, he could see no point in doing otherwise. Instead, he spotted the far more valuable potential of winning accord and even friendship from those he had bested. They were not always attainable, but the times when they were proved useful. And the Maharaja displayed constant goodwill towards his own subjects, of whatever ethnic or religious group. His benevolence fitted well with his generous disposition and his grand strategy of unity.

Ranjit Singh was also a genius at combining apparently inconsistent attitudes. Ranjit the uneducated and outdoor-loving boy became a keen student of the largely academic pursuit of administration. Ranjit the provenly devout Sikh was blithely disobedient to some fundamental Sikh teachings. Rarely other than modestly attired himself, he expected his courtiers to dress with spectacular opulence. He lived in conditions that were simple and even dangerous to his health while maximising the magnificence and splendour of the Darbar over which he presided. He was decisive and habitually blunt in communication with his courtiers, yet liked to consult them and consider their opinions. Opposed to capital punishment for civilians, he occasionally ordered bodily mutilations and even allowed a miscreant to be beaten to death.

Yet Ranjit was never so contradictory as to be a hypocrite. His attitudes were ultimately explicable and they enhanced rather than undermined the trust that he built up. People knew where they stood with him. That did not make him predictable; his lively imagination and ambitious policy agenda meant that he frequently embarked on unexpected pursuits. That was his right as the legally appointed ruler with absolute power, and it does not alter the fact that he could be trusted to be himself. Nothing proves the point about his integrity better than the fact that his closest adviser at the start, Fakir Aziz-ud-din, was still there displaying selfless loyalty right at the end, and that the Darbar remained supportive throughout. Some aides might have been –

indeed, were – incompetent or grasping, but none was ever shown to have plotted against him.

This corporate loyalty made for a rule that was impressively long by any standards. In the nineteenth century, when personal life expectancy was in any case relatively short, to have led an expanding, warring country for 40 years was an amazing achievement. This, more than anything, proves Ranjit's sheer quality of character and personality.

Is there one period of his reign that could be termed better than others? Perhaps the seven or eight years up to early 1835 (when he suffered his third stroke) were outstanding. During that time Ranjit Singh fought off the last serious challenge to his rule, that of Syed Ahmed; in the process he neutralised the threat from Afghanistan, and held his first summit meeting with a governor-general of British-ruled India, Lord Bentinck. But historians have rightly been wary of making value judgements. Instead of focusing on particular scenes or acts, scholars have tended to cast their eyes across the entire play. They saw it as a dynamic production from start to finish, which can be best assessed as a whole.

Ranjit Singh continued to offer meaning to people after he died. As with many really powerful rulers, he was such a legend in his own lifetime that when his body died, his spirit lived on, inspiring men and women at all levels in all their daily doings. Many Sikhs simply could not accept that he had gone. Their sense of loss was not fully realised until a decade later when, on 11 March 1849, the Second Anglo-Sikh War was concluded. On that grim day, many soldiers mournfully declared while surrendering their weapons, 'Aj Ranjit Singh mar gaya' ('Today Ranjit Singh has died').

In many ways Ranjit Singh continues to be recognised today. For instance, the provincial government of Punjab in India offers the prestigious Maharaja Ranjit Singh Award for feats of exceptional excellence and achievement in sport at any level – Olympic, world championship, international, national. Instituted in 1978, the award comprises a trophy figure of Ranjit Singh, a citation and a sum of one lac in rupees (about £1,000 in 2016 values). The first person to win the Maharaja Ranjit Singh Award was Pargat Singh, who captained the Indian hockey team at the Barcelona and Atlanta Olympics.

The surest proof of a ruler's reputation lies in what people say, and continue to say, long after he or she has departed. British writers led the field in producing a stream of admiring (if patronising) books about Ranjit Singh and about the Punjab in the nineteenth century. Some anti-imperialist observers might take the sardonic view that the British could afford their praise, for they had consistently got the better of him; but, as this book has shown, Ranjit Singh generally got as good a deal out of the British as they got from him. Whatever opinion may be held about the British in India, the fact was that they *were* there and had to be taken seriously and handled on their own tough-minded and wily terms. Ranjit Singh knew full well how deceit featured in their diplomacy and necessarily used some himself in handling them.

Asian writers have naturally been respectful about him, basking in the fact that the subcontinent produced a political and military figure who was the equal of any of his time. Indeed, many have overpraised him, portraying him as an infinitely wise man who made no political errors and whose shortcomings as a human being could be glossed over. Yet it in no way detracts from Ranjit Singh's singular contribution to Punjabi history to declare his deficiencies. They pale into significance against his monumental success in creating a thriving mixed society. He successfully led a varied community from a minority group within it. There is no evidence that either the large Hindu or larger still Muslim sections of the Punjab felt antagonistic towards him. They did not share the Sikhs' adulation of him: Punjab ethnic tensions – like others elsewhere – are inherent and long-lasting. But Ranjit always discouraged ethnic and religious ill-feeling and inspired his countrymen and women to do likewise. It was his supreme, if temporary, achievement.

In sum, he was, quite simply, a very great man.

POSTSCRIPT

MAHARAJA DULEEP SINGH

The life of Ranjit Singh's last son marks a complete break from his father's life, but is such an extraordinary story that it deserves a postscript.

Prince Duleep was born a year before his father's death. With Ranjit being terminally ill, he could hardly have got to know his eighth and last son at all. The Prince lived his first years of life happily amid the rich background of the court and the beautiful Mughal palaces of Lahore. He enjoyed falconry and, like the other royal children, rode the best horses and elephants in the country and could choose from costumes and trays of jewels. The boy received his education from two tutors, one of whom taught Persian for court business and the other Gurmukhi for reading and following recitations from the Guru Granth Sahib. Duleep learnt to shoot guns and bows, and was trained in the art of command by being given a troop of 60 boys. The love of his mother and his uncle Jawahar Singh surrounded him. In 1846 the new British Resident Sir Henry Lawrence found himself charmed by Duleep, now Maharaja, and was kind to him, organising magic lantern parties and other events.

At first, the boy-Maharaja was insulated from the struggles behind the scenes. He was protected from the real world beyond the palace, his every need instantly attended to. Yet his cocooned lifestyle could only have meant that he was hit all the harder when the brutalities of politics invaded two years into his kingship. A few weeks after his seventh birthday, he was forced to experience the violent murder of his uncle. When Jawahar appeared before several army officers accompanied by the Maharaja and Rani

Jindan, the Rani had quickly assessed what the men were up to. But despite her loud pleas, a soldier stabbed Jawahar to death – only minutes after his uncle had been holding Duleep in his arms.

Three months later the First Anglo-Sikh War broke out. With Duleep still Maharaja after the conclusion of hostilities, he was in a position to carry out a political act that annoyed Henry Lawrence. At the annual Hindu festival of Dussera in 1847, Duleep Singh publicly disregarded British expectations that he would honour Tej Singh as his commander-in-chief. The British believed, probably rightly, that Rani Jindan had encouraged Duleep to make the snub. At any rate, Lawrence reacted ruthlessly and had both Duleep and his mother confined and forbade contact between them.

Devastated, Rani Jindan pointed out that Duleep was not only very young but had no other close relatives. She demanded to know into whose care he had been entrusted. She warned that if justice was not done she would appeal to London. But the Rani had already surrendered authority to the British and events were proceeding towards the Second Anglo-Sikh War. The significant responsibility of protecting and educating Duleep Singh was eventually placed in the hands of a British doctor (later Sir) John Login, and his wife Lena. Login had served as an army medical officer; he was later in charge of the Toshakhana (Royal Treasury) at the Fort of Lahore, from where he retrieved the Koh-i-Noor diamond and had it taken to the governor-general. The diamond was then shipped to England.[1] After the Punjab's annexation, the young Maharaja himself would similarly end up in England, though not before living a few fateful years in exile in Fatehgarh, on the banks of the Ganges. Fatehgarh was a centre of Christian missionary activity, with churches, orphanages, schools, a carpet factory and a village of Indian Christian converts. Duleep's household staff was part-European and part-Indian. He lived in a house which he shared with Sher Singh's widow Rani Dukno and with their son, Sahdev Singh. The relatives' presence at least would have ameliorated the melancholy experience of being in exile. Duleep was allowed elephants and hawks and accorded a guard of honour. But any hopes the British might have entertained that Duleep would forget about his mother were dashed. He asked eagerly for information about her, and her influence on him remained strong.

The material privileges hardly made up for the human deprivations imposed by the British. Restrictions on who he was allowed to meet weakened his health, and he was often sent to Landour in the Lower Himalayas to convalesce. After several days' travel, he would remain for weeks at a time in a grand building called The Castle, which had been lavishly furnished for him. But physical comfort could not make up for emotional pain.

Another high-handed measure the British took with Duleep was over his religion. The Logins had taken on the role of the boy's parents, and both were devout Christians. Their influence was reinforced by two British boys being Duleep's closest friends in Fatehgarh: one of them was the son of a Christian missionary. In addition, the British textbooks Duleep studied were full of Christian messages. One of his servants, Bhajan Lal, was a Brahmin convert to Christianity and read to him from the Bible. As an intelligent young man who showed interest in all sorts of subjects and people, Duleep was affected by the Christian context of his life. Eventually, in March 1853 and under Bhajan Lal's tutelage, he converted.

Duleep Singh's conversion to Christianity in artificial circumstances inevitably aroused controversy. Was it genuine? Or was it a response to psychological pressure? Certainly his decision was freely made in the sense that he willingly went through the procedures, even reportedly overriding resistance from his servants and sister-in-law, plus hesitation on the part of some British staff. And he acted with customary generosity in financially supporting the Christian mission schools in the area.

Duleep's situation was now transformed. Having converted and been inducted into British traditions and customs, it was only natural for him to visit Britain. He set sail in April 1854. He took with him a Bible which Dalhousie had given him, in which was inscribed: *This holy book in which he has been led by God's grace to find an inheritance richer by far than all earthly kingdoms is presented with sincere respect and regard by his faithful friend* – a 'friend' who had cost him his kingdom.

After arriving in London, Duleep was quickly granted a royal audience. Queen Victoria immediately took to Duleep and kept him near to her on state occasions. She also invited him to family occasions, when she sketched him and Prince Albert photographed him. A bizarre incident with lasting consequences occurred during one painting session. While the Maharaja was standing in his costume on a plinth, a party of yeoman warders entered with an official carrying a box containing the Koh-i-Noor. Victoria showed Duleep the stone, newly cut, which he took over to a window to inspect. Duleep then handed the diamond back to the queen, as if making a presentation, apparently (according to British records) adding that it gave him much pleasure to be able to make the gift in person. The official account of the event, in effect turning a theft into a 'gift', sounds extremely convenient from London's point of view. Whether or not the event was stage-managed, we are told that Duleep's act of 'presenting' the diamond sealed the friendship between him and the British queen.[2]

Initially, Duleep lived mainly in or near to London. He also had the use of Castle Menzies in Perthshire, which the Logins provided, and then another large Scottish residence, plus a place in Yorkshire. He came to enjoy the opulent lifestyle of a British gentleman, being known for his lavish pursuits, shooting parties and a predilection for dressing in Highland costume.

In the late 1850s Duleep asked to return to India. However, that was in the immediate aftermath of the 1857 First Indian War of Independence, when the British certainly did not want a famous ex-Maharaja ruffling the tense peace. Instead, the East India Company suggested that he tour on the European mainland, which he did with the Logins. But Duleep was not to be deflected from his aim. In 1859 he was granted his wish to rescue his now ageing mother from her exile in Nepal. Inevitably, his return caused pandemonium in some places. In Calcutta he was inundated with visits by ex-members of the Darbar and by soldiers from Sikh regiments. He could find nowhere suitable for his mother to live, and his own movements were curtailed by the government. All in all, it was an unhappy experience.

But at least he was reunited with his mother. In order to remain in close contact, they decided to live in Britain. Rani Jindan went to great lengths to adapt to this alien environment. She lived in a smart home in London, wore British-style clothes and went to church. She also encouraged Duleep to take a British wife. But their re-acquaintance was to be brief: in 1863 she died. After returning her body to India for cremation, the Maharaja determined to fulfil her wish that he should marry. However, he did not limit his field to British women. He eventually chose a part-German, part-Ethiopian mission-educated teenage girl called Bamba Muller, whom he met in Cairo. After their marriage in 1864, he took his 16-year-old bride home to a freshly acquired estate at Elveden near Thetford in Norfolk, which he had been able to purchase with the help of a mortgage provided by the India Office.[3] Duleep fell in love with Elveden and transformed the rundown estate into an efficient, modern game preserve and made its house a semi-oriental palace. He decorated the halls with mosaics and put up huge oil paintings, including ones of Ranjit Singh and Sher Singh. Naturally, jewellery was everywhere too.

Duleep and Bamba had six surviving children (another child died in infancy), three sons and three daughters. The sons were noted for their range of costumes, which included Sikh clothes, and had uncut hair. Duleep invited Edward, Prince of Wales, to shoots and received Sikh visitors as well. He loved his family life at Elveden, where he rebuilt the church, some cottages and a school with such generosity that the prospect of his leaving the village caused the rector to fear for the well-being of the village's poor.

The large new home and family, plus Duleep's spending on the poor, strained his finances. He sought an increase to his pension. Queen Victoria asked the India Office to consider the matter and Duleep's well-placed British friends also supported him in his wish. The India Office was at first obstructive, believing Duleep to have been too extravagant. Eventually, however, it was agreed that he should be loaned £57,000 on condition that after his death his estate at Elveden would be sold. Duleep reacted to the decision by spending more of his time at a much smaller house in London.

This setback tilted Duleep's mixed feelings for his British present and his Asian past sharply towards the latter. The tension had, in fact, become noticeable in the 1860s when he was with Rani Jindan. Now, India Office parsimony exacerbated his grievance over the loss of his kingdom. In 1882 the dispute became public when Duleep wrote an anguished letter to *The Times* newspaper. Two years later Duleep's growing animosity towards British officialdom increased still further. Thakur Singh Sandhanwalia – a relative from the same family that had committed almost unspeakable cruelties towards his brother Sher Singh and his family – stayed with Duleep in London and reintroduced him to the tenets of Sikhism. Under Thakur Singh's influence, Duleep began again to feel the strong sway of his first religion, and recalled Rani Jindan telling him of rumours that he had been mentioned in prophecies by Guru Gobind Singh. He decided to reconvert and go home. The British tried to stop him returning to the Punjab by offering him another £50,000 but Duleep stuck to his wish and in 1886 sailed east with his family and servants. He claimed that he intended to place himself as the prophesied moral head of the Sikh people, to reinvigorate the religion and purify it of the less desirable Hindu influences that still clung to it. But above all he was interested in recovering his lost kingdom in the Punjab and in giving substance to his title of 'Maharaja' once again.

The British now showed the newly assertive Maharaja yet another iron fist. After his ship stopped at the coaling station of Aden where the writ of the British Raj began, he was barred from proceeding further. Duleep made the agonising decision to send his family back to England while he himself, now too angry with the imperial power to live in its homeland again, would go to Paris. The British allowed his Pahul (re-initiation to Sikhism) to proceed before he left Aden. Once in Paris he again agitated to return to the Punjab, saying he would be content just to have his private estates there and a seat on the Council of India. He tried to persuade the British that his presence would help their cause because it would douse the feelings of ill-will among Indians and he would behave loyally towards the crown and the empire. Indeed, his Punjabi origins, his later British lifestyle and continuing respect for many English traditions meant that no one was better acquainted than he was with both the Punjab and Britain.

But the British still found the idea of Duleep being anywhere near the subcontinent intolerable. His hopes dashed, events now took another extraordinary turn: he entered the world of political intrigue. Thakur Singh had created a large secret movement in the Punjab with which Duleep now linked up. The Sikh conspirators discussed how to pursue their aims. Two models presented themselves: Irish nationalism (Paris had many Irish nationalists) and Russian imperialism in south Asia. Duleep travelled to Russia using the passport of an Irishman. Naturally the British had kept an eye on his movements, and an agent stole much of his money in Berlin. Once in Russia, though, he was championed by a conservative anti-British journalist and newspaper editor, Michael Katkoff. He introduced Duleep to Jemal al-Din al-Afghani, who was dedicated to the pan-Islamic anti-colonial movement.

Thus the Maharaja whose life had once been at the top of formal politics, then removed from politics altogether, now found himself among an assorted band of Sikhs, Irish republicans, a Russian reactionary and an Afghan left-wing agitator. They devised a plan for a combined Russo-Afghan force to invade India and precipitate revolts by the Sikh regiments and nobles, supplemented by mutinies among Irish elements in the British forces. British attempts at suppression would be contained by Bengalis sabotaging the Indian railways and Egyptians cutting the Suez Canal, Britain's communications link with her eastern empire.

It was a bizarre, hopelessly ambitious plan by a motley collection of people each with his own interests in mind, with little prospect of success. The Russian government's interest was really to use Duleep as a pawn to persuade the British to make life difficult for anti-Tsarist dissidents in London, while the Irish nationalists, too weak to make a big impact at this time, were concerned almost entirely with their home affairs. Then Katkoff, Duleep's principal Russian backer, and Thakur Singh both died. With little money left, Duleep's dream of making an impact of some kind on the Punjab ended. Perhaps worst of all, Princess Bamba died in 1887 aged only 48, her health having suffered from her unsettled life. Duleep might well have added to Bamba's woes by taking a mistress, Ada Douglas Wetherill, whom he later married and by whom he had two girls. Having been Duleep's mistress in Britain, Ada had gone to join him in Paris; she also went with him to Russia.

No less surprisingly, the Maharaja's own health began to fail and he had a severe stroke in 1890. Several British friends who had helped care for his children went to see him, and the aged Victoria met with him while on holiday in Nice. In October 1893, Duleep died in Paris aged 55. He had not wanted to return to Britain, in life or in death, but his body was brought back across the Channel, taken to Norfolk and buried, according to Christian rites, in Elveden Church, beside the grave of his first wife Maharani Bamba and one of their sons.[4] That was almost the end of his line: although Duleep's children married, none of them produced children of their own.

In 1999, the Prince of Wales unveiled a statue of the Maharaja at Butten Island in the River Thet, which runs through Thetford, the town which had benefited so much from his and later his sons' generosity – a belated recognition by the British monarchy of Duleep's status and importance.

NOTES

Introduction

1. John William Kaye, *The Life and Correspondence of Charles, Lord Metcalfe* (Smith Elder & Co., 1858), p 149.

Chapter 1. The Foundations

1. Khushwant Singh, 'The Sikhs', in Joseph M. Kitagawa (ed), *The Religious Traditions of Asia: Religion, History, and Culture* (Routledge/Curzon, 2002), p 114.
2. K.S. Duggal, *Ranjit Singh: A Secular Sikh Sovereign* (Abhinav Publications, 1989), pp 14–18.
3. Balwant Singh, *The Army of Maharaja Ranjit Singh* (Lahore Book Shop, 1932), p 15.
4. Gurmatas involved meetings of Sikhs in Amritsar who discussed religious and political issues with a view to resolving them. Resolutions had to be carried unanimously. They then became gurmatas (decisions of the Guru) and were binding on all Sikhs.
5. Indu Banga, *Agrarian System of the Sikhs: Late 18th and Early 19th Century* (Monohar, 1978), p 21.

Chapter 2. Ranjit's Early Years and Entry into Power

1. George Forster, *A Journey from Bengal to England through the Northern part of India, Kashmire, Afghanistan, and Persia, and into Russia by the Caspian Sea*, 2 vols. (London, 1808).
2. Some sources claim his birth date was 2 November.
3. J.S. Grewal, *The Reign of Maharaja Ranjit Singh: Structure of Power, Economy and Society* (Patiala, 1981), p 2.

4. Hira Singh (ed), *Maharaja Ranjit Singh: Being Tributes to the Memory of the Great Monarch* (Lahore: University Sikh Association, 1939), p 13.

5. J.S. Grewal, *The New Cambridge History of India: The Sikhs of the Punjab* (Cambridge University Press, 1994), p 3.

6. Khushwant Singh, 'The Sikhs', p 39.

7. H. Heras and S.N. Prasad (eds), *Fort William–India House Correspondence* (Government of India, 1974), paras. 74 and 75 of despatch dated 31 August 1800 (p 566). The index to this book suggests that the main British motive was fear of Afghanistan. The entry 'Afghanistan' refers to correspondence concerning 'defensive measures against attack of' and 'threat of invasion by' (p 628).

8. Duggal, *Ranjit Singh*, p 63.

Chapter 3. Reaching Out Beyond Lahore

1. T.R. Sharma (ed), *Maharajah Ranjit Singh: Ruler and Warrior* (Panjab University, Chandigarh, 2005), p 31.

2. Grewal, *Cambridge History*, p 5.

3. Narendra Krishna Sinha, *Ranjit Singh* (A.R. Mukherjee, 1951), appendix C.

4. Bikrama Jit Hasrat, *Life and Times of Ranjit Singh: A Saga of Benevolent Despotism* (Nabha: Hasrat, 1977), p 44.

5. Manveen Sandhu, *Maharaja Ranjit Singh, Personalitas Extraordinaire* (S.S. Sandhu, 2007), p 71.

6. Fakir Syed Waheed-ud-din, *The Real Ranjit Singh* (Punjabi University, Patiala, 2001), p 130.

7. Hasrat, *Life and Times*, p 46.

8. It is not surprising that many have wished to change the name from 'Kanjari' as this is nowadays a Punjabi swear-word, similar to 'whore'. In 2008, Moran and Pul Kanjari were given fresh publicity through Manveen Sandhu's play, *Moran Sarkar*, which was staged in Amritsar. Sadly, Manveen Sandhu and her husband were killed in a motor accident in 2009.

9. Waheed-ud-din, *The Real Ranjit Singh*, p 131.

10. Sharma (ed), *Maharajah Ranjit Singh*, p 47. Sharma gave the European's name as Charles Gouch.

11. *Memoirs of Alexander Gardner, Soldier and Traveller*, ed Major Hugh Pearse (William Blackwood & Sons, 1898), p 199. By the end of Ranjit's reign cash salaries had become the most general method of

payment in the army (Gulshan Lall Chopra, *The Panjab as a Sovereign State 1799–1839* (Uttar Chand Kapur & Sons, 1928), p 109). However, it appears that delays in payment led to open mutiny in some regiments. See W.G. Osborne, *The Court and Camp of Ranjit Singh* (Mahbub Alam, 1895), p 33.

12. Sita Ram Kohli, *Maharajah Ranjit Singh* (GNDU, 2002), p 170.
13. *Jagir*: a small territory granted by the ruler to an army chieftain for a short term in recognition of his military service.
14. Khalsa College, *Maharajah Ranjit Singh: First Death Centenary* (Amritsar: Khalsa College, 1939), p 67.
15. Lepel Griffin, *Ranjit Singh* (Oxford: Clarendon, 1893), p 144.
16. Chopra, *The Panjab*, p 80.
17. Radha Sharma, *The Lahore Darbar* (GNDU, 2001), p 5.
18. S.P. Singh and Harish Sharma (eds), *Europeans and Maharaja Ranjit Singh* (GNDU, 2001), p 40.
19. Chopra, *The Panjab*, p 147.
20. Kohli, *Maharajah Ranjit Singh*, pp 164–5.
21. Grewal, *Cambridge History*, pp 101ff.
22. *Ibid.*, p 4.
23. Radha Sharma, *The Lahore Darbar*, p 3.
24. Waheed-ud-din, *The Real Ranjit Singh*, p 25.
25. Roshan Lal Ahuja, *The Story of Ranjit Singh* (Amritsar, n.d.), p 18.
26. D.R. Sood, *Ranjit Singh* (National Book Trust, 1968), p 93.
27. Not everyone believed he was particularly religious. One British writer from almost a century ago described him as 'dissolute in morals', while S.N. Banerjee regarded his attachment to Sikhism as sincere but criticised him for rapacity and licentiousness. The modern-day Pakistani research scholar and expert on inter-faith relations in the Punjab Dr Akhtar Sandhu has pointed out that Ranjit Singh smoked openly, in violation of Sikh opposition to this practice. H.G. Rawlinson, *Buddha, Ashoka, Akbar, Shivaji and Ranjit Singh: A Study in Indian History* (Essess Publications, 1980, reprint), p 187; S.N. Banerjee, *Ranjit Singh* (Lahore: Atma Ram & Sons, Lahore, 1931), p 71; and interview with Akhtar Sandhu, 21 August 2008.
28. Fauja Singh, *State and Society under Ranjit Singh* (Master Publishers, 1982), pp 54–5.
29. Surinder Singh Johar, *The Life Story of Maharaja Ranjit Singh* (Delhi: Arsee Publishers, 2001), p 23.

30. 'Death penalty' in this context refers to human beings. It should, however, be noted that Hindus equate cow-killing with capital punishment, and cow-killing was widely practised in the Punjab. (Interview, Akhtar Sandhu, 21 August 2008.)
31. It is noticeable that all eight of Ranjit's known children were boys. Without wishing to add to the gossip that inevitably attached to him as a ruler, it is reasonable to reiterate that female infanticide was common across the subcontinent at this time.
32. Waheed-ud-din, *The Real Ranjit Singh*, p 113.

Chapter 4. Enter the British

1. Khushwant Singh, 'The Sikhs', p 63.
2. British Library, India Office Registry file IOR/F/4/239/5472, letter dated 26 September 1807.
3. M.L. Ahluwalia (ed), *India's Foreign Policy Series – Select Documents: Ranjit Singh–Metcalfe Negotiations* (M.S. Ashoka International Publishers, 1982), pp 362–3.
4. Khushwant Singh, 'The Sikhs', p 74.
5. British Library, India Office Registry file IOR/H/592, titled 'Charles Metcalfe's Mission to Lahore', letter, 20 June 1808. Subsequent quotations up to the reference to IOR/H/593 are also taken from this file.
6. Khushwant Singh, 'The Sikhs', p 78.
7. The British used Calcutta as their Indian capital and continued to do so into the twentieth century.
8. British Library, India Office Registry file IOR/H/593, titled 'Charles Metcalfe's mission to Lahore', letter, 13 September 1808. Subsequent quotations up to the reference to IOR/H/595 are also taken from this file.
9. Edward Thompson, *The Life of Charles, Lord Metcalfe* (Faber & Faber, 1937), p 83.
10. Khushwant Singh, 'The Sikhs', p 79.
11. *Ibid.*, p 84.
12. *Ibid.*, p 85. Edward Thompson asserted that Metcalfe had three Eurasian sons by a Sikh woman whom he met at Ranjit Singh's court; he deduced the identity from the fact that the eldest boy was born in 1809. See Thompson, *Life of Metcalfe*, pp 101–2.
13. Ahluwalia (ed), *Select Documents*, pp 424–5.

14. Aristotle's teachings in the third century BCE profoundly influenced not only Christian philosophy but that of other faiths, including Islam.

15. Khushwant Singh notes that Metcalfe took umbrage ('The Sikhs', p 92). Although the British records do not say this in so many words, that is in keeping with their usual reticence.

16. British Library, India Office Registry file IOR/H/595, titled 'Charles Metcalfe's mission to Lahore', letter, 3 June 1809.

17. Kaye, *Life and Correspondence of Metcalfe*, pp 23–5.

18. The episode showed how seriously Ranjit regarded British might, which is important to note because some writers have claimed that the evident superiority and discipline of the sepoys, who were outnumbered, had impressed him so much that he decided to introduce Europeans and European methods to the army. However, while the incident might have reinforced Ranjit's inclination to learn from others, he was already well aware of British strength and the training and discipline that went into it.

19. British Library, India Office Registry file IOR/H/595, letters, 17 and 18 April 1809.

20. S.R. Bakshi, *History of the Punjab* (New Delhi: Anmol Publications, 1991), p 55.

21. Jean-Marie Lafont, *Maharaja Ranjit Singh: The French Connections* (GNDU, 2001), p 4.

Chapter 5. The Second Decade

1. Khushwant Singh, 'The Sikhs', p 96.

2. Ranjit Singh made several requests for weapons from the British. For instance, at various times over 1813 and 1814 he sought flints and muskets, once so insistently that in March 1813 Ochterlony reported his request for 1,000 muskets and 20,000 flints as being 'highly objectionable' in tone. Nonetheless, the British stretched their rules to accommodate his requests, as an internal letter of 30 September 1814 shows: '[W]e approve of your having so far deviated from the regulations in force regarding the prohibition of the exportation of arms as to agree to furnish … 500 muskets (British Library, India Office Registry file IOR/F/425/10406). Ranjit Singh's requests for British weaponry represented the important unpublicised side of the Punjabi/British relationship.

3. Khushwant Singh, 'The Sikhs', p 109.
4. N.B. Sen, *Maharaja Ranjit Singh & Koh-i-noor Diamond: The Brightest Jewel in the British Crown* (New Delhi: New Book Society of India, 2001), ch. 9.
5. Khushwant Singh, 'The Sikhs', pp 108–9.
6. K.S. Duggal, *Maharajah Ranjit Singh: The Last to Lay Arms* (Abhinav Publications, 2001), ch. 10.
7. Today, this famous gun stands outside the Lahore Museum.
8. H.L.O. Garrett and G.L. Chopra, *Events at the Court of Ranjit Singh* (Punjab Government Record Office, 1935), pp 8, 25, 26, 36, 74, 75, 151, 152, 203, 247, 270, 280, 281.

Chapter 6. At the Midpoint: The Flourishing State

1. Hasrat, *Life and Times*, p 297.
2. Khalsa College, *Maharajah Ranjit Singh*, ch. 6.
3. Khushwant Singh indicates thus. However, Syed Waheed-ud-din implies that Bhawani Das was in post until his death in 1834. Khushwant Singh, 'The Sikhs', p 128; Waheed-ud-din, *The Real Ranjit Singh*, p 81.
4. Kirpal Singh, *The Historical Study of Maharaja Ranjit Singh's Times* (National Book Shop, 2002, 2nd edn), pp 78ff.
5. Lehna Singh initially maintained influence at court during the fraught years after Ranjit's death, but he lost favour after Sher Singh's assassination in 1843 and moved to Calcutta. He served the Punjab again under the British until his death in 1854.
6. J.S. Grewal and Indu Banga, *Maharajah Ranjit Singh and His Times* (GNDU, 1980), pp 94ff.
7. Narendra Krishna Sinha, *Ranjit Singh*, pp 142–3.
8. Grewal and Banga, *Maharajah Ranjit Singh*, p 155.
9. For instance, Narendra Krishna Sinha, *Ranjit Singh*, p 147. N.M. Khilnani has also argued that trade thrived and people flourished despite the 'cumbrous and grinding' nature of the revenue-raising systems: *British Power in the Punjab* (Asia Publishing House, 1972), p 116.
10. Chapter 9 covers the Maharaja's interest in the arts.
11. Grewal and Banga, *Maharajah Ranjit Singh*, pp 138ff; and Grewal, *Cambridge History*, p 13.
12. Grewal, *Cambridge History*, p 22.

13. *Ibid.,* pp 32ff.
14. Jasbir Singh Ahluwalia and Param Bakhshish Singh (eds), *An Overview of Maharaja Ranjit Singh and His Times* (Balbir Singh Batia, Punjabi University, Patiala, 2001), p 1.
15. Banerjee, *Ranjit Singh,* ch. 4.
16. Khalsa College, *Maharajah Ranjit Singh,* p 144.
17. Grewal and Banga, *Maharajah Ranjit Singh,* pp 253ff.
18. For example, Srinagar, Peshawar, Dera Ghazi Khan, Dera Ismail Khan, Bannu, Jhelum Pind Dadan Khan and Khushab in the north, Hafizabad near Gujranwala, Gujranwala itself, Gujrat, Sialkot, Batala and Dera Baba Nanak near Amritsar, and Kangra.
19. Charles, Baron von Hügel, *Kashmir under Maharaja Ranjit Singh,* ed D.C. Sharma (New Delhi: Atlantic Publishers & Distributors, 1984), preface, pp 6, 69.
20. Roshan Lal Ahuja, *The Story of Ranjit Singh,* pp 45–6.
21. Ahluwalia and Singh, *An Overview,* p 112.
22. T.R. Sharma (ed), *Maharajah Ranjit Singh,* pp 61ff.
23. *Ibid.,* p 52.
24. Hira Singh (ed), *Maharaja Ranjit Singh: Tributes,* p 91.
25. Devinder Kumar Verma, *Foreigners at the Court of Maharajah Ranjit Singh* (Arun Publications, 2006), ch. 1.
26. Khushwant Singh, 'The Sikhs', p 139.

Chapter 7. Secularism and Tales of the Hero

1. S.P. Singh and Jasbir Singh Sabar (eds), *The Rule of Maharajah Ranjit Singh: Nature and Relevance* (GNDU, 2001), pp 24ff.
2. Griffin, *Ranjit Singh,* pp 122–3.
3. Balwant Singh, *The Army of Maharaja Ranjit Singh,* p 22.
4. Khalsa College, *Maharajah Ranjit Singh,* p 209.
5. Joginder Singh Kairon, *Tales around Maharaja Ranjit Singh* (GNDU, 2001), pp 21ff. The tales include the aforementioned episode with the calligrapher, though the account has the Maharaja coming across him riding out of Lahore with his transcribed Qur'an and telling him that he would pay more than whatever price he wanted for it.
6. The Punjabi word 'paras' means 'Philosopher's Stone'.

Chapter 8. The Third Decade

1. Khushwant Singh, 'The Sikhs', pp 142, 155.

2. Although Ranjit Singh revered Amritsar, he was always clear that he had been right to make Lahore the Punjab's capital as part of his balancing of group interests.

3. Originally Carl von Hügel.

4. Almost all writers on Ranjit Singh have been careful not to describe Leili as male or female. One exception was Griffin, who surmised from Hügel's description that Leili was male whereas, Griffin wrote, Sikhs had spoken of Leili as a mare. Griffin concluded from this that the creature Yar Mohammad surrendered might not have been Leili at all (Griffin, *Ranjit Singh*, p 104).

5. Khushwant Singh, 'The Sikhs', p 164.

6. *Memoirs of Alexander Gardner*, pp 171–2.

7. The description of Ellenborough was made later by the future governor-general of India, Lord Dalhousie: *Private Letters of the Marquess of Dalhousie*, ed J.G.A. Baird (William Blackwood & Sons, 1911), despatch from Malta, 17 March 1858, p 410.

8. C.H. Philips, *The East India Company 1784–1834* (Manchester University Press, 1968, reprint), pp 261ff.

9. Ellenborough's tactless manner did not prevent him from later becoming governor-general of India.

10. Alexander Burnes, *Travels into Bokhara*, vol. 1 (London: John Murray, 1834), p 76.

11. Hasrat, *Life and Times*, p 147.

Chapter 9. A Grand Summit of Equals and Ranjit's Nobles

1. British imperial rulers officially used the term 'native' in its accurate sense of meaning indigenous person. As time went on, however, the term was applied more pejoratively throughout the British Empire.

2. Quotation taken from Khushwant Singh, 'The Sikhs', p 173.

3. *Ibid.*, p 174.

4. Duggal, *Ranjit Singh*, p 118.

5. Inderyas Bhatti, 'Nobility under the Lahore Darbar (1799–1849)', M.Phil. dissertation, Guru Nanak Dev University, Amritsar. I am grateful for Dr H.S. Chopra's assistance.

6. This issue of a distinction in socio-political status is a grey area in the historiography. For example, Fateh Singh Ahluwalia is commonly termed a 'vassal' by leading Punjabi historians, such as J.S. Grewal, but he could equally be considered as one of the key nobles of the

Punjab (at least for the first half of Ranjit Singh's reign).

7. Examples are: Gaus Khan, Quteb Khan Akhrotia, Raushan Khan, Ahmad Shah, Ilahi Baksh, Ibadullah, Ghulam Mohammad Khan, Mazhar Ali Beg and Sayyad Imam Shah.

8. The cut of the Sikh uniform was also likely inspired by Allard, and the army medal was based on the style of one of Allard's medals, given to him by Napoleon himself, the Legion of Honour.

9. Antonio Sorrentino and Maurizio Taddei, *Napoli e l'India* (Naples, 1990), p 275.

10. Singh and Sharma, *Europeans and Maharaja Ranjit Singh*, pp 24–8.

Chapter 10. Afghan and British Provocation

1. Nalwa's name became so feared that thereafter generations of Pathan mothers employed it to quieten their children by warning them that he was coming.

2. Khushwant Singh, 'The Sikhs', p 216.

3. Lajpat Rai Nair, *Sir William Macnaghten's Correspondence Relating to the Tripartite Treaty* (Punjab Government Records Office, 1942), p 15. The three-month delay in replying was not necessarily a deliberate snub to Dost Mohammad. At this time even the most urgent of communications could be unavoidably slow, and Dost's letter did not fall into the highest category of priority.

4. *Ibid.*

5. *Ibid.*

6. Khushwant Singh, 'The Sikhs', p 197.

7. Lajpat Rai Nair, *Sir William Macnaghten's Correspondence*, pp 18, 20. The British distorted Burnes's pro-Dost reports because they did not fit in with Britain's policy to back Shah Shuja against him. Burnes's references to Dost's ability, his hold over Afghanistan, desire for friendship with Britain rather than Russia or Persia, and his apparent readiness to settle his quarrel with Ranjit Singh were all expunged from a top-level 'Blue Book'. Burnes swallowed his disappointment and reconciled himself to backing Shah Shuja. See Penderel Moon, *The British Conquest and Dominion of India* (Duckworth & Co., 1989), p 504. Dost, however, was embittered; as he noted in an intercepted letter: 'I have not abandoned the British; but the British have abandoned me'. See Algernon Law (ed), *India under Lord Ellenborough: A Selection of Hitherto Unpublished Papers and Secret Despatches of*

Edward Earl of Ellenborough (London: John Murray, 1926), p 20.

8. Khushwant Singh, 'The Sikhs', p 204.

9. *Ibid.*, pp 206–7; Hasrat, *Life and Times*, pp 167–71.

10. Lajpat Rail Nair, *Sir William Macnaghten's Correspondence*, p 45. However, Khushwant Singh states that, after hearing the proposals, Aziz-ud-din and Bhai Ram Singh were the only two courtiers who wanted to cooperate with the British; all the rest were opposed. It is reasonable to conclude, therefore, that Ranjit's choice of two initial negotiators fell on one who favoured cooperation and one who did not (Khushwant Singh, 'The Sikhs', p 206).

11. *Ibid.*, p 59.

12. *Ibid.*, pp 45, 58.

13. *Ibid.*, p 42.

14. Khushwant Singh, 'The Sikhs', p 207.

15. Lajpat Rai Nair, *Sir William Macnaghten's Correspondence*, pp 61ff.

16. Khushwant Singh, 'The Sikhs', p 207.

17. Lajpat Rai Nair, *Sir William Macnaghten's Correspondence*, p 91.

18. Law (ed), *India under Lord Ellenborough*, p 19.

Chapter 11. Fateful Conclusion with the British

1. Khushwant Singh, 'The Sikhs', pp 209ff.

2. Shahamat Ali, *The Sikhs and Afghans in connexion with India and Persia, immediately before and after the death of Ranjeet Singh – from the Journal of an Expedition to Kabul through the Panjab and the Khaiber Pass* (John Murray, 1847), pp 11–12.

3. T.R. Sharma (ed), *Maharajah Ranjit Singh*, p 56; Hasrat, *Life and Times*, p 177.

4. Shahamat Ali, *The Sikhs and Afghans*, pp 140–1, 222ff.

5. Hasrat, *Life and Times*, pp 189–90.

6. Henry Steinbach, *The Punjaub: Being a Brief Account of the Country of the Sikhs* (Smith, Elder & Co., 1846), pp 17–19.

7. Leopold von Orlich, *Travels in India, Including Sinde and the Punjab* (London: Longman, Brown, Green, and Longmans, 1845), pp 171–2.

Chapter 12. Vicious Aftermath

1. *Memoirs of Alexander Gardner*, pp 212ff. Alexander Gardner claimed to have witnessed many of the events following Ranjit's death, including this quoted exchange and Chet Singh's murder by a gleeful

Dhian Singh Dogra. We should accord the account of Gardner considerable regard without being able to wholly endorse it because it is largely uncorroborated.

2. Again, we are dependent upon Alexander Gardner's memoirs for much of this account, and Gardner was, by his own account, not present at all that happened. See *Memoirs of Alexander Gardner*, pp 246–9.

3. Khilnani, *British Power in the Punjab*, p 15.

4. The Nepalese government operated a generally pro-British policy, which was notably displayed in 1857 when it supported Britain during the Indian rebellion. Dost Mohammad Khan also supported Britain to the extent of not helping the rebels. He had gradually shed his opposition to the British after they annexed the Punjab and in 1855 made an alliance with them.

Postscript: Maharaja Duleep Singh

1. John Lord, *The Maharajas* (Hutchinson, 1972), p 23.

2. The way in which the British obtained the Koh-i-Noor and their unwillingness to consider returning the diamond to its land of origin continues to rankle with many Indians. The post-independence government of Prime Minister Jawaharlal Nehru came under pressure to demand its return but Nehru decided to play down the issue out of gratitude for the better side of British rule. The Koh-i-Noor now has pride of place among the British crown jewels. See N.B. Sen, *Maharaja Ranjit Singh & Koh-i-noor Diamond*, preface.

3. The India Office had absorbed the functions of the East India Company and exercised administrative responsibility for India from London.

4. Although burying Duleep alongside members of his closest family can be seen as a mark of respect and humanity, his Christian burial showed disregard for his re-found Sikhism.

BIBLIOGRAPHY

Ahluwalia, M.L. (ed), *India's Foreign Policy Series – Select Documents: Ranjit Singh–Metcalfe Negotiations* (M.S. Ashoka International Publishers, 1982)

Ahuja, Roshan Lal, *The Story of Ranjit Singh* (Amritsar, n.d.)

Ali, Shahamat, *The Sikhs and Afghans in connexion with India and Persia, immediately before and after the death of Ranjeet Singh – from the Journal of an Expedition to Kabul through the Panjab and the Khaiber Pass* (John Murray, 1847)

Baird, J.G.A. (ed), *Private Letters of the Marquess of Dalhousie* (William Blackwood & Sons, 1911)

Bakshi, S.R., *History of the Punjab* (New Delhi: Anmol Publications, 1991)

Banerjee, S.N., *Ranjit Singh* (Lahore: Atma Ram & Sons, Lahore, 1931)

Banga, Indu, *Agrarian System of the Sikhs: Late 18th and Early 19th Century* (Monohar, 1978)

Bhatti, Inderyas, 'Nobility under the Lahore Darbar (1799–1849)', M.Phil. dissertation, Guru Nanak Dev University, Amritsar

British Library, India Office Registry files IOR/F/4/239/5472, IOR/F/425/10406, IOR/H/592, IOR/H/593, IOR/H/595

Burnes, Alexander, *Travels into Bokhara*, vol. 1 (London: John Murray, 1834)

Chopra, Gulshan Lall, *The Panjab as a Sovereign State 1799–1839* (Uttar Chand Kapur & Sons, 1928)

Duggal, K.S., *Ranjit Singh: A Secular Sikh Sovereign* (Abhinav Publications, 1989)

___, *Maharajah Ranjit Singh: The Last to Lay Arms* (Abhinav Publications, 2001)

211

Forster, George, *A Journey from Bengal to England through the Northern part of India, Kashmire, Afghanistan, and Persia, and into Russia by the Caspian Sea*, 2 vols. (London, 1808)

Garrett, H.L.O. and G.L. Chopra, *Events at the Court of Ranjit Singh* (Punjab Government Record Office, 1935)

Grewal, J.S., *The Reign of Maharaja Ranjit Singh: Structure of Power, Economy and Society* (Patiala, 1981)

___, *The New Cambridge History of India: The Sikhs of the Punjab* (Cambridge University Press, 1994)

___ and Indu Banga, *Maharajah Ranjit Singh and His Times* (GNDU, 1980)

Griffin, Lepel, *Ranjit Singh* (Oxford: Clarendon, 1893)

Hasrat, Bikrama Jit, *Life and Times of Ranjit Singh: A Saga of Benevolent Despotism* (Nabha: Hasrat, 1977)

Heras, H. and S.N. Prasad (eds), *Fort William–India House Correspondence* (Government of India, 1974)

Hügel, Charles, Baron von, *Kashmir under Maharaja Ranjit Singh*, ed D.C. Sharma (New Delhi: Atlantic Publishers & Distributors, 1984)

Kaye, John William, *The Life and Correspondence of Charles, Lord Metcalfe* (Smith Elder & Co., 1858)

Khalsa College, *Maharajah Ranjit Singh: First Death Centenary* (Amritsar: Khalsa College, 1939)

Khilnani, N.M., *British Power in the Punjab* (Asia Publishing House, 1972)

Kohli, Sita Ram, *Maharajah Ranjit Singh* (GNDU, 2002)

Lafont, Jean-Marie, *Maharaja Ranjit Singh: The French Connections* (GNDU, 2001)

Law, Algernon (ed), *India under Lord Ellenborough: A Selection of Hitherto Unpublished Papers and Secret Despatches of Edward Earl of Ellenborough* (London: John Murray, 1926)

Lord, John, *The Maharajas* (Hutchinson, 1972)

Moon, Penderel, *The British Conquest and Dominion of India* (Duckworth & Co., 1989)

Nair, Lajpat Rai, *Sir William Macnaghten's Correspondence Relating to the Tripartite Treaty* (Punjab Government Records Office, 1942)

Orlich, Leopold von, *Travels in India, Including Sinde and the Punjab* (London: Longman, Brown, Green, and Longmans, 1845)

Osborne, W.G., *The Court and Camp of Ranjit Singh* (Mahbub Alam, 1895)

Pearse, Major Hugh (ed), *Memoirs of Alexander Gardner, Soldier and Traveller* (William Blackwood & Sons, 1898)

Philips, C.H., *The East India Company 1784–1834* (Manchester University Press, 1968, reprint)

Rawlinson, H.G., *Buddha, Ashoka, Akbar, Shivaji and Ranjit Singh: A Study in Indian History* (Essess Publications, 1980, reprint)

Sandhu, Manveen, *Maharaja Ranjit Singh, Personalitas Extraordinaire* (S.S. Sandhu, 2007)

Sen, N.B., *Maharaja Ranjit Singh & Koh-i-noor Diamond: The Brightest Jewel in the British Crown* (New Delhi: New Book Society of India, 2001)

Sharma, Radha, *The Lahore Darbar* (GNDU, 2001)

Sharma, T.R. (ed), *Maharajah Ranjit Singh: Ruler and Warrior* (Panjab University, Chandigarh, 2005)

Singh, Ahluwalia Jasbir and Param Bakhshish Singh (eds), *An Overview of Maharaja Ranjit Singh and His Times* (Balbir Singh Batia, Punjabi University, Patiala, 2001)

Singh, Balwant, *The Army of Maharaja Ranjit Singh* (Lahore Book Shop, 1932)

Singh, Fauja, *State and Society under Ranjit Singh* (Master Publishers, 1982)

Singh, Hira (ed), *Maharaja Ranjit Singh: Being Tributes to the Memory of the Great Monarch* (Lahore: University Sikh Association, 1939)

Singh Johar, Surinder, *The Life Story of Maharaja Ranjit Singh* (Delhi: Arsee Publishers, 2001)

Singh Kairon, Joginder, *Tales around Maharaja Ranjit Singh* (GNDU, 2001)

Singh, Khushwant, 'The Sikhs', in Joseph M. Kitagawa (ed), *The Religious Traditions of Asia: Religion, History, and Culture* (Routledge/Curzon, 2002)

Singh, Kirpal, *The Historical Study of Maharaja Ranjit Singh's Times* (National Book Shop, 2002, 2nd edn)

Singh, S.P. and Harish Sharma (eds), *Europeans and Maharaja Ranjit Singh* (GNDU, 2001)

___ and Jasbir Singh Sabar (eds), *The Rule of Maharajah Ranjit Singh: Nature and Relevance* (GNDU, 2001)

Sinha, Narendra Krishna, *Ranjit Singh* (A.R. Mukherjee, 1951)

Sood, D.R., *Ranjit Singh* (National Book Trust, 1968)

Sorrentino, Antonio and Maurizio Taddei, *Napoli e l'India* (Naples, 1990)

Steinbach, Henry, *The Punjaub: Being a Brief Account of the Country of the Sikhs* (Smith, Elder & Co., 1846)

Thompson, Edward, *The Life of Charles, Lord Metcalfe* (Faber & Faber, 1937)

Verma, Devinder Kumar, *Foreigners at the Court of Maharajah Ranjit Singh* (Arun Publications, 2006)

Waheed-ud-din, Fakir Syed, *The Real Ranjit Singh* (Punjabi University, Patiala, 2001)

INDEX

1. A portrait of the Maharaja sitting in a chair. Painted on paper.

2. A painting showing Ranjit Singh's tomb in Lahore; a water-colour with pen and ink borders.

3. A portrait of the Maharaja with an attendant bearing a fly-whisk and supplicant; painted in gouache on paper.

4. This portrait of the Maharaja seated on a terrace gives a good indication of his blind eye; painted in gouache on paper.

5. The funeral of Ranjit Singh, depicting suttee, the Maharaja's body being on the funeral pyre with some of his wives; a group of men are also present grieving while helping with the ceremony. Painted on paper.

6. Ranjit Singh seated with a flower in his hand and his foot on a stool; a watercolour with pen and ink borders.

7. A meeting between Ranjit Singh and the Maratha leader Jaswant Rao Holkar, seated on a mat. This would have been from 1805, when Holkar sought refuge in the Punjab following his defeat by the British. Holkar is in the centre of the portrait while a rather unlikely looking Ranjit Singh is dressed in red.

8. This painting shows Ranjit Singh on a Western-style chair with his legs tucked beneath him, the manner in which he was often seen by European visitors to his court. He is shown with Hira Singh, who was introduced to the Maharaja by his father, Dhian Singh Dogra. Ranjit Singh regarded Hira favourably, almost as a son. Opaque watercolour and gold on paper.

9. This award, the Order of Merit with a portrait of Ranjit Singh,
was introduced by him (see Chapter 9).

12. (facing). Prince Nau Nihal Singh, Ranjit Singh's favourite grandson, sits on a Western-
style chair typical of those in use at the Sikh court. His Hindu companion Dhian Singh
Dogra, Ranjit Singh's prime minister, is seated at his feet. After Ranjit Singh's death in 1839,
Nau Nihal's father, Kharak Singh, became Maharaja, but was soon the victim of plotting at
the court and was poisoned. On the day of his death Nau Nihal Singh also died, quite possibly through murder involving Dhian Singh, though this was never proved.

10. This watercolour portrait shows Ranjit Singh with a halo and with a parasol held over his head by a bearer, indicating his royal status. The Maharaja is shown from his right to conceal his blind eye, the result of the childhood smallpox that also disfigured his skin. The portrait was probably painted in about 1838.

11. A goldsmith, Hafez Muhammad Multani, made this splendid throne for Ranjit Singh, probably between 1820 and 1830. Whereas in Europe royal furniture is usually simply gilded, creating the effect of gold without incurring the cost, in the Indian subcontinent the reverse was true and thrones were decorated

with richly worked sheets of gold. The dis tive cusped base of this throne comprises two tiers of lotus petals. The lotus is a sym of purity and creation and has traditionall been used as a seat or throne for Hindu gc However, the octagonal shape of the thron is based on courtly furniture of the Mugha Their many-sided furniture provided mod for thrones, footstools and tables througho northern India.

13. Although the name Ranjit Singh was very well known in the northern region of the Indian subcontinent during his reign, few outside the Punjab ever saw him or his likeness. Lacking a true image from which to copy a likeness, the carver of this ivory statuette (who may have worked in Delhi, a major centre of the craft) gave the Maharaja the majestic appearance and jewellery of a Mughal emperor. In reality, Ranjit was renowned for his simple dress. (Carved ivory with traces of gold and pigment.)

14. This opaque watercolour on paper, probably from about 1835, again typifies the style associated with the court of Ranjit Singh. It depicts Gulab Singh of Jammu taking his bath prior to worship. Gulab Singh was one of the many Hindus in the army of court of Lahore. However, his loyalty to the state did not survive the death of Ranjit Singh. He passed military intelligence to the British during the First Anglo-Sikh War in 1845–46, for which he was rewarded by being made ruler of Kashmir in addition to remaining ruler of the adjacent kingdom of Jammu.

15. Ranjit Singh is shown here with traditional emblems of royalty, a parasol held over his head and a turban jewel. The painting was formerly in the collection of Queen Mary, and English inscriptions on paintings in the same group suggest that the first (unknown) British owner acquired the series between October 1839 and November 1840. Opaque watercolour and gold on paper.

16. This painting depicts Dhian Singh Dogra on horseback. He, too, is shown with traditional emblems of royalty, a parasol held over his head, and a turban jewel. As principal minister in the Punjab, Dhian Singh was the most powerful person in the kingdom after Ranjit Singh.

17. In this painting, Dhian Singh Dogra kneels on a carpet against a bolster, facing his younger brother, Suchet Singh. Both of these members of the Hindu Dogra family were rewarded with high office and titles under Ranjit Singh, but they contributed to the turmoil of the region following his death.

18. This drawing depicts a Sikh *sardar*, a title originally meaning 'chieftain' or 'headman' in Persian but which came to be used routinely for the dignitaries of the Darbar, the court of Ranjit Singh. The court attracted artists from around the Punjab who worked for new patrons, who might be Sikh, Hindu or Muslim, or even Europeans in the service of the Maharaja. Drawing done in ink on paper and lightly painted in body colour.

19. A further painting of a Sikh *sardar* in typically striking attire.

20. Prince Kharak Singh succeeded his father as the second Sikh Maharaja of the Punjab in June 1839. His frail constitution and naive personality left him unable to withstand the plotting against him that took place as rival factions at court jostled for power. He was slowly poisoned and died on 5 November 1840. Opaque watercolour and gold on paper.

21. A young man sits on a gold chair facing a youth who holds out his hands deferentially before him. Both wear turban jewels, the insignia of royalty introduced by the Mughal emperors but, by the nineteenth century, also often worn by senior members of regional courts. It is possible that the seated man is Ranjit Singh's grandson Hira Singh, who had been honoured with the title of Raja by him in 1816. The young men's cut hair indicates that they are not Sikhs; Hira Singh was a member of the Hindu Dogra family, which was highly influential at Ranjit Singh's court. Whoever it was sitting on the chair most probably enjoyed a certain status. Opaque watercolour and gold on paper.

22. This opaque watercolour and gold on paper shows Ranjit Singh riding through a flower-sprinkled landscape on a white stallion that is bedecked with gold chains and turban jewels. The Maharaja is dressed in saffron-coloured clothes with a brocade short coat, his only jewels being long ropes of pearls and a bazuband, or ornament for the upper arm. He is surrounded by companions, many of whom carry insignia of royalty such as weapons wrapped in cloth. Most important of these is the parasol – the ancient emblem of kings – that shades Ranjit Singh's head. The painting was given to the V&A in 1955 by Mrs L.M. Rivett-Carnac on behalf of the Van Cortlandt family. According to family tradition, this was one of a pair of portraits made for Ranjit Singh by his court artist and presented by him to Mrs Rivett-Carnac's grandfather, Colonel Henry Charles Van Cortlandt, the other copy being kept by the Maharaja. Van Cortlandt (1814–88) entered Ranjit Singh's service in 1832, and after the first Anglo-Sikh War (1845–46) commanded Sikh detachments under the British. (Victoria and Albert Museum)

23. The painting depicts a Sikh *sardar* with a black shield strapped to his back receiving petitions on a terrace. He has been identified as Lehna Singh Majithia by W.G. Archer in his book *Paintings of the Sikhs* (HMSO, London, 1966, p 142). Lehna Singh was an immensely able member of the court and a talented scientist. The painting was probably done in Lahore or Amritsar, the major cities of the kingdom, between about 1835 and 1840. Opaque watercolour and gold on paper.

24. This albumen print painting shows the gateway to the Ram Bagh in the north-east of Lahore. The Ram Bagh was laid out by the order of Ranjit Singh and, like the Shalimar gardens in Lahore, was intended to provide a haven of tranquillity. The gateway, with its two imposing octagonal towers, was known as a 'bunga' and was one of several built during Ranjit Singh's reign for the use of dignitaries visiting Amritsar.

25. Hira Singh sits on a Western-style chair. Dressed in a slate blue turban, green shawl, white coat and orange trousers, the terrace on which he sits has a dark green carpet edged with pink, patterned with floral motifs in white, red and green. His attendant is in white with a green turban. This albumen print painting was also in the collection of Lord Auckland (governor-general of India 1836–42) and brought back by him to England in 1842, and was given to the museum in 1953 by Lord Auckland's great-nephew, O.E. Dickinson.

26. The photographer Samuel Bourne took this photograph from the Shish Mahal of Lahore Fort in 1864. Rising over the landscape and dominating the scene is the Badshahi Mosque. Its imposing gateway facing the marble pavilion in the Hazuri Bagh is just visible on the left. In the foreground an assortment of artillery lies in one corner of the Shish Mahal's marble court. Overlooking the graceful curved roof of the Naulakha pavilion nearby is Ranjit Singh's tomb.

27. This further image of Prince Nau Nihal Singh portrays him sitting on an oval rug of deep blue edged with bright yellow. He wears a green turban, yellow trousers, yellow shawl and mauve coat. His right arm is outside the sleeve and his left hand rests on his left knee. Smallpox scars are visible on his face. This painting was formerly owned by Queen Mary, wife of George V. From English inscriptions on related paintings from the same source, it is thought that they were all made between October 1839 and November 1840, when Nau Nihal Singh died.

28. This photograph shows the marble pavilion that was built by Ranjit Singh in 1818 to provide a cool garden retreat where he could take refuge from the heat and, in the background, the imposing Fort of Lahore.

29. This drawing on paper is of Dina Nath, a civil administrator and counsellor of great influence and importance at the court for over three decades. He was perhaps particularly as finance minister under Ranjit Singh. Dina Nath became a member of the Regency Council of Dulip Singh, the last ruler of the kingdom. In this lightly drawn portrait that was probably done between about 1835 and 1845 he is depicted sitting on the ground holding a petition, with his pen case and a bundle of documents before him.

30. This photograph was taken from Ranjit Singh's palace in Lahore. It focuses on his tomb, and manages to capture a number of carts positioned in the courtyard. This gives a sense of activity rarely seen in early photographs. The fuzziness surrounding the carts would have been caused by people or livestock moving around the well.

31. This portrait depicts Maharaja Gulab Singh of Jammu and Kashmir with his small grandson and an attendant, who stands behind him holding a fan of peacock feathers. The artist was William Carpenter (1819–99), who was born in London and was the son of the artist and miniaturist Margaret Sarah Carpenter and William Hookham Carpenter, Keeper of Prints and Drawings at the British Museum. William Carpenter first visited Indian in 1850 to paint portraits and make studies of Indian life and scenery. He remained there until the Great Mutiny, or First War of Independence, caused him to return to England in 1857. This was one of 134 works bought from the artist by the South Kensington Museum in 1880. The following year, the museum held an exhibition of Carpenter's Indian paintings.

Gulab Singh, born in 1792, was an influential member of the court of Maharaja Ranjit Singh, the first Sikh Maharaja of the Panjab (r. 1801–39) who made Gulab Singh Raja of Jammu in 1822. He was a loyal servant of Ranjit Singh, but intrigued against his successors and finally allied himself with the British during the first Anglo-Sikh War (1845–46). For this he was given extensive territories seized from the Sikh kingdom. The portrait was done in about 1855, after the second Anglo-Sikh War and the annexation of the Panjab to the British Empire in 1849.

9 781350 337138